# She Flies On

*A White Southern Christian Debutante Wakes Up*

## CARTER HEYWARD

Church Publishing
NEW YORK

She comes sailing on the wind,
Her wings flashing in the sun;
On a journey just begun, She flies on.
And in the passage of Her flight,
Her song rings out through the night,
Full of laughter, full of light, She flies on!

—Gordon Light,
"She Comes Sailing on the Wind"

For Bev and Sue

like none other

Unless otherwise noted, the Scripture quotations contained herein are from the New Revised Standard Version Bible, copyright © 1989 by the Division of Christian Educa-tion of the National Council of Churches of Christ in the U.S.A. Used by permission. All rights reserved.

Words and music for "She Comes Sailing on the Wind" by Gordon Light, © Common Cup Company, 1985. Used by permission.

Church Publishing
19 East 34th Street
New York, NY 10016
*www.churchpublishing.org*

Cover photo by Beverly Hall Photography, Nantucket, Massachusetts
Cover design by Jennifer Kopec, 2Pug Design
Typeset by Rose Design

Library of Congress Cataloging-in-Publication Data

Names: Heyward, Carter author.
Title: She flies on : a white southern Christian debutante wakes up / Carter
  Heyward.
Description: New York : Church Publishing, 2017. | Includes bibliographical
  references.
Identifiers: LCCN 2016054006 (print) | LCCN 2017007397 (ebook) | ISBN
  9780819233530 (pbk.) | ISBN 9780819233547 (ebook)
Subjects: LCSH: Christianity. | Non-church-affiliated people.
Classification: LCC BR121.3 .H49 2017 (print) | LCC BR121.3 (ebook) | DDC
  230/.3092—dc23
LC record available at https://lccn.loc.gov/2016054006

Printed in the United States of America

# Contents

# Acknowledgments

Many thanks to my editor, Nancy Bryan, Ryan Masteller, and others on the editorial staff at Church Publishing for their support, and to Darlene O'Dell, Hal Wildung, Bonnie Engelhardt, David Conolly, and Angela Moloney for reading the manuscript and making suggestions. Special thanks to photographers Albert Dulin and Beverly Hall, both friends of many years, for a number of the photos in the book. Thanks also to the loved ones and friends who appear in these pages, as well as to some others who, walking and talking with me in the woods, barns, kitchens, and coffee shops of the North Carolina mountains over the last couple of years, inspired this writing and may not know it: Michael Wainwright, Kathleen Barnes, Sheila Mooney, Robert Kilgore, Hilary Dirlam, Jim Lewis, LaVonda Blackwell, Mary Gordon, Webb Brown, Jennifer Henley, Eleanor Mockridge, Denise Jones, Carmen Kelling, Peggy McGoldrick, Sandi Thompson, Lillie Ware, Kris Woodaman, and Josh Rood. Y'all are the best!

# Prologue

In the basement, tucked away among scores of old photos, is a rumpled sepia image of a six-year-old me, proudly beholding a turtle in a cardboard box (see p. 137). I'm wearing a baseball cap over pigtails, and a pair of shorts, no shirt, my face fixed in contemplation. If I were kneeling beside a bed, head bowed before a cross or a picture of Jesus, you'd assume I was praying. In this book, I will be telling you how I have spiraled back round to those early days when something in me knew that the turtle was a sacred creature. Indeed, the old photo reminds me today that, once upon a time, I knelt on the ground and prayed to the Spirit who greeted me in her small, tough, scarred, shelled body. Hello, God.

I always feared I was crazy. Note the past tense. Not that I know today that I'm not; I just no longer fear it. A sweet gift of aging is perspective. The accumulation of time can help frame our lives. We can become clearer and more confident and move beyond caring much about some things, like how our adversaries may regard us, as we care more about other things—doing what we can to help raise up younger folks to take care of one another, themselves, and the whole created earth and its many varied creatures, human and other. The younger ones increasingly become our love and our legacy.

What we say, or refuse to say, about God and the world can matter a great deal to us as we get older, and perhaps also to those who are coming along behind us on the journey. But our presentations—on paper or virtual pages, Facebook or blogs, fading photos or airbrushed portraits—are never entirely the right, much less the only, words or images that might do some justice to ourselves, the world, and the elusive Spirit swirling around and among us. Much as we may think we know, try hard as we may to remember, our offerings of truth are always partial and fragmented. Still, we must speak or write or otherwise let people know what we believe. We stay silent at the expense of not only our souls—where the Sacred stirs within us and within our communities— but also the strength and well-being of our societies and the whole earth.

Because so much is at stake, we do indeed need to speak or write, preach or sing, paint or compose, or somehow express what we value, what we honestly think about what is going on around us and within us. With this in mind, I decided early in my seventieth year that it was time to write another book, as much for the younger folk, my nephews, nieces, and their generation, as anyone else. But whoever you may be, whatever your age or identity, your religious affiliation, if any, or your politics, I am writing to you.

This book will tell you how I, one small human on planet earth, have experienced the Sacred, or God, or Spirit, and what I've come to believe over the years. I will be telling you how my mind has changed, and how it has not. I'm not out to proselytize or convince you, but to merely recount and describe my adventures over seventy years with "something" that moves and pushes and yearns through us, and with us, and beyond us, connecting our lives—yours and mine—not only with each other in ways that can be noticed through eyes of faith but also in ways that we cannot, I truly believe, fully imagine.

I see the Spirit in the turtle at whom I worshipfully gazed as a child, but not until I looked at the crumpled up photo recently did I notice the shadow of the photographer, which became for me another image of God—the power who produces the picture yet whose presence often goes undetected. And then, of course, there are the trees and the ground. A whole book could be written about that one photograph. Even so, the photograph images a tiny fraction of how much God there is in every frame of life and, from another perspective, how much creatureliness—human and other—there is in God.

So this book is about God and turtles and kids. It is about strong spiritual, social, and political efforts to transform and heal the wounds of racism and sexism, economic inequality and environmental distress, and rigid definitions of gender. It's about a Father God and His only Son who have played both protective and damaging roles in my life and in the lives of other people and creatures throughout the history of the church and world. It's a book about the tenacious, wicked, woman-denying, sexually out of control, shape of patriarchal religion to this day, a violent state of affairs that has driven millions of strong women beyond the bounds of organized religion.

This is a book about women's ordination and "coming out." It is about godding (a word I adapted decades ago from the works of Paul Tillich and Mary Daly). It's about godding through the love and power of good parenting and great teachers. It's about the "power of the erotic and the love of God" on a collision course with God the Father and Jesus Christ, as traditionally constructed by church fathers. It's about Jesus-Liberator, simultaneously angry and compassionate, bringing down structures of oppression and leading movements for liberation close to home and around the world.

This is a book about transformative spiritual friendship and relational mutuality at many levels of our life together. The book is about horses as priests, an image that surprised my friend Tom, an Episcopal bishop, when I told him about the Sacred Power meeting me through my deepening relationship with my mare, "Red." It's about the spirits in the hills of western North Carolina, where I hope to spend my last years here on this bruised, brave earth. The book is about the music I have always enjoyed as backdrop and sometimes foreground to the days of my life that have been best.

It's about many things, this book, but mainly about God.

By God, I do not mean a far off deity who creates us and then leaves us on our own. I do not refer to a paternalistic or maternalistic God who oversees us like a parent or a bishop. I most definitely am not thinking of a traditionally "Christian" God, to whom we are taught to look up and pray for particular blessings because we either do or, more often, do not deserve His blessings.

By God, I mean our power for generating right, or mutual, relation, a theme I explored some thirty-five years ago in my doctoral dissertation, which was published in 1982 as *The Redemption of God: A Theology of Mutual Relation*.[1]

After forty years of ministry as a proudly "irregular" Episcopal priest and more than thirty as a Christian feminist theologian, teaching various liberation and systematic theologies—some interesting, some compelling, some boring—I am no longer much concerned with academic theologies. I retired from that world in 2005 and have been glad to leave that work to communities of sister and brother academics, who will publish, debate, and teach their scholarship to each new generation of students.

But "theology" is not simply an academic discipline and it need not be inaccessible to everyone except scholars in religion. When I was getting my PhD in theology at Union Theological Seminary in New

York City in the late 1970s, my savvy academic advisor Tom F. Driver
said something to me that shaped my work as a theologian. Exhausted
from reading the books of academic theologians, mainly white European men, day and night, week upon week, I made an appointment to
meet with Tom Driver. I was discouraged. There was so much I didn't
know, so many men and so little time. "I will never know all of this!"
I sighed. "I'll never be able to learn what all of these men thought!" I
handed him a list of about a hundred theologians whose names had
appeared in the footnotes of the books I'd been reading. Tom took the
list, looked it over, smiled, and handed the list back to me with a question, "Who are these people?" This was Tom's cryptic, lighthearted
way of helping me relax. He was letting me know that I need not worry
about such academic trivia; after all, even he had no idea who these
men on my list were.

And so, I am happy to say that, more than ten years after my retirement as a professor, I am still a theologian from the tips of my toes, to
borrow an expression from my wonderful horse-loving pal and sister
theologian Gretchen Grimshaw. I enjoy thinking about God. I am energized by critical thinking, and I aspire to approach theology honestly,
respectfully, intelligently and, from moment to moment, whimsically. I
do better when I take neither my notions about "God" nor myself too
seriously—and neither as absolute, or final.

There was a woman whose name I don't remember but whose
words have never left me. She was a member of St. Clement's Episcopal
Church in New York City's Times Square where I did my field work
as a seminarian at Union Theological Seminary in the early 1970s. She
and I were discussing the creed and our difficulties with it. The woman
said, "The only faith statement I can truthfully make is, 'I believe in
God'—and I can only say that in sign language."

It's more or less true that there's no such thing as a new idea about
God or anything else, so I don't assume that anything in these pages is
either new or entirely mine. In fact, one of the basic themes you will
encounter here is the centrality of our relation, connection, and mutuality to any experience or understanding we may have of the Sacred, or of
life itself. One of the implications of a relational theology is that all that
we are, all that we do, and all that we think is connected and, therefore,
relative to everything else. No one, no idea, no thing, stands alone, on

its own, ever. This is as true of God and Jesus as it is of you and me and our ideas.

"In the beginning is relation."[2] Jewish social mystic Martin Buber's simple observation holds the clue to everything. The source of our very being, our human being, our creature being, is relation. Our bodies and those of planets and stars begin in relation. There is no thing outside of relation to every thing else. This means that we are relatives—I and thou, you and me—like it or not. You are my cousin, my mother, my brother, whether we share gender or racial or ethnic or religious or ideological or species identities. Love me, fear me, welcome me, hate me, give me life or death. You have the power, and so do I, through our relation.

Readers familiar with identity politics,[3] in which the particularity of our race, gender, or ethnicity matters to our worldview, may wonder how this fits with our radical relationality, in which no dimension of who we are stands alone, on its own, apart from others. Like so much in life, it's a both-and, not an either-or. That I am a woman matters a great deal, to me and to many. It always has, always will. That I am a woman matters not one whit apart from everything else that I am and apart from others. These statements are equally true.

Two of the people with whom, in the course of my life, I have most consciously and explicitly explored "mutual relation" as a theological foundation and ethical imperative have died—my beloved Bev, with whom I shared vigorous academic explorations in the late 1960s, and a life journey together beginning in the early 1980s; and Sister Angela, who joined me on a spiritual quest in the early 1990s. You will meet them both in these pages. Each is in some mystical realm a co-author to what I am writing.

My third companion in wrestling intellectually through the meanings, challenges, and politics of mutuality has been Janet Surrey, a "spiritual friend."[4] Jan and I met in 1987. At the time I was teaching feminist liberation theology at the Episcopal Divinity School in Cambridge, Massachusetts, and Jan was a clinical psychologist on the staff of McLean Hospital in neighboring Belmont. Almost immediately, we realized each other's passion for mutuality and admitted that each of us was discouraged by the dearth of mutual relation in our respective professional realms. In fact each of us had been fantasizing about switching fields of inquiry, Jan moving into theology, me into psychology. "No!" each of us warned the other. "Don't do that!" We quickly disabused each other of any romantic notions we had about the other's profession.

In the past ten years, Jan has become an insight dialogue dharma instructor. Over thirty years, she has also become one of my most cherished friends and a sister sojourner in seeking to build mutuality wherever we can in life. As a draft of this book was nearing completion in the summer of 2015, Jan and I went hiking in the Great Smoky Mountains in celebration of our seventieth birthdays. Over five days we hiked, sat together in meditation, ate simply, pondered the state of the world in the immediate aftermath of the Charleston massacre, listened to President Obama's inspired eulogy at shooting victim Rev. Clementa Pinckney's funeral, and talked a lot about aging and loss. We shared grief and sorrow, and we also found a great deal of gratitude and peace together. Our shared "obsession" with mutuality, as Jan herself has written, has drawn us both about as deeply as humans can go into thinking about what I, as a Christian, would call God—the Spirit that I have long believed is our power for generating right, or mutual, relation in all arenas of our life together in this world.

As we hiked, I told Jan about my horse Red's message to me from the great beyond—Red died in 2013: "Lift up your feet!" Red tells me every morning as I begin the day. As we hiked on, Jan added, "Yes—lift, move, place." Lift up your feet. Move them. Place them. A way of relating to the earth. A way of relating to one another. A simple mantra. Lift. Move. Place. The way to walk the path we're on, making mutuality as we go.

As we walk the path, we come eventually to see more clearly, as if from a mountain peak: we see ourselves together. We see that we really are one family of earth-creatures. We notice the Spirit weaving among us, binding us together. We realize that, in the beginning and in the end, what we do as characters here on earth makes little or no difference, because God is God, and Life is Life, and Life includes Death, and Death precedes Life. And so on we go, sisters and brothers, in relation to one another and everything else, now and forever more. Blessed be.

But please do not take the preceding paragraph out of context and contend that I am suggesting in this book that the shape of our lives doesn't matter. Because it does. What we do with our lives—lifting, moving, placing our feet—makes all the difference in the world to those who live with us on planet earth, humans and other creatures, and what we do with our lives matters to us, how we experience and understand the value and meanings of our own lives. What we do matters more than we can possibly imagine because each of us so deeply yearns for love—to love and to be loved, to experience the joys and happiness of right, mutual relation, here on earth while we are here.

Indeed, the Creator may be weaving all of our lives—past present future—together, somehow forgiving and transforming the damages we have done into what She eternally yearns for Her creation to be. And perhaps, in the Wisdom of God, everything we call "good" and everything we call "evil" is truly and radically relative, so fundamentally in relation are our lives and deaths to all that has been and all that will be. God's glorious ways of weaving our lives together, in all the goodness and the evil that we do in this world, is beyond our capacities to even imagine, much less know. But we are responsible to do everything we can to treat one another, and ourselves, as beloved sisters and brothers who were born to share this time and space. The evil done in our fear and greed may not have the last word in God's eternal realm, but too often it is the last awful act, word, or image experienced by human beings and other creatures in this world.

So here and now, we have a task—to help give shape and voice to the Sacred, Her wisdom and Her compassion, Her love and Her liberation, so that we creatures can more fully enjoy and celebrate Her presence and Her movement in our midst, whoever and wherever we are today.

Books are linear in shape, moving from beginning to end, much like we usually think of ourselves creeping along in chronological time. With this in mind, I urge you not to imagine that the perspectives in this book, or the theological images, or the stories themselves, which are told more or less in chronological order, can be appreciated or understood fully in chronological order. Everything that is important in this book, if read in the spirit in which I offer it, should burst out of chronological time into *kairos*, or God's time, which I explore more fully in part one.

If you read this book from beginning to end, which is a good way to read it, please do not be confined to its linear shape or to the literal meanings of any of its words. If there is some truth here, it should slip off the page into your voices and dreams and songs, and weave its way into the fabrics of your lives and of our life together, its meanings evolving as it thrives and eventually dies, giving way to deeper or other truths.

## THE TRINITY AND THE SHAPE OF THIS BOOK

For many Christians, the Trinity makes little sense. It is a tradition passed on to us via the historic creeds such as the Nicene (325/381 CE) and Athanasian (probably late fourth century CE).[5] Especially among Roman Catholics, Orthodox, and the more "catholic" Protestant communions such as the Anglican/Episcopal and Lutheran, belief in the Trinity is assumed to be essential to the faith, but the doctrine is obscured by abstraction. Sometimes referred to theologically as a formula, the doctrine of the Trinity surely defies most Christians' best abilities to reason or imagine: God is Father, Son, and Spirit—three in one, one in three, and that is that.

But that is not simply that. What on earth could possibly have given rise to such an elusive piece of theology? As a doctrine of faith and a liturgical centerpiece, the Trinity is emblematic of the alienation from the institutional church of many of Jesus's most loving friends.

But there is an important intuition in this particular Christian teaching. Despite its obscure philosophical origins, it has been, from the beginning, a metaphor for an intuition of the relationality at the heart of God. However abstract, the Trinity is an image of relation— the relationality of all that is good and wise, beautiful, and true.

It is an image of God rooted in an intuition of relation—the same intuition that the Jewish philosopher Martin Buber would explore two millennia later in *I and Thou*. The Trinity represents the connectedness of all that is Sacred.

Along these lines, Augustine of Hippo, one of the most influential theologians in Christian history, described the Spirit as the love between the Father and the Son.[6]

This is metaphor, poetry, imagination—but why "Father and Son"? Why not "Mother and Child"? Why not "Creator and Creation"? Why not simply "I and Thou"? Why is Christianity rooted in the iconic patriarchal relationship?

Why, indeed. The doctrine of the Trinity images a Father-Son relationship because Christian theology, from its beginning, has been androcentric, male-centered, at its core. It would not have occurred to the
fathers of Christianity—or their Hebrew forebears—to conceptualize
God in any way other than masculine. Insofar as these theologians were
attempting to stay true to Scripture, their personal and relational images
of God were profoundly patriarchal. The doctrine of the Trinity was for-
mulated by churchmen and philosophers who could only imagine God
as a reflection of their maleness, which was, and is, the basis of patriarchy itself. Any other images—especially those affirming strong women
or femaleness as sacred or virtuous—were unthinkable to early church
fathers, and so too to most Christian men and women up to the present.

Nonetheless, the primary impulse behind the Trinity has been radically relational all along. Despite its male-dominated origins and history and its static formulation—Father, Son, Spirit—something in the
doctrine of the Trinity pushes, always pushes, beyond the doctrine itself
and beyond all doctrines. This "something" is the relational character of
God, the movement of the Sacred to connect, the energy of the Spirit to
reach beyond itself toward the other, the irrepressibility of the power of
God, or Love, to expand and forever move us into new places in which
we are likely to be uncomfortable, all the more so if we are wed to static,
unchanging experiences and images of God.

This book is shaped around the primary intuition or impulse
behind the doctrine of the Trinity—the radical relationality of God,
which calls, lures, pushes, urges us beyond where we are now, and who
we are now, toward that for which we are never fully prepared. Basic to
my evolving faith is that the most deeply healing and fully liberating
energies of Christianity, and of all religions, spin us beyond doctrine
into emerging opportunities for spiritual yearning and ever-deepening
gratitude.

In this spirit, parts one and two attempt to illustrate how my experiences and understandings of God as Father and Son have affected, both
positively and negatively, my life and those of others in the world. Part
three is an effort to describe the Spirit bursting through our lives, spiritualities, and theologies—and carrying us beyond our comfort zones,
beyond familiar ground, beyond organized religion, and most assuredly
beyond the theological and liturgical authority of Christianity's Trinity.

Does this mean that I have "left the church"? This question follows me around in my work among Christians, and I am happy to answer it. I seldom "go to church" because I have become weary of the patriarchal shape of liturgy and mainstream Christian theology even in relatively liberal, justice-loving denominations like the Episcopal Church. Attending church usually wears me down and depresses my own best energies. So I seek to find or build community, essential as a relational basis for life itself. I find community wherever I can, sometimes through Christian churches and other religious organizations, but often through the NAACP, the Democratic Party, and with other writers, horse people, musicians, friends and neighbors, Christians and others, who yearn and work for a more justice-loving society and world. Whatever the context and community, I am still a Jesus-person, an older white woman who loves the story of the man from Nazareth whom I experience as a brother and friend, and whose sacred Spirit does indeed "walk and talk" with me, as the old hymn affirms.

I am shaping this book in a loosely sketched chronological order and employing Trinitarian images because a rather traditionally shaped— although liberal, feminist, LGBTQ, and liberationist—Christian faith has provided the basis for much of my life personally and professionally. It has been interesting to study my own life, as well as aspects of the world and God, through the lenses of the Trinity. As you move along through these pages, perhaps you will be able to connect your life experiences with mine and catch glimpses of the Sacred as She shapes our lives in relation to the world around us.

Part one is a bittersweet exploration of my early years, the childhood years, in which I found meaning in relation to God as Father. I do not mean that Jesus and the Spirit were absent from the first thirty years of my life any more than that the experience of God as Father or Mother or Parent has played no role in the last four decades. My faith is rooted in an ever-deepening belief that the relationality of God has permeated my life and the life of the world, from beginning to end. Part one is intended both to tell stories about God that correspond, roughly and imprecisely, to my own childhood and young adulthood, and to challenge the patriarchal authority projected onto God as "Father" for over two millennia of Christian history. I am suggesting in this book, and especially in part one, that the image of God as Father is steeped in our childhood as a human race and as Christians. I am hoping not to be harsh, but I do believe that we humans need to grow up.

Part two presents some images of Incarnation. As a Christian doctrine, "incarnation" historically has referred either solely or primarily to the Incarnation—the in-flesh-ment—of God in the man Jesus of Nazareth. For many decades, I have focused my own theological work on helping expand our understandings of incarnation so as to include all humans and other creatures, each and all of us bearers of God and able "to god"—to participate in the ongoing movement of God in making right, mutual relation throughout the whole creation. In part two, I offer thirteen images of incarnation, snapshots of how I have experienced God as embodied in people, movements, events, and creation itself.

Part three is intended to illuminate the movement of the Spirit, who is bursting open many categories and assumptions that have shaped our lives and grounded the work of theologians and religious leaders. The Spirit is never finished with us, even when we die. Part three is meant to suggest the ongoing, eternal movement of God the Spirit through and beyond the cosmos as we know it (or imagine we do). Part three has been a challenge to write—more truthfully to *stop* writing—because just when I've been ready to turn this manuscript in for publication, something else happens in the world, the nation, or my own life, that illuminates what, I believe, the Spirit is moving us to do, or not to do, at this time in our life together.

At the beginning of each of the three parts is a brief theological reflection on the Trinity—Father, Son, Spirit. Those who wish not to be bothered with thinking about the Trinity can easily skip these introductory pieces and move on. Those who share my curiosity about how the Christian Trinity has come into being and what differences, for better and worse, it has made in the lives of Christians over two millennia might want to read the pages at the beginning of each part.

About this book and the 2016 election in the United States: I finished the first draft in late summer 2015 and *She Flies On* was accepted that fall for publication in 2017. This gave me time to take care of editing and notes and to revise the manuscript. What I could not have anticipated was the terrifying, turbulent character of the presidential race, its debates and primaries beginning just about the time I submitted the first draft to the publisher. Much less had I imagined the results of the election.

Interestingly, Trump's election notwithstanding, something had become apparent to me as I set out in the fall 2016 to revise the early draft: without much revision at all, part three already explored a number of the most important issues and disturbing dynamics being unleashed in the 2016 presidential race as well as down-ticket competitions. I had only to add a few words here and there to reflect the current—and ongoing—state of our life together in this nation and world and in our local communities. These dynamics, their roots and significance, infuse the shape and substance of the book in its entirety, not only part three.

*She Flies On* reflects the relational character of God as I have experienced Her dynamic spiritual movement. Traditional Christian theology refers to the basis of this sacred dynamic relational movement as the Trinity—Father, Son, and Spirit. This book tells you why, over the years, this androcentric language has seemed to me increasingly small, restrictive, and oppressive not only to women and girls, but also to men and boys, and to the Creator and Her glorious creation.

# Part One

## Through The Eyes Of A Child

Our birth is but a sleep and a forgetting:
The soul that rises with us, our life's star,
   Hath had elsewhere its setting,
    And cometh from afar.
   Not in entire forgetfulness,
   And not in utter nakedness,
But trailing clouds of glory, do we come
   From God, who is our home:
Heaven lies about us in our infancy.

—William Wordsworth,
from "Intimations of Immortality"[7]

# The Father

It's so simple—the Father—so utterly right, so powerful beyond words, an image reflecting deep-seated human yearning for One who is older and wiser to take care of us, to help us, to love us. The image of our Father God can convey much tender loving care. But this same image is also a projection of men's aspirations to control women and the world, an image of God that has done unspeakable damage to humans, especially women and girls, and other beings. Please hear me: It's not that the image of God the Father is wrong. "He" is just too small, too tiny, too limited an image of the Sacred. "He" is also too often, and too globally, violent as a social construct, functioning as a mighty theological and political tool of male domination and violence against women and children and even against the earth itself.

Of course, God the Father has always been presented by the liberal Christian communities in which I've lived and worked not as a literal description of God but rather as metaphor, a poetic way of imaging the unimaginable, that which liberal Protestant theologian Paul Tillich described as "God beyond God." My brother priest and friend, Presiding Bishop Michael Curry, reminds us of the Buddhist teaching that the word "God" must always be understood as the finger pointing at the moon, never as the moon itself. So too with the word "Father."

But let me be clear. When we speak of "God the Father," or pray to "our Father God," or lift up our hearts in Holy Communion to an "Almighty Father," this explicitly gendered image of the Sacred cannot be legitimized simply as metaphor, a finger pointing at the moon. Here is why: a basic course in the sociology of knowledge teaches that language is socially and historically constructed—formed on the basis of our very real lives as people in particular societies. In ancient as well as contemporary societies, "father" references the male head of family—the human family, the church family, our personal families.

Words carry power. "God the Father" is not simply language, because language itself is not simple. Words shape the world and our lives as people in the world. "God the Father" places maleness at the top of creation. The word "father" denotes the headship of creation and cosmos. This gendered language implies a divine order of creation, in which the male exercises headship over the female.

Recognizing the historic power of this "father" language, some of the most vitriolic and honest opponents of women's ordination in the Episcopal Church were 100 percent correct. They were neither exaggerating nor silly to insist, in the words of one male priest, "God is our Father, and so shall be His priests!" In the 1970s, many of us regarded this language as limited and sexist and, therefore, as silly but also dangerous. In the struggle for women's ordination, we could not dismiss it politically or spiritually, because it was hurting and diminishing women, men, and the church itself. I would have said, and I'm sure I did say at some point, that this sexist language, which reflected oppressive and cruel relationships between the genders, also diminished God, our Spirit of Life and Love and Justice. Sexism still functions in this way throughout the religions of the world, including Christianity. Male supremacy, buoyed by language about "God the Father" continues to batter women and girls throughout the church and all around the world.

I can think of no feminist, liberation, or liberal Christian theologian who has seriously argued that God as Father is in any way a necessary or even defensible theological construct. Yet, as recently as Easter Sunday 2015, I attended the Eucharist at my home parish where we reaffirmed our faith in God the Father. I stood and softly spoke words I most emphatically do not believe except in a limited way. Because this language carries such pain, alienation, and a history of such violence against women, the use of Father-language in worship is tantamount to participating in my own oppression and that of my sisters throughout the world—regardless of how other women might regard it.

More often than I care to admit, I have allowed myself to be seduced by the argument that when we say one of the ancient creeds or pray to our "heavenly Father," we are simply affirming our historic connections to those who have gone before, including generations of Christians who, over the years, have affirmed their faith in God the Father. Today, I would insist that indeed we are affirming our connections to a tradition of male domination and female subordination, all in the image of God.

But we might wish, today, to plead that in our prayers to our Father, we are standing with our brothers and sisters throughout the world who pray to the Father and, too often, are being slaughtered for their faith, alongside Muslims, Jews, and other faithful religious communities caught up in the horrific violence being waged at this time by practitioners of a wretched perversion of Islam. Make no mistake, ISIS, the Taliban, and other distortions of Islam are not rooted in the life and teachings of the Prophet but rather in the rage, violence, and confused identities of a generation of young men and women who also imagine that their deity is a sword-wielding Super-Man, quintessential Patriarch, Master of Control, Terror, and Fear.

So yes, I believe it can be argued, legitimately and compassionately, that we can, and even should, lift up our prayers in solidarity with our sister and brother Christians and with people of all faith traditions who are being persecuted for their faith. But it is not an either/or. Praying with other Christians does not relieve us of our responsibility to do whatever we can, in our own times and places—literally our churches and homes and throughout our lives—to un-mask an image of God the Father as the Male Head of a patriarchal family. That responsibility includes pointing out the connections to violence against those perceived to be a threat to power, whether Palestinian families in the West Bank having their homes bulldozed by the state, Coptic Christians in Egypt being beheaded by ISIS, European Jews still today targeted by neo-Nazis in the Netherlands, or disobedient daughters and gay sons in conservative Christian families and churches who are punished, disowned, or worse, here in the United States, in the name of God the Father.

# Falling into Good and Evil

In 1945, at the end of what is sometimes referred to by Americans as the "Good War," the Spirit of Love and Justice and Compassion for All had been battered and bombed, gassed and blown up, and torn all to pieces. It was a terrible time, filled with pain and sorrow, as war is always terrible and sorrowful. But, true to Her eternal form, God was being liberated and lugged on the shoulders of strong soldiers to Her new beginnings. And, somehow, in the midst of all this terror and hope, a whole bunch of human babies fell out of that universal womb into infancy on this terrestrial ball.

That is how it always begins for God, and that is how it began for me and all the other babies who arrived in 1945.

Over the years, some of the most vocal critics of feminist theology have read my work, and that of other feminists, as "narcissistic" because we use experience as a primary source for theology and because, in statements like the one above, it may appear that I, as one feminist theologian, am comparing myself to God.

But I ask you: Does any theologian or artist, any scientist or poet, any framer of words about anything under the sun, not draw on her or his experience as a primary basis for, and source of, her work? For example, in *The Emperor of All Maladies: A Biography of Cancer*, [8] Siddhartha Mukherjee draws extensively from his own experience—his perceptions and interpretations, his choices and opportunities and encounters—as oncologist, surgeon, researcher, and the particular person he is to help him make sense of one of the most devastating, challenging, and baffling phenomena in human history: cancer.

Ah, but you may ask, how then can we ever know the errors of our ways, our experiments, or our ideas about God or cancer or anything else if we base most of what we claim on our experience, or if our own judgment is the standard by which we measure truth and falsehood, good and evil?

This is a hugely important moral question.

The key here is that you are as important to my understandings of God and the world as I am. My experiences of matters of life and death include almost constant, interactive engagement with your experiences of such matters. This is as much the case for any relatively wise claims we might make about God as it is for the discoveries of research oncologists like Siddhartha Mukherjee, whose ongoing experience, personally and professionally, is forever being challenged, corrected, and sharpened by the research—and experiences—of others.

But still, am I comparing myself to God when I say things like, "That is how it begins for God, and that is how it begins for me" or, as in these pages, I suggest that we are called to learn how to see ourselves and the world "through the eyes of God"?

Most people, including theologians, take words literally rather than metaphorically. Many assume that, when we personalize God, when we attribute agency to "Him" or "Her," when we assume that God has power to act "like us"—to create, destroy, love, hate—we are actually imagining both God and ourselves chiefly as individual "persons." For example, we assume that, when we are being good, we bear some resemblance to a supernatural version of our human selves. Or we imagine that if we are learning to see the world "through the eyes of God," we are like school children imitating a wise teacher who has eyes like ours but also greater wisdom and who, therefore, can see more deeply and fully and further than our young, inexperienced eyes can see.

But God cannot be understood literally to look or think like us, to be made in our image, any more than we are literally made in God's image. The Sacred cannot be boxed into the limits of our imaginations. God is not a "person" like me or like you—nor is She unlike either of us. God is not a turtle, horse, rattlesnake, or blue spruce tree, either. He is neither like, nor unlike, any person, creature, or species. To speak of God as a father or a mother, a child or a teacher, a friend or an enemy, an animal or a plant, a rock or an ocean, or to refer to God as "Her" or "Him," does not mean, literally, that God is a supernatural person—like us, but bigger and wiser and invisible—or that God is any one of us.

When the German political theologian Dorothee Soelle contended, as she often did, that "God's hands are our hands in the world," she did not mean that God is some giant being with hands, or that she, Dorothee, was God, or that I am God, or that you are God in any static or absolute sense. Soelle was attempting to convey throughout her life as a poet, theologian, and activist that God does indeed act through us in the world to make justice and bring peace and that, in this way, we are all God-bearers to the extent that we make justice and bring peace.

My effort here is something very much like my friend Dorothee's. Neither she nor I have imagined ourselves to be better, or smarter, or closer to God than any other creature, and neither Dorothee nor I have imagined that there is any "God" who thinks that we are better, or smarter, or closer to God than any other earth creature.

To the contrary, the great Spirit of Life, our source of making justice-love and the root of our compassion, is not a giant human being with whom we, as individuals, can compare, much less identify, ourselves. This reality—the essentially collective, social, relational character of God—ought to prevent any of us from imagining that any *one* of us is God.

I am not God and neither are you, but neither are we "un-godly," because God is the Spirit moving between us, infusing each of us with an impulse to connect. God is the wellspring of our yearning to love, here and now and everywhere, forever and ever. This vibrant Spirit God was the ground of Jesus's being, as it also the ground of your being and mine.

So when I say that this is how it began for God and for me—as I came squeezing out of my mother's womb into life—I am neither comparing nor identifying myself with a personal God. What I am doing is what artists and poets do: suggesting metaphorically that the Spirit of Love is born again and again in times of great trouble and times of great joy.

As Elie Wiesel suggests in *Night*,[9] God is indeed the small, Jewish boy hanging on the gallows at Auschwitz, just as God was the young Jewish man hanged on a cross between two thieves. This same God was the Allied liberators who rescued prisoners from the Nazi death camps, just as She was the women who came to the tomb to pay tribute to their crucified friend and found that the tomb was empty.

And the two thieves, flanking Jesus, where were they in relation to God? In what sense were they also God? More challenging to our sensibilities—theologically and ethically—where in relation to God were the Nazi exterminators, Hitler, Eichmann, and those who followed their evil lead? These terrible questions about good and evil, about God and "the devil," will be lingering over these pages, much as they haunt our life together. I believe that any worthwhile theology is necessarily pressed by such questions to which, very often, our human imaginations have no answers.

As a sister concerned about good and evil in our common life and world, I am not saying that God is everyone in every moment, because there are surely people, events, and processes that are un-godly or evil in particular historical moments. I am not saying that God is, or is in, everyone and everything all the time. I am suggesting that God is never far away, never entirely absent from anyone or anything and that, even in relation to the most egregious human behavior, those acts and attitudes that are evil beyond dispute, God is only one heart-beat, one courageous creature, one movement for justice, or one well-placed word away. I am suggesting, moreover, that in God's eternal ongoing Spirit, evil is only relatively problematic because the darkness does not overcome the light, ever. How this can possibly be true is not ours to know or even to imagine at this moment, but I believe it to be true and deep in my soul, I know it is. I regard this as a terrible and sacred mystery.

I also believe that we humans need to be spiritually concerned with doing all in our power to feed the hungry, clothe the naked, shelter those without homes, welcome the strangers, care for the sick and elderly and those with special needs, set the prisoners free, become advocates for the earth, bring hope to one another and, in the prophetic words of the Hebrew prophet Amos (5:24), let justice roll down like waters, and righteousness like an ever-flowing stream.

To live this way, immersed in God's Spirit, is to live counter-culturally to the ways many of us have been raised in the United States, at least those of us who have benefitted from white privilege. To live in God—in right relation to one another and all others—we consciously commit ourselves to learning to work together, collectively involved in struggling for, and celebrating, the justice-love we are forging in our life together on this planet.

Because I am one person and you are another, it is easy for us to mistake the radicality and depth to which God, our sacred root, calls us. Throughout this book, I will be referring to God as our power to create, generate, or struggle for right or mutual relation whether we are individual people writing/reading a book or nations, races, religions, genders, cultures, or species.

One of my primary efforts in these pages is to call attention to the stunning, sparking presence and movement of the Sacred all around us, between us, and within each of us as we help shed light on forces of evil present in our life together.

Without regard for the evil and its ugliness, the vision of who we are in right relation to one another has always been—and will be forever—accessible to each and every gathering and person, regardless of our religious or spiritual traditions, insofar as we are open to this vision, to being drawn to it, and to sharing it. I submit that whether we are Christian or Jew, Muslim or Buddhist, Hindu or Sikh, pagan or "other," we can learn to see one another—and notice our shared worth and beauty—through the eyes of God.

This happens as we wake up and begin to see who we are, as sisters, brothers, siblings, on a shared journey. We notice that what makes us most deeply and honestly human is our capacity to share whatever is good and that, in this sharing—which is what it means to love one another—we are "godding,"[10] a word I use to promote an understanding of God as active verb (to god) rather than as a noun, much less a proper name.

Indeed, that is how it begins for God, morning by morning, and day by day, something womanist ethicist Katie G. Cannon would say[11]—and that is how it began for me, a kid in the mountains of North Carolina in the late 1940s and early 1950s.

# Kindness

From the outset, I was lavished with the beauty and goodness of the Spirit of Life and Joy. Each day brought wonder and adventure. Daddy and Mama and I had a fine time—just the three of us and the animals for the first six years—and a spacious yard around our small house in the mountains of western North Carolina. An apple orchard and raspberry bushes grew on one side, a field of wildflowers stretched as far as I could see in front of the house, and a thick woods lay beyond the creek that ran behind the house.

In this setting, I was raised on idealized expectations of what our life together should be: an opportunity to share kindness and goodness with each other. Cruelty and violence should have no place whatsoever. You might think that my surroundings would have left me unprepared for the evil in our midst. But they did indeed prepare me, probably as well as a child can be prepared, to begin to cope with the violence and terror that invariably shape our experiences as human beings.

I was introduced to God by parents who believed that He was a kind and caring Father—and God was a mighty "He" in those days. Yet there was never any overbearing emphasis on the maleness or masculinity of either Bob Heyward, "Daddy" to me, or the Father-God, who I must have assumed was somewhat like my daddy. Fortunately for my life—and religious assumptions—Daddy was a good model for a Father God. There was nothing harsh or authoritarian or abusive about my father. He was a good humored, modest, and kind man—exceptionally so, I would learn over the years.

Of course my father was not perfect. He lacked confidence in himself, probably because—as I would write decades later—he was a lousy patriarch[12] in a social, religious, and cultural context that expected men to throw their weight around. This was not Bob Heyward. He did not rule over us. The only way we could tell if he was angry was that, once in a blue moon, he'd say "damn it!" or bang his fist on the table and storm out of the room. Seldom was his anger directed at us kids. It was never directed at our mother.

The idea of any father—divine or human—who would hurt people or reject them was simply unthinkable. I suppose I heard the biblical stories about God choosing the people of Israel to drive out the

Canaanites, but I don't think it much impressed me. The God in whom I was learning to put my faith was an inclusive, caring Super Spirit who would always make space for everyone and every creature. I can thank my own father for helping plant in my young consciousness these early seeds of a universally loving Presence.

Decades later, one of my male colleagues at the Episcopal Divinity School would suggest, in all seriousness, that my sister-priest Sue Hiatt and I must have had "bad fathers," given how much we advocated inclusive language in liturgy. "What do you have against your fathers?" our colleague snapped. That night over supper, Sue Hiatt and I gave thanks to the patient Sophia who looked over us and prompted us to smile as we considered the depths of the theological misogyny and collegial stupidity of otherwise intelligent, affable men.

As a kid, I imaged Jesus much like a brother—older than me, but not too old to hang out with and play with. I figured he must have been a little bit like Luther, my mother's younger brother, eighteen years my senior and a most interesting guy, a journalist with an intense interest in the world. I adored Luther—"Unkie," I called him. I admired his spirit of inclusivity, his acceptance of so many different sorts of people. I also loved to hear him laugh his deep chuckle. Like my father, Luther would start telling a joke and then begin laughing at his own joke, unable to finish it.

In a family dominated by conservative Democrats and moderate Republicans, none of them very interested in politics, Luther stood out. In the early 1950s, he was a liberal and an outspoken Democrat. Luther thought everyone should belong to a political party. "How do you expect people to do what you want them to unless you work with them?" he would ask my parents. Luther was also respectful of "colored" people and of the people in Morocco, where he'd worked as a journalist. He seemed to think that people on the whole were excellent, intelligent, and worthwhile. I didn't know it at the time, but Luther apparently had little use for religion even back in the 1950s.

The main theological lessons I carried from these very early years was that God the Father was a wonderfully kind supernatural Spirit who loved, accepted, and welcomed every living creature and was glad each one of us was who and what we were. I learned that Jesus was God's son and a most interesting character, young and full of energy for life and that, like his father, he welcomed and affirmed everyone, including Africans like the ones Luther had met in Morocco and like the "colored" people we saw from time to time in our town but didn't seem to know very well, except for one or two like Bessie, who helped Mama take care of me, and Jeff, who helped Daddy take care of the yard.

But what about Mama? Was I learning that my mother was like God or that God was like my mother? And myself, a girl child—was I like God? Was God like me? Could I ever be as much like Jesus as a boy or a young man like my uncle could be? I doubt that these gendered questions surfaced in my child's mind, though a couple of decades later, my mother told me that I'd told her and my father that I thought I might be a priest when I grew up. They had to tell me that this wouldn't be possible because only boys could become priests. I have no recollection of that conversation or of having any thoughts or feelings about my gender, or God's, when I was a very young child.

However, gender assumptions don't need to be spoken very often to take hold.

Simply through the experiences and observations of being alive, reinforced by historical and cultural precedence, I was surely learning that my father and my uncle were more like God and Jesus than my mother or me, even though I knew that my mother was one of the most loving human beings on earth.

I grew up in what I once would have described as a moderately conservative Christian family, but I have come to realize that mine was an unusually open-minded and socially progressive white Christian family in the US South. My siblings and I were taught by our parents that most humans are good, decent, loving folks, and that all of us—all people, with enough encouragement and support—can be kind and caring. There was never any question that the Heyward kids, all three of us—Carter, Robbie, Ann—were simply expected to be kind to all humans and animals, period.

The conservative dimensions of our social and religious upbringing had much to do with sexuality (especially for girls and women, of course) and with basic customs of Southern etiquette—saying "yes ma'am" and "yes sir," not using bad words, helping older people, especially women, lift things and making a place for them at the head of the line, and reluctantly accepting—without really approving of—social segregation by race and class. Never, however, were Robbie, Ann, and I taught that Christians had any hotline to God, or that the Bible was the only "Word of God," or that the Bible must be taken literally, or that you had to "accept Jesus Christ as your Lord" to be "saved." For that matter, nobody ever said anything to us about "being saved." Thank God.

I was an Episcopalian, and still am, in the broad streams of Anglican tradition, which are basically universalist. By universalist, I mean an assumption that God loves all humans and creatures, without exception, and that no one has to be a Christian or a member of any other religious tradition in order to be chosen by God because we all are chosen, simply that. This spiritual universalism was planted very early in my life. Its seeds were not primarily in what I was being taught at church about Jesus or God, but rather in what I was learning at home about the worth of human beings and creature beings. If God had been given any other name by my parents, it would have been kindness.

In this world of human kindness, evil was quite the exception. When I was three or four, I tripped and fell on the new puppy, my Christmas present. I was startled, then mortified, to see that the puppy was dead—and because of me. My first experience of death. My parents were sad, not angry. They assured me it wasn't my fault, and that I had done nothing wrong because I had not meant to do it. I remember it as a deeply sad moment and, even now, when I think of it, my body trembles. Me, killing a puppy.

Still, I believed my parents, who were clear that if something was an accident, like my killing the puppy, it wasn't evil or even wrong. It was just very sad. My father and I buried the puppy in the back yard and he told me that that before long we would get another puppy. We did, and except for the decade and a half when I was in college and graduate school, I have always had dogs, creatures who have been among my close friends. Other animal lovers know how deeply true this is.

As I grew up, I would learn that philosophers sometimes refer to death and loss and accidents as natural rather than as social or moral evil.[13] It would take a book to begin to explore this distinction. For our purposes, let me say clearly that the death of the puppy, like the falling of leaves each year, is not evil in any moral or ethical sense. I think it is not evil at all but simply a dimension of life that reflects the sadness that all humans and other animals as well experience in the course of our lives.

It's just as well that most parents try to protect children from realizing the amount of death, loss, and sadness woven into the texture of human and creature life and, I have come to believe, woven also into the texture of God.

# Evil All Around

But social or moral evil—to my way of thinking, real evil—was around, lurking nearby. In discussing evil, I mean something quite distinct from the death of the puppy. I mean something that is neither accidental nor natural, and something that moves us beyond sadness. Over the years I've come to believe that evil is not the absence of God, but rather is an assault on God. Evil batters Love, rapes Sophia/Wisdom, violates whatever is kind or compassionate or vulnerable. Evil executes the Sacred and wages war against God's Spirit, time and again throughout history.

There is only one solution to evil—one gift common to us all—by which we can struggle, often with remarkable power, to crush or transform the evil in our world: Love, the healing, liberating force that many of us call "God."

Many may recognize love simply as kindness, compassion, patience, or any number of other spiritual gifts, because Love, God, the Sacred takes many forms, from one situation to another. In a very real sense, the God who is Love is an eternal shape-shifter. The moment we think we have the right word or image or picture of God, the view shifts. We are likely to be thrown off balance because God suddenly is somewhere we weren't expecting, and we may not recognize Her, or Him, or It.

When I was about four or five, my best friend Elliott told me her cousin Wimberly had been murdered, shot by her jealous boyfriend. I had never before heard of murder. I must have sensed, or been told, that this was a terrible thing, this murder. It was my first recognition of evil at a personal level, something that can happen to people like Wimberly, Elliott, or me.

I doubt that it occurred to me that evil was something I could do to someone else. I imagined that evil was an awful stranger who could do horrible things to people, like murder them, and want to and mean to. There was nothing accidental about evil. In my childhood, *Grimm's Fairy Tales* was my best sourcebook for imagining evil—the wolf eating Little Red Riding Hood, the witch trying to eat Hansel and Gretel, Cinderella's nasty stepsisters trying to do her in.

I might also have learned something about evil if anyone had read to me the parts of the Bible that detail ways in which the faithful people of God treated their enemies: slaying them, showing no mercy, and willing to kill their own children to please God—e.g, Abraham's willingness to sacrifice Isaac, Jepthhath's actual sacrifice of his daughter. All of this wickedness was done at the behest of a supposedly good God. Without realizing the anti-Jewish character of their accusations, Christians are likely to say, well, but that was the "Old Testament God." Not so fast. Jesus was himself a devoted Jew who believed in this very same God's word. Although mostly portrayed as a man of love, forgiveness, and compassion, Jesus was no stranger to outbursts against unbelievers and even, on one occasion, we are told, in a fit of anger because it produced no fruit, cursed a fig tree at the side of the road, causing it to wither and die. (Matt. 21:18–22)

But it would be in the wider, broader social realm of life that I would find myself falling into the snares of evil.

From as far back as I can remember, I had known that something was wrong with the way white people treated "colored" people. I also had figured out that I was part of the problem, because I had hurt our maid Bessie when, in her presence, my best friend Elliott and I had sung the jump-rope jingle: "eenie meenie minie mo, catch a nigger[14] by its toe  . . . "Bessie left work that day, and I never saw her again. To this day, I wonder where she went and what she told her family and friends. I have thought from time to time about trying to find her, but then I never knew Bessie's last name, since she was "colored" and I was white and it was 1949 in North Carolina. There it was—evil, huge and heavy, bearing down on a young black woman, hurt and angry, and a little white girl, baffled and becoming aware of my own involvement with evil. I was about four at the time.

Yet this act was accidental too, wasn't it? Did I mean to hurt Bessie any more than I meant to kill the puppy? Of course not, so what was the difference? Why would one be evil and the other not? I wouldn't have made a distinction when I was a child, but I do now.

Falling on the puppy and killing it was an accident and a terrible event for me, my parents, and the poor puppy. It was a sad day, but it was not evil. It had no moral implication. The hurtful jingle, however, with the word "nigger" in it, was a cultural carrier of the evil of slavery and its ongoing effects through Jim Crow. In singing this rhyme, I was perpetuating the legacy of white racism. Though I didn't understand what I was singing, or why it was wrong, I was, even at a very young age, mouthing evil.

As in the puppy incident, I was innocent in that I didn't intend to do anything hurtful to anyone. But later, especially in my work with colleagues of color, I would learn the difference between intent and impact,[15] which has helped me think about this childhood incident with Bessie and the "n" word. My intention was innocent enough. Regardless, the impact of the incident was obviously hurtful to Bessie and an early wake-up call to me. My parents never discussed this event with me—I never knew what, if anything, Bessie told them other than that I had hurt her feelings. All I knew at the time, and all I know now, is that Bessie had been hurt by my action, my words. My parents told me this, and I believed it and felt sad and guilty, because I had not intended to hurt anyone.

This was my first lesson about the important, critical difference between intent and impact, a lesson still lost on many of my brother and sister Americans who insist that they are not racist or sexist or homophobic or whatever regardless of the impact of their actions and words. Through this early incident and its impact on me, as well as on Bessie, I had stepped into the adult world of morality—questions of good and evil—and had glimpsed my own ability to dabble, through innocence and ignorance, in evil.

Around this same time, when I was about five, I watched through the glass panes in the front door as the sheriff shot over the head of our yardman Jeff and forced him to run down the road for his life. I had told my mother that Jeff had touched me between my legs in exchange for prizes from Cracker Jack boxes, and my father had called Sheriff Keeling, who had come and told Jeff that if he ever came back into the county, he would be "one dead nigger."[16] Years later, I heard that Bill Keeling, the sheriff, had shot himself. Gunshots and evil in the air, then as now.

Sometime around 1950, I was joined by an imaginary playmate. I named her "Sofie Couch" and insisted she have a place at our family table for meals, so my mother would set out a placemat for her. Sofie was a little colored girl, my age. She and I hung out together quite a bit in those days. I don't really remember what we discussed, but I imagine we talked some about Bessie and Jeff and Sheriff Keeling. I do remember that, sadly, Sofie didn't go to kindergarten or first grade with me. I remember excitedly telling her what I was learning in school, without any awareness of the racial significance of the segregation—even in my imagination—that would have kept her out.

That was what I knew about evil by the time I was six: a tale of murder, two tales involving guns, the ubiquitous presence of racism and segregation, though, in 1950, I had not heard these words—"racism," "segregation"—and my own sense, as a child, of being part of the problem.

I also, of course, had begun to learn something about sexual abuse through Jeff's having molested me, another manifestation of evil, then and now. I recall being horribly upset as I watched Sheriff Keeling shoot at this "colored" man and heard him shout over and over "you nigger" as Jeff ran for his life. The awful racism in that moment was what made it so evil in my mind.

As for the sexual abuse, my mother told me it would be best if we never talked about it. But I did talk about it—with my friend Elliott and with Sophie Couch. And I've talked about it over the years from time to time. It was not a source of trauma in my life—not like Bessie walking away or Jeff being shot it—but I was aware in my body and soul that something bad had happened.

I am clear, however, about several things regarding Jeff's abuse of me: it was unfortunate that my parents didn't want me to talk to them about the incident, because they could have told me what I had to figure out on my own: that what had happened to me should not have happened, that Jeff was wrong, that it was not my fault, and that this bad experience could be left behind and did not have to shape the rest of my life.

Except for these few memorable events, I had a mostly storybook life as an only child for six years, then as a big sister to two babies. Playing with and helping care for the dogs, befriending a black snake, catching crawfish in the creek by the house, snacking on apples with Elliott as we sat munching in our tree house, flying on foot through the meadow pretending we were horses. I was a golden palomino and Elliott was a black stallion, even though she was a girl. All of these adventures I shared with Elliot and other kid-friends, with Sophie Couch, and with the animals, and the babies, Robbie and Ann, when they arrived.

# Death

As for death, it was there, too, and not just the death of the puppy or Wimberly's murder. Every night, often with one or both parents kneeling beside me, I prayed, "Now I lay me down to sleep, I pray the Lord my soul to keep. If I should die before I wake, I pray the Lord my soul to take." I remember laughing with other kids as we tried to figure out who "If-I-should-die" was, imagining it was some funny lady! I was taught to pray this every night and for years I did, believing that there was a part of me—my soul, which I guess I thought was something like the angel part—that would go to heaven to be with God when, or if, I died. It was more an *if* than a *when* because the possibility of my dying seemed utterly unreal and remote.

I'd heard of a man drowning in a lake when his car plunged into it. Rainbow Lake was not far from our home in Hendersonville, North Carolina. To this day, when I drive into Hendersonville, I wonder about that lake, which I've never been able to find, and that man. Obviously, the story impressed itself on my child's mind—making me somewhat leery of big bodies of water into which a car, or a person, might fall and disappear.

The only other death I'd heard about in the early 1950s was of a child my own age, my cousin Lexie, who, in my mind, lived very far away, in Pennsylvania. I had never met Lexie, but I knew that his mother, Isabel, my mother's first cousin, had a little boy my age. I had seen his picture and knew who he was when the accident happened. Lexie had been killed when the body of an old car fell on top of him while he was playing. The way I remember this story, which my mother told me, is that Isabel had leapt through a window and singlehandedly lifted the car off of her little boy. My sister remembers this story differently and probably more accurately. She recalls that Mama told us that cousin Isabel had watched a man lift the car off of her little boy. In either version, this dramatic event—tragic and heroic—had made quite an impression on me when I was five or six. Even Lexie's death, however, seemed far-removed from my life in the rolling Blue Ridge Mountains of western North Carolina.

I had never personally known anyone who had died, and in those days—late 1940s, early 1950s—we didn't have television shows or movies in which we might see a dead body lying on the ground or watch someone get shot or get sick and die. I suppose my first "sight" of a human death was in the early 1950s when we got our first television set, watching cowboys shoot each other, or shoot Indians, on shows like *The Lone Ranger*. In my child's mind, human death remained a fantasy, like a movie.

And, indeed, a few years later, two fleeting, exciting, and terrible images of death bounded into my childhood consciousness on the big screen. The year was 1954, I was nine years old, and the movie was Hollywood's spectacular 1939 adaptation of Margaret Mitchell's *Gone with the Wind*. Even though, on the screen, soldiers were falling everywhere in battle, the first death to hit me hard in this film was little Bonnie's, when she fell from her pony and was killed. I remember this scene vividly, probably because Bonnie was a girl about my age who loved animals. But I remember with a much greater emotional urgency the scene in which the weeping black "Mammy" reports to "Miss Scarlett" that "Mister Rhett done gone and kilt that poor pony!" To me, the violent death of the pony, not shown on screen, but simply reported by Mammy, was the single most horrifying and memorable image of death up to that point in my life. I took that memory with me from *Gone with the Wind* and, at least a decade before I began to think about the racialized meanings of the story and its presentation, I loathed Rhett Butler for having "kilt that poor pony."

Looking back, I think this was an early moment in my life in which I connected death with human-waged, intentional violence, not accidental and not simply a mistake, but a choice and a moral problem, the fact and presence of evil in the world. Following by several years the murder of Elliott's cousin Wimberly, Hollywood reinforced the connection in my mind between evil and violence and death.

*Gone with the Wind* notwithstanding, like most white middle-class kids in 1950s United States, I was sheltered from many experiences and images of suffering and death. No war, no violence, no serious illness crossed my path. The first death of someone I actually knew was my Granddaddy Heyward in 1960. I have no recollection of how he died, except that he had been sick. He lived on the South Carolina coast, at Myrtle Beach, where he was a fisherman. My parents, siblings, and I lived several hours' drive away in Charlotte and, throughout the

1950s, we had visited Granddaddy and Etrulia, his second wife and our step-grandmother, every year. Neither Granddaddy nor Etrulia were especially warm or emotionally forthcoming, so my siblings and I did not feel close to our paternal grandparents. Still, we liked them and knew that they liked us and always welcomed us into their home in Myrtle Beach. Etrulia always had a fresh lemon pound cake, a Heyward favorite, waiting on the kitchen counter for our arrival.

When Granddaddy Heyward died, none of us Heyward kids attended his funeral, even though, at fifteen, I was certainly old enough to understand that my father's father, my grandfather, had died and that funerals and the big lunch or reception that routinely follows, at least in the US South, are when folks come together, as family and friends, to say goodbye to someone who has been important to them, to share stories and feelings, and to help each other come to terms with this death. Daddy's father and Etrulia, whom Granddaddy had married when our father was still a small boy, had both been extremely important to him. That in itself might have been enough to warrant the three Heyward children's attendance at the funeral of their father's father.

But in those days, there was a prevailing notion that children should be spared from knowing much, if anything, about death—its sadness, finality, inevitability.

I can almost hear my mother's voice, "Children should be allowed to be children." Throughout her long life, Mary Ann Heyward epitomized innocence. She described her own childhood as happy, even exuberant, and she believed strongly that the less negativity humans are exposed to, the better. I think of Mama every time I put on a "Life is Good" t-shirt, because that pithy slogan pretty much sums her approach to each new day, in which death has no good place, and evil, even less.

Cushioned by childhood innocence and a mother renowned for her optimism, connected somehow to a denial of death and evil, and shielded by being white and middle-class from the systemic violence waged against those black or brown or poor, I approached adolescence without much fear of—or preparation for—suffering and death. Such difficult experiences seemed to me far away and mostly unreal, the stuff of history or fiction.

For me as a child, God was perfect, and I loved Him. I loved Elliott and Sofie and the animals and my parents and the babies when they arrived. I loved Jesus and St. James, patron saint of the local Episcopal church, which was covered with ivy and had stained glass windows and was a quiet place to sit and think.

In my spiritual imagination, God would always be there, taking care of us, everyone, all people "red and yellow, black and white" though I don't think I knew who "red and yellow" people were and we did not call "colored" people "black" in those days. But I knew, definitely, that God was taking care of all people and all other creatures too, including the turtle and dogs and the shiny black snake who slithered around in the grass at our feet.

I had learned in church and at home that God was our Father, but I intuited that God was also a Spirit in all of us, earth and plants and animals and people. That seemed obvious. I trusted my parents and the priest and teachers at church who taught that God was our perfect Father but also, throughout my life, especially when outside, I experienced a Spirit much closer, a vibrant energy animating every rock and person.

I have some memory of knowing full well at age six that God the Father did not like the way we white people treated colored people, and I knew that it shouldn't be this way. I was shocked and horrified by evil, including my own involvement in cruelty to other humans, like Bessie and Jeff.

To this day, I remember believing deep in my little girl bones that somehow, someday, some way, the God-energy that was all around, the Spirit in the land and humans and other creatures, would swell up and take charge and make everything good and beautiful and happy for colored people as well as white people.

# Cold War

On Easter Sunday, 2015, I went to church with my beloved friend, Brownie troop leader, and "second mom" Ann Elliot, who was almost ninety-five. I sat beside her eldest child, JoAnn, and several of Ann's other family members, in the first pew at St. Martin's Episcopal Church in Charlotte, the church where I had spent much time during my teen years, following my family's move from the mountains back to North Carolina's largest city. Sitting in the pew, I glanced left and there, reminding me of those days a half-century before, hung the old St. Martin's banner, which I had helped to make, the iconic symbol of a cloak split down the middle by St. Martin of Tours so it could be shared with a beggar. The banner is still standing there near the sanctuary, still bright and evocative. It made me smile. I bowed my head and listened to the string quartet play Mozart before the festive processional.

As I sat there, my mind wandered back to earlier times at St. Martin's, when this church had been a refuge for me as a teenager. The Easter service—with its glorious music and traditional prayers to the Father and Son—spun me back to the late 1950s and my adolescence in a world in which I had not been an easy fit. As my anxieties had deepened in my teen years and I wondered where I belonged, if I belonged anywhere, my theology had become more conservative, largely as a coping mechanism. By age sixteen, in 1961, I was an ardent Episcopalian, accepting Christianity's patriarchal roots. God the Father and Jesus Christ His Only Son our Lord had become lifeguards for me—and the church a mighty fortress from a tsunami of race, class, and, primary for me at the time, gender confusion.

In order to better understand this movement in my life and faith as a young teen, let's travel back even further in time to the culture of the Cold War, in the early 1950s, which had begun to shape my generation's lives and spiritualities not long after the end of the Second World War. Although I had never heard his name in our home or church, Senator Joseph McCarthy of Wisconsin had lurked like a giant predator in the background of the whole society in the early 1950s. Later I would learn that McCarthy had equated communism with an un-godliness that, he had insisted, was threatening to topple not only the political system of the United States but also its moorings in God.

I don't recall anyone around me ever mentioning McCarthy and I have no personal memory of his damaging deeds, but he was there in our midst in the 1950s and his fear-based presence filled the air. My generation was shaped by the culture of this Cold War—at least we white, middle-class, Christian kids in the US South. We were breathing in a doctrine of anti-communism stronger than anything we could possibly have been learning at home or church to help us temper or reject it.

Much like terrorism stirs our fears today, the widespread fear of communism and hatred of our communist enemies was in the air in the 1950s. We needed to be afraid of Russians and any communists who might be hiding here in the United States. I didn't know any communists, at least I didn't think I did, and I really didn't want to know any.

By the time I was ten or eleven, I was an ardent anti-communist, and this was in no small part *because* I was enthusiastically pro-God. Somehow the connection got made: Communists are atheists. For me, as a child, they were linked: Christians were anti-communist. I was anti-communist, because communists hated God, right? It would never have occurred to me that this was largely propaganda being manufactured by politicians and military leaders who needed people to fear and hate communists.

A few years earlier, in 1952, as a seven-year-old, I had favored Adlai Stevenson for president and taken his part in a debate in my second grade class. Like my mother, I argued that Mr. Stevenson's being divorced should have nothing to do with his being president and that he was smarter than "Ike," the patriotic general, who was my father's favorite. Thanks no doubt to my uncle Luther and his older sister, my mother, Mary Ann, I was on my way early toward becoming a good Democrat if, in those days, a cautious one. By the time I was nine or ten, God appeared to me more and more like a good, patriotic, American man: thoroughly anti-communist, culturally conservative (rather prudish), a gentleman, the man in charge. When Congress added the words "under God" to the Pledge of Allegiance on Flag Day in 1954, I was all for it!

The Cold War was ubiquitous in the early to mid-1950s. With its symbolic fallout shelters that would have saved nobody from a nuclear attack, its message was that, in the United States, patriotism and Christian faith were, together, the key to our goodness and power as a nation and to the health and happiness of families and individuals—and that all this goodness was under attack simply because communism existed in Russia and maybe other places, too. This gung-ho "America and God" rhetoric met us everywhere—in school each day, where we said the Pledge of Allegiance and prayed together—Christian prayers, I am quite sure—and on television which, by the mid-1950s, was becoming a staple in white middle-class homes.

My own family was not intensely patriotic or religious, but moderately so. I have no recollection, and neither do my siblings, of either parent being especially concerned about communism, though they cared about both God and country. They were good citizens and good Christians—low key, without any major investment in raising their children to be especially patriotic or religious, though they no doubt assumed we would be proud Americans and they surely hoped we would be good Christians. There was also no question that being kind had more to do, for Bob and Mary Ann Heyward, with being good Christians (or Jews, or whatever people were) than with being especially patriotic.

We prayed together most mornings at breakfast—"family prayer," my parents called it—which I usually enjoyed, unless I was in a hurry to get to school. Our prayers were open-ended and suggestive, never dogmatic or preachy. They strengthened my assumption that God was in charge and that communists and other evil people would not get us. For the most part, I didn't think too much about it or worry about it. A white, middle-class, Christian kid, I felt safe everywhere—at home, school, church, and outside doing cartwheels with my friends, running around after my toddler siblings, and helping care for our dogs.

As a salesman for Esso, my father was transferred from time to time. We moved in 1954, when I was nine, from the mountains of North Carolina back to Charlotte, where I'd been born and where my maternal grandmother, Nana, lived. Charlotte was one of the largest cities in the South at the time, with a population of about three hundred thousand. We no longer lived in a rural setting with fields and woods all around. I badly missed the outdoors, the amazing creatures and daily opportunities to revel in nature. In the 1950s, my parents purchased several different modest ranch-style houses. Like many white middle-class families, we moved a couple of times even within the same city into somewhat larger houses each time, as we kids were growing and taking up more space.

When I was in the sixth grade, in 1956 we moved to Paw Creek, a rural setting in a tiny community near Charlotte, where Daddy had become the superintendent of an oil storage facility. I was delighted to have lots of yard and space to run around as well as two new adopted dogs, "Esso," a German shepherd who guarded the storage facility, and a small stray whom daddy named "Extra." Plus our parents gave us a tiny yellow duck, "Peppy," as an Easter present. Within a year Peppy had grown large and white and feathery and followed us kids everywhere, inside the house and out. One Sunday our family took the grown duck Peppy to a lake in a popular park in Charlotte and left him there to join the other ducks. I remember all three of us Heyward kids berating our poor father on the trip home for making us give up our pet duck, even though I knew deep inside that Daddy was right— Peppy needed to be in a place where she, or he, could be a duck. Life in Paw Creek, basically a country crossroad, was an adventure for our family, especially the three kids. It was a very good time for me since, from my earliest childhood days in the North Carolina mountains, I had developed a preference for country living.

Less than two years after moving to Paw Creek, we moved back to Charlotte when our father was transferred again by Esso. In each new place, in four different elementary schools between first and sixth grades, I thoroughly enjoyed school. I made friends easily, was an excellent student, proud to bring home almost straight As on each report card, and was a talented athlete—excelling in softball, kickball, acrobatics, and running. I could hit home runs, catch flies, stand on my head, walk on my hands, do back flips, and outrun most of the other girls— and boys. I was tall for my age and sturdy, never very shapely and not at all feminine in style. I was a tomboy through and through. I adored my life as a kid, up until my early teens.

# Gender Confusion

By the time I was eleven or twelve, however, the comforts and charms of my childhood were coming to a close. The spirit of the confident, happy little girl had begun to crack apart in ways invisible to others and largely to myself. I was still a good student, smart and athletic, who loved family, friends, animals, and God. But I was also an awkward pre-teen, feeling ugly and unattractive, with big buck teeth and braces, an acned face like most of my friends, and a tall, sturdy body, more androgynous than most girls my age. I was torn between wanting to fit in—to be a pretty teenage girl, popular with boys—and eager to get away from the whole damn thing, wanting no part of it.

This was when the binging and purging set in. Psychologists would name this disease bulimia and look for a cause, often blaming it on early childhood sexual abuse. But I have always assumed that bulimia for me had little if anything to do with having been touched inappropriately by Jeff the yardman when I was five years old and everything to do with being an androgynous girl who felt like a misfit as I entered my teens.

Not surprisingly, I think, this was the moment—pre-adolescence—when I turned earnestly to a traditional, Anglo-Catholic understanding of the Trinitarian God—Father, Son, and Spirit—for comfort and even salvation from being an ugly young female duckling who really didn't want to be part of the flock in which I found myself.

# Race, Class, Gender—An Unholy Trinity of Injustice

In childhood, I'd been confused and concerned primarily about racism, although the word was not much used among white folks in the 1950s. Why did white people apparently assume that we were smarter and generally "better" than colored people? How were we supposed to live this way and be good Christians? By the time I was six or eight, it had become apparent to me that white supremacy, by whatever name or no name at all, was most definitely not the will of God, whether God was our Father or more simply the Spirit of all life and goodness—my two childhood, and not entirely compatible, assumptions about God.

By the time I approached adolescence in the mid-1950s, I was still concerned but no longer confused about race. Clearly, white supremacy was wrong and it needed to be undone. I had no idea what to do about it, but I knew something should be done and I was ready in body and soul for the civil rights movement which was coming to a head. After all, Brown v. Board of Education had been decided by the Supreme Court in 1954 and, as an architect of the movement and one of its strategists, Rosa Parks had sat down on that Montgomery bus in 1955.

Similarly, as a young girl I did not understand how class functions in the United States nor did I grasp the extent to which both of my parents were suffering from class injustice and injuries. My father suffered—not greatly, I think, but chronically—from a sense of inadequacy in relation to my mother's more apparent class privilege. My mother always seemed to feel a bit inadequate in relation to some of her high school and college friends who had "married up" and who lived in the Myers Park section of Charlotte, in those days the primary neighborhood of huge old houses with gorgeous oak and elm trees lining the streets.

My parents' class injuries I would come to recognize more than a decade later, in the early 1970s, when Christian social ethics professor Beverly Harrison introduced us to *The Hidden Injuries of Class*[17] an assigned text in one of her courses. Meanwhile, in my preteen years, I enjoyed the class privilege that came my way—being sent to summer camp by my grandmother, taking horseback riding lessons, belonging to a swim club, eating out with my family in restaurants on a regular basis, going to the beach on family vacations, and being proud that my father's family had descended directly from Thomas Heyward, one of the signers of the Declaration of Independence. Not surprisingly, the Heywards failed to mention—in fact they probably didn't know—that my paternal grandmother, Othello Long, was a direct descendant of Anne Hutchinson (1591–1643) who, as punishment for her free spirited religious leadership among the Puritans, had been banished from the Massachusetts Bay Colony in 1638.[18] Ancestor, indeed!

As I entered my teen years, I was suffering from hidden injuries of class but without much cognitive awareness. I was experiencing some of the connotations of both race and class insofar as these dynamics were intersecting with gender assumptions; each reinforcing the other and giving it a particular shape. For example, I picked up cultural cues from white upper-class women and girls, and so aspired to be thin, well-versed in etiquette, and ladylike, yet not sexually active until I would marry "Mr. Right" someday, take his name, be his wife, and have his children.

This gender-script, feverishly reinforced by class and race, became chaotic and crazy-making for me. In relation to gender, my anxiety soared and my confidence plummeted. Throughout junior high school, I felt as if I had landed on an unwelcoming planet, distant from the beloved earth of my childhood. There was nothing "feminine" about me, and yet I was not a boy and had no desire to be. I just wanted to be myself, and I didn't seem to be a very satisfactory girl-self. I disliked the way girls dressed and I detested the unmistakable messages that we were supposed to be "young ladies," soft-spoken and polite in all situations and deferential to boys. Boys were expected—by parents, teachers, clergy—to be the leaders in every class, every sport, every game, every dance, all facets of life, as far as I could tell.

Good girls knew their place. If boys were involved, our place was always second. Boys had more fun. They could play sports and folks applauded; they could run around almost nude and folks cheered them on; they didn't have to worry about how they looked, at least not in the ways girls did; and they could ask whomever they wished to go do something fun, like have a picnic or even something un-fun like go to a dance. If you were a boy, the world was a welcoming place, or so it seemed to me. But I was stuck with being a girl and I despised being stuck in a gendered role. I hated not being able to do what boys do in the world, and I resented the fact that dressing more like boys (comfortably, casually, and skimpily) wasn't acceptable for girls at school, church, on the street, or at the beach. My style as a young teen, and to this day, was much more boyish and androgynous.

Had I lived my teens in a trans-world where people were open to an expansion of the gender binary, I might have lived more freely—crossing over back and forth between identifying primarily as girl, as boy, as both, or as neither. Or perhaps I'd have been delighted to be a girl in a non-gendered-scripted world, because the problem for me was not, then or now, about anatomical parts and how they fit together but rather the absurd roles that girls, and boys, were—and continue to be—socialized to play. In a world making space for greater gender imagination, I'd have resisted getting stuck in a gender category. If I'd had the confidence to make such a claim, and I dare say I would have in such a brilliant world, I'd have insisted that the transcendence of gender identities was truly, mind-bogglingly, an image of God! Looking back, I believe I'd have been not only right about both myself and God but profoundly and radically and wonderfully right.

However, at thirteen, I had no stronger desire than for some gender clarity. It was as if my life depended on my being clearly, unambiguously, one gender or the other. I was a girl. So in the midst of this dis-ease, as throwing up became a daily ritual, and dieting and exercising became routine, I sought refuge in four places—academics, sports, music, and church: I was just fine in my school work, though not in every subject. To this day I remember a comical looking skirt I made in a home economics class we girls were funneled into as ninth graders. My olive green skirt looked like a potato sack. I also failed algebra that same year—and why? I had always loved math but something in me was no longer letting me succeed in areas dominated either by girls (home economics) or boys (math and science). In sports, I was okay, though not as nimble and swift as I'd been as a kid, and, of course, nobody much cared about helping girls excel in sports. In music, I had some talent, almost none as a piano student, but I did like singing in the church choir and had a booming alto voice that would serve me well in high school musicals a couple of years later.

It was in church, more than anyplace else, that I took comfort in what I experienced as God's love. In church, I was happy just sitting or kneeling in the presence of our Father and His Son Jesus, the Christ, who took care of my spirit, assuring me that, regardless of how I felt, I was a much loved and very good person. As an Episcopalian, I was able to make a private confession on a regular basis—and tell the priest about my "sins," like binging and purging and "playing marriage" with another girl, with whom I first began to explore sexual touching at about age fourteen. No question, by this time, sin had become for me a problem associated with bodily pleasure—eating too much, making myself throw up, touching my own or my friend's breasts and enjoying it. When I did these things, I assumed I was doing something wrong, unpleasing to my Father God. I figured I was getting to know myself as a sinner.

Mr. Moore, my priest in the late 1950s, clearly liked and affirmed me and my two best friends, also Episcopalians who would make their confessions, too. In junior high school, all three of us were social misfits in one way or another. One of these girls was a musical prodigy who had no use for teenage nonsense and wanted to be a nun; the other was beautiful, but too smart for most boys. All three of us were unusually interested in religion and good in our school work. We formed a society, which we named the "Silly Scholars," and we celebrated Holy Communion with each other in my family's back yard, consecrating Vienna sausages and coconut milk as the body and blood of Christ.

As critical as I've become over the years of the patriarchal shape of Christianity and its theological foundations, beginning with its male-identified Trinity and its Father God, I cannot write an honest theological essay without acknowledging the extent to which I may personally owe both my personal anguish and my life to this ancient—though badly misshaped and mistaken—theological doctrine of a Father God and His Only Son our Lord Jesus Christ. I cherished and clung to this doctrine and, when I was fourteen, even "gave my life to Christ" at a Billy Graham rally in the Charlotte Coliseum.

So how can the doctrine of God the Father be both life-giving and death-dealing? How can patriarchal Christianity, or any male-dominated religion, save the life of a teenage girl who clings to it for emotional salvation from the confusion and anguish that the religion itself has generated? How, for God's sake, can an androcentric religious tradition that breeds leaders who sexually and spiritually abuse women and children dare to offer itself as a spiritual haven for anyone, especially women and children? What are we to make of a patriarchal deity who requires a girl's father—the mighty warrior Jephthath the Gileadite—to kill her in order to keep his promise to slaughter the first person to come out of his house when he returns home from war? (Judg. 11:1–40) What are we to make of a Father God whose love for the world has been shaped, doctrinally, around the violent sacrifice of his own child?

The fathers of the church and of every patriarchal religion on earth have much to answer for to the women and girls who inhabit this planet. We women have not been perceived by the fathers of these misogynist traditions as fully human beings, as much "in the image of God," and as deserving of freedom and choices as any of our fathers, or brothers. I am proud to stand with countless strong women in today's world.[19]

The problem with the Christian faith I practiced as a fourteen-year-old girl was not the kindly, accepting character of the Father God or His Son Jesus. The problem was that God, Jesus, and I were locked by gender role expectations and static historically-constructed images into something less than who we really are: I was yearning to be more than girls thought we could be, yearning to grow into a fuller stature of myself than I could imagine, given the terribly limited vocational and relational paths open to females. And poor God was surely yearning in Her mystical mysterious ways to be seen and known for who God really is and always has been. And Jesus? Surely His ongoing spirit yearns to be recognized as the Jewish brother and friend and lover of neighbor that He was in His own time and place.

I perceived the God of my teen years as a glorified male. He was experienced by me, as He is has customarily been experienced by Christians, in the image of ruling class men who, inverting the truth, have imagined themselves, and themselves alone, to have been created fully in the image of our Father God. While my one small life was being diminished by a religion whose God images are too small, the constrictions placed upon God have universal consequences, mostly damaging and damning to women and girls, but also damaging to all humans and to the earth and its many, varied creatures. Generation upon generation, the Creator of the Universe has been at best trivialized and more often cast out, even condemned, whenever She presents Herself as our mother or our Sophia, our sister or bigender sibling, our daughter or our lover.[20]

Moreover, whenever God pushes entirely beyond gender images and bursts forth as a star or swirls about as a storm or makes the ground shake as a herd of stampeding elephants or crawls through the grass as a turtle, Christians often nod and wink, affirming these images as colorful and creative, but seldom celebrating, much less worshipping, our sister and brother earth-creatures as compelling manifestations of the Spirit. Nor does it occur to many of us to imagine that God is literally, not only metaphorically, our power to generate right relation, mutuality or love, between and among ourselves.

If any of these God-images had been presented to me when I was fourteen or fifteen, I'd have been astonished. I might or might not have been open to recognizing and acknowledging the Sacred in any forms or images other than Father and Son and a rather bland Holy Spirit. No doubt, I would have been most receptive had such possibilities been raised by a priest or bishop, so under the sway was I of traditional Christianity and its spokesmen. As it was, God was my Father, and Jesus was His Only Son, our Lord and Christ, and the Holy Spirit was something of an afterthought, probably for church fathers like Origen and Augustine, definitely for me. My parents neither understood nor shared my intense devotion to the church and its very traditional teachings. It didn't worry them, however, because they saw no harm in it and, more importantly, because I seemed happy when going to church or returning home from making my confession or attending youth group.

My parents also didn't grasp the depth of my difficulty with matters of gender. They both tried to encourage me in every way they knew: Mama urged me to wear whatever clothes I wished and never suggested that I should be more interested in homemaking, cooking, sewing, typing, or other activities generally associated with girls. My mother was, however, concerned about my weight because, she said, I seemed unhappy with my size.

From high school to this very day, I have been a medium-sized person, neither larger nor smaller than most girls and women of my generation, culture, race, and class. Over time, I have been either "stocky," not obese, or sometimes rather thin, but never by the anorexic standards by which white middle and upper-class women and girls have judged ourselves and each other. In other words, I've been basically a healthy-sized, though never glamorously super-thin or shapely sized female throughout my life. I bring this up because, over the years, I have spent too much precious time worrying about, and even thinking about, being "too fat," a curse of patriarchal norms shaped by dominant-race and -class men and accepted by vast numbers of women.

My deeply caring mother was sincere in her advocacy of my well-being. The bottom line was this: Mary Ann Heyward wanted her kids to be happy. Like most other white middle-class mothers of teenage girls in the 1950s and 1960s, she assumed that happy meant thin, which many women of my generation recognize today as a dangerous assumption. However, since standards for female beauty are a foundation of a male-dominated, androcentric society, they continue to be set by men. In this white patriarchal society, thinness lingers on as a standard for female beauty, and girls and women continue to be beaten down physically, emotionally, and spiritually by this heavy measuring rod. In my teen years and early twenties, my sweet, non-patriarchal father seemed at ease with whatever size and shape I was and with whomever I seemed to be becoming, physically and mentally. Whatever I wanted to be, and with whomever, seemed okay to my father, although ten years later he would have fleeting misgivings about my having women lovers.

Because neither of my parents realized the depth of my distress, neither realized how badly I needed someone to help me become more fully myself. By the grace of God, someone appeared in 1960. That someone was Miss Betty Smith, who taught world history to tenth graders and who would become one of the most significant mentors and friends in my life. Betty Smith was, hands down, the best teacher I ever had at any level of schooling, and also, in many ways, one of the best priests, tapping the Sacred Spirit in me, which is what priests who are good at their jobs do. Miss Smith was in fact an Episcopal laywoman and, as far as I knew, not very churchy, which was helpful to me since it enabled me to realize how Spirit-filled a rather secular minded person could be. Even though she and I attended the same church, I didn't associate Miss Smith with church or religion.

Her gift to me was her faith in me, her faith in the real me, in all of my gender confusion and in all of my passion for racial justice and in all of my classroom questions about the state of the world. Why were the leaders of our country so worried about Fidel Castro? What did it mean that the United States was "the leader of the free world"? Who were we leading and what did "free" mean and how could we talk about being "free" given the situation of Negroes in our country? These were the kinds of questions Miss Smith encouraged and insisted that we wrestle with. For any reader who might assume, on the basis of such questions, that such a teacher would have been a liberal Democrat in 1960, think again. Years later, Betty Smith told me she had voted for Richard Nixon in the 1960 election. She was simply a very good, provocative teacher who dared her students to think outside the box.

One of my proudest moments was when I received an A+ on an essay I wrote on the Congo, in which I said that it seemed to me it didn't really matter whether the Congo became communist or capitalist; that it should become whatever might best help it feed and care for all of its people. "I want to congratulate you, Carter," Miss Smith wrote, "for daring to think your own thoughts in a world in which few do." An ecstatic fifteen-year-old, I ran home from the bus stop that afternoon waving my paper in the air to show Mama and, later, Daddy when he came home from work. They were proud and, like me, thought Betty Smith was about the best thing that had happened to me!

A dozen years later, after I had graduated from high school, college, and seminary, Miss Smith located me. She had married and moved away from Charlotte to Long Island and had been excited to read about the ordination of women in the Episcopal Church—and to see that one of those first women was me. She invited me to her home, which became the first of many visits between us over decades to come. We became fast friends and mutual advocates as women wrestling with forces of sexism and various forms of abuse and injustice in our own lives and in the lives of those closest to us.

One of our ongoing conversations was about God and the church. She had left the church because it had let her down years earlier by trivializing her experience of an abusive relationship with a man, a phenomenon common to women seeking counsel and support from male clergy. Betty Smith was extraordinarily interested in what I thought about God and how my mind had changed from my high school years when I had been such an earnest young Episcopalian. She was perhaps the first person to hear me talk about why, as a young teen, I had been so attached to a conservative and traditional understanding of God the Father.

When Betty and I met again as adults, in 1975, I was a newly ordained priest, a young feminist theologian, and a woman ready to do whatever I could—as priest, scholar, and teacher—to put the Father in his place, and the Son in his. Betty was thrilled about this evolution in my religious thinking. For four decades, until her death from cancer several years ago, Betty and I spoke from time to time of our shared desire to encourage women—mothers, sisters, siblings, daughters, students, clients, friends, and lovers—to step forward and take their rightful places as sources of, and participants in, the Sacred.

Looking back to Betty Smith's role in my life as a tenth grader, I see clearly that she, more than any other individual, brought God into my life by calling forth who I really was: a bright, inquisitive kid with a budding passion for justice and no desire or intention to be defined by gender. I was kneeling before my Father God in church and accepting Jesus as my Lord and Savior, and this was all well and fine. But all the while it was Betty who was blessing me most fully with the real presence of that which is most Holy, and it was she who set me on the path to becoming myself.

# Yearning for Mutuality/
# Yearning for God

In 1962, while I was a camp counselor, I developed a crush on the female director of the camp. When I told her about my feelings for her, she told me not to speak of this again, and she avoided being around me throughout the rest of the camp session.

That same year, the Episcopal bishop of the Diocese of North Carolina told me, and the other teenage officers of the Episcopal Young Churchmen, that we were being "disrespectful" of his authority in our insistence that the diocese integrate its camp, there and then, not later. Nine years later, in 1971, that same bishop turned me down for ordination as an Episcopal deacon because, he said, "You have an authority problem." Apparently at least one of my aunts agreed with this bishop. When my parents told Aunt Jo that I had stood up for integrating the diocesan camp and asked her not to brag about it, she exclaimed, "Brag? I'm ashamed she's related to me!"

In 1965, I went to see the movie *The Sound of Music* when it opened in Charlotte. I was twenty and, like countless young women and men, fell madly in love with Julie Andrews. Looking back, I know I didn't so much want to hold hands with Julie Andrews, even in my dreams, as to *be* the Julie Andrews who met me through the character of "Maria," a charming young woman who was yearning for love, for God, and for a better world.

About a year later, a college professor literally stopped speaking to me about anything, even materials related to the course I was taking from her, rather than risk talking with me about my sexual feelings for her. As with the camp counselor, I was yearning to be heard and instead was met with a silent, unmistakable, "Go away!"

At about this same time, in 1966, as a college junior, I began to take to heart the radical theologies of men like the heroic Dietrich Bonhoeffer, murdered by Hitler in 1945; the bold Anglican Bishop J.A.T. Robinson, whose small book *Honest to God* had stirred a controversy in the Episcopal Church in the late 1960s; and several of the American "Death of God" theologians. Like Bonhoeffer and Robinson, these men were not rejecting "God" per se but rather the notion of a "God above us" who rules over, or controls, us.[21] I didn't comprehend at the time that my strong attractions to these theologians—as well as to people like the counselor, the professor, and Julie Andrews; and to struggles for justice, like the integration of the camp—were rooted in my yearning for the Spirit of Mutuality. I was yearning to experience One who truly makes justice roll down like waters. Did I intuit that She would help move me beyond the patriarchal Father God of my childhood and early teen years?

# Yearning and *Kairos*: Experiencing "Time"

In order to understand our yearning for God, we need to look at the role of "time" in our lives and our yearning. We can't experience the many dimensions of God, Sacred Spirit, or ourselves if we imagine that we are trekking along a one-dimensional line from past to present to future. If this is how we experience "time," we are unlikely to be able to imagine ourselves, other humans, the creation, or God in the fullness of who any of us is, or of who we are as a global community.

In order to be able to notice the various aspects of ourselves—our physical selves, our minds, our dreams, our communities, our interests—and the Spirit that connects us, we must help each other look honestly at our lives in the *present*. We must also reach into the *past*, to draw strength from whatever has been and from those who have gone before us, and we must dare to imagine a *future* that is not here yet in order to imagine what we and those who come after us might become. This "tri-focal" spiritual vision—what was, what is, what will be—is only possible through an experience of *kairos*, God's time, in which our lives and our consciousness can open up into many dimensions of past, present, and future, sometimes all in the same moment, and in ways that move us beyond the empirical and rational.

Edward Schillebeecxk (1914–2009), a Belgian Dominican theologian, suggested that, in God, we meet and are involved with the future. In other words, God comes to us from the future. When I read Schillebeexck in graduate school, I couldn't understand him. His ideas seemed too heady and obscure, but I've come to imagine that, perhaps, Schillebeecxk knew something that eludes most Western Christians much of the time: we are living in several dimensions of time in every moment of our lives. In each moment, the past and future are mingled, which may be why we sometimes experience ourselves as dragged down and depressed or, conversely, buoyed and uplifted by energies we don't fully understand.

Looking back to my late teens and throughout my twenties, I spent a fair amount of my waking and probably my sleeping life as well in *kairos*—God's time—yearning for something I could not name: authentic

40

connection with those who represented in some way the "me" that I could be if I were living fully as myself, participating in mutually empowering relationships throughout my life—including past and future—both in my personal relationships and more impersonal, social, and distant relationships with people of other races and cultures as well as creatures of other species. Of course, it would be another decade or so—the late '70s and '80s—before I could begin to articulate this theologically, but this is what I was yearning for in my teens and twenties: to glimpse, and begin to generate, mutual relation with and in God, other humans, and other creatures, all involved—rolled up together—in our past, present, and future.

Such yearning always moves from some deeply human and divine place in us, our soul, where the most fully human/creaturely and the most fully Sacred energies converge and are one. The soul is the source of our yearning for God, our yearning to build more fully mutual relation with God and one another. This yearning transcends—cuts across—our religions, cultures, languages, nations, ages, politics, and genders. Perhaps our yearning for mutuality transcends even our species. I doubt we can know much about this cross-species connection except in relation to certain of our creature-companions with whom we relate as if they were like us—mostly other mammals, sometimes birds. But if we are paying attention to the integrity of the earth and sky, we can well imagine the mutually interdependent, interactive web of life in which we participate.[22]

Our souls are wellsprings in each of us—and our communities—from which we draw intuition that our life here on earth has many dimensions. In other words, we sense soulfully that there's more to each moment than we can see with the naked eye—more about ourselves and others, more about the world and God, more than the present time and place.

# *Kairos*: Where Augustine and I Disagree

One of the great architects of Christian theology was Augustine (354–430 CE), Bishop of Hippo, a town on the northeast coast of contemporary Libya. The Western Christian church has long celebrated his brilliance and faithfulness. In his forties, Augustine seems to have been yearning for God—a tale he recounts in his *Confessions* (397–400 CE). During what we might term a "midlife crisis," Augustine came to Christianity from the radically dualistic Manichean philosophy in which good and evil were eternally at war with each other. Rejecting this dualism, Augustine turned to a God whom he experienced as radically good and, through the resurrection of Jesus Christ, victorious over all evil—now and forever. God's victory over evil, Augustine taught as a young man, was both here and now, in the present world at the present time, and eternal—that is, in the future that awaits us in each moment and which, in the fullness of time, will be our eternal home, or heaven.

In the *Confessions*, which details Augustine's conversion to Christianity, his early experiences are of "God's transcendence as God's radical immanence," Tom Driver's definition of "transcendence."[23] In such an experience of God's transcendence, time and space are being woven together in the mystery of God's Spirit. God is not only here, but also there, just as God is not only now, but also in past and future. Augustine the convert seemed to affirm this radical sense of God's transcendence: God's presence and movement not only in history but before and after, under and above, around and within, every moment and place of his life and all life. This was the younger, less dualistic Augustine.

Most of us, however, have difficulty living in more non-dualistic patterns in which we can see links and notice passages between ideas that we experience as contradictory, ideas of good and evil, God and humanity, male and female. It isn't really surprising therefore that, as Augustine incurred greater responsibility for exercising authority in the church, his theological teachings became more dualistic, easier to both live with and transmit. It is also not surprising that Augustine's more dualistic comprehensions of God and the world eventually became the foundation of Western Christian orthodoxy which, in effect, became more dualistic, a milder version of the radical split between good and evil that, earlier in his life, Augustine had abandoned.

Thus, for the older Augustine, bishop of Hippo, and subsequently for the Western Christian church itself, the radicality of God's good presence and God's *kairos* with us here and now is obscured by a spiritualized vision of a future realm of God—a time and a place that awaits us somewhere else, further along, outside life and history as we know it. Western Christians are heirs of this dualistic split between earth and heaven, a split laid bare by Augustine in *The City of God*.

This dualism forms the basis of much spirituality that arises in realms of human suffering, such as slavery and Jim Crow experiences of African Americans. Negro spirituals abound with the belief that further along, we can lay down our burdens.[24] As we anticipate an increase in human pain and earth suffering at home and abroad, and as we commit ourselves to the struggles against injustice and despair under Trump and other demagogues on this planet, spiritualities that affirm the sacredness of other realms and times call to me—though in more mystical, less dualistic ways.[25] I explore the connections between mysticism and resistance more fully in parts two and three of this book.

As I understand him, the older Augustine seemed to have lost the vibrant spirituality of the younger convert. The older man does not seem to affirm the kairotic dimensions of God as radically present here and now—the soaring, sparking, spiraling movements that turn our chronological experiences of past, present, and future upside down and inside out. The older, more established, Augustine, bishop of Hippo, did not appear to believe that, in *kairos*, we find ourselves in the present moment, meeting the past and being met by the future, because the bishop seemed unable to get beyond the linear shape of human experience.

For Bishop Augustine, *chronos* and *kairos* characterized not only different realms but also separate ones. In what the church has generally considered his major theological work, *The City of God* (426 CE), Augustine speculated that, while we live now in the "City of Man" under the realm of *chronos*, we will gather someday, after life in this world, in the "City of God," the realm of *kairos*, which we often refer to as "eternity."[26]

For the later Augustine, these realms of God and humanity, *kairos* and *chronos*, were different realms separated by time and space. In my experience, these realms are different, often overlapping, never entirely separate. They are woven together—mystically, mysteriously, magically—which is how, in our often mundane daily work and play, we can nonetheless see or hear or touch God in ways that surprise us and sometimes change our lives.

The movement in Augustine's spirituality and theology has been interesting to me because it is the reverse of my own spiritual experience and theological transformation. Insofar as I understand Augustine as a Christian theologian, I read his younger theological affirmations as freer and more liberating than his mature work. In my life, the opposite has been true. The younger Augustine and I, in my later years, seem to me rather close in our affirmations of time as a weaving together of *chronos* and *kairos*, linear time and eternity—in which we experience other people and creatures, including our ancestors, those who've gone before, and perhaps those who are coming along from the future, as being involved with us today, wherever we are and whatever may be happening.

In this spirit of mystical time, and as I began to build my library in feminist theologies, I read Isabel Allende's *The House of the Spirits* (1982) several times. Allende offers a vibrant counterpoint to Augustine's separate realms of *kairos* and *chronos*. She presents an imaginative portrayal of a family of Chilean women over three generations, in which those who have died accompany and empower their loved ones here on earth. I found this tale and its presentation of spirits compelling and, like all good fiction, a window into some truth: the presence of spirits who seemed to me, as to Isabel Allende, lively and powerful and real.

As a young woman, I encountered such spirits at the core of my being through *kairos*, which was not—as Bishop Augustine might have assumed—primarily an eternity or heaven awaiting me beyond the grave, but rather a vigorous resource of power, love, and courage for my life, and the wellspring of a yearning for God, here and now, a Spirit that I sensed in the turtle but could not quite understand as really, fully present. In my teens, I was reaching to imagine—yearning to believe—that God was as present in a turtle, or in my teenage girl body-self, as in a heavenly Father! But I could not quite get there. The yearning was strong, but so too was my inability to crawl outside the box of traditional patriarchal Christianity.

Had I been alone in this teenage yearning, I doubt I could have survived it, because the experience was too intense and often too bleak for me to have endured. Throughout my teen years and twenties, I was accompanied by particular spirits who kept me, not only physically alive, though surely they played some part in that, but mentally and spiritually vibrant. I have already told you about Betty Smith, a powerful spiritual force in my early life. I have spoken of my parents, who never failed to be there for their kids and remained throughout their lives primary wellsprings of God's Spirit. I have told you about my crush on Julie Andrews and what it meant. Other spirits—humans and other creatures, those past and present and yet to come, both fictional and nonfictional—have also played a part. Such a community of saints has been present with me throughout my life. Through eyes of faith or perhaps simply a strong sense of spiritual intuition, such empowering community is present to all persons and creatures.

The spirits of those whom I have loved and who have loved me, together with countless other spirits, many whom I don't recognize, but who somehow know me well, conspire to keep me vibrant and in touch. In the poetic language of Brian Andreas, "Most people don't know there are angels whose only job is to make sure you don't get too comfortable & fall asleep & miss your life."[27] The spirits, perhaps they are angels, demonstrate that every event, relationship, and process has chronological and kairotic dimensions.

The spirits also warn that we will miss *kairos* entirely unless we are open to all that is seen, unseen, and startlingly real, however large and significant or small and incidental each moment may seem to us. We cannot ever realize all of *kairos'* many dimensions, but we can catch a few intimations and glimpses of what God is doing in the present moment if we are open.

# Sexual Yearning

As for many young women, sexuality was for me the most obvious site of yearning in my late teens and early twenties. I felt sexual, but I didn't have any sense of what to do about it or of what it meant, nor did it occur to me that it had as much to with God as with the scary possibility of having sex with anyone, male or female or even myself.

I had no clue:

Was I a lesbian woman running away from my own truest sexual identity?

Was I a bisexual woman who could not imagine that this was a natural way of being human?

Was I a heterosexual woman so alienated from my body and sexuality that I couldn't imagine being sexual with a boy?

Was I too hurt by being unpopular with boys to even imagine myself as heterosexual in years to come?

A decade later, when I came out as lesbian to them, my parents feared it was the latter—that I had been too hurt by boys to be able to enjoy being heterosexual. As we would learn, many psychologists offered this as a classic reason for why girls and women become lesbian: we have been rejected by boys and men; or we had weak fathers and overbearing mothers, or perhaps the other way around? In any case, lesbians got used to hearing that "all we needed was a good man" or, more crudely, in angry, public, sexist discourse, "a good fuck."

In retrospect, it's clear to me that this disturbing period of my life had little to do with whether I was lesbian or straight and much to do with my inability to understand—emotionally, spiritually, intellectually, or physically—my sexual confusion as my yearning for, and confusion about, God. I was out of sorts with myself, the world around me, and God—and, dear reader, do keep in mind that, over time, I would come to realize that God is our power for generating mutuality. By the time my life was at least half over, well into my fifties, I would finally see clearly that this is what I had been yearning for from the beginning: to realize mutuality as a great spiritual power and a moral goal surpassing all others and, therefore, to be grateful for my life as a sacred opportunity to join in the struggles for mutuality.

But in my teens and twenties, I was out of sorts with myself, the world, and God because I was imagining both myself and God as rather static "identities" rather than as living, breathing movements. Thus, my ideals of both God and myself—and mutuality itself— seemed out of reach. Where, after all, was there any true mutuality in our life together?

Certainly not between white people and people of color. Not between the richer and poorer in our life together. Not between Christians and people of other, or no, religious traditions. And definitely not between men and women, although Bob and Mary Ann Heyward had about as much mutuality as a married, heterosexual couple could have had in the latter half of the twentieth century—and both of them suffered for it socially. The degree to which they related mutually—sharing responsibility for managing their relationship and family—prevented them from modeling very well the sexist assumptions about men needing to be in control of women (and families) and women needing to support their men by being deferential. Neither of my parents would play out their gender-scripts much better than I did, but this was not something we were ever able to discuss, even in my family, which, I came to realize, shared feelings and ideas more honestly and frequently than most of my friends' families seemed to.

If God is indeed our power for generating mutuality, as I have come passionately to believe, I was unable to pray to such a God in my teens and early twenties, because I was not yet capable of that understanding. By the time I was a young adult, I knew that mutuality was an ethical ideal, and I knew that God had something to do with it. Indeed, the one real and magnificent God was becoming foundational to my spiritual journeying as a young woman, but I still couldn't quite believe it.

I couldn't believe that God was simply our active power to love, or to create mutuality, in our lives and in the world, never perfectly, never completely, yet with full and grateful hearts. Miss Betty Smith had embodied this mutuality—the love of God—in beautiful, life-affirming ways for me, as had my parents, Mary Ann and Bob. But none of these loving people knew how fully and truly they, along with my good friends and our animal companions, were bringing God into my life. In the language of Christian theology, those who loved and respected me were, like Jesus, incarnating God in my life.

I had no idea that prayer was simply the yearning to "speak" to such a God—such a life-affirming power of love and mutuality—and to "talk with" this Spirit. I had no idea that prayer was, and is, an opening of ourselves to this creative, liberating energy that is always present, always a possibility, for us to imagine. I had no idea that prayer was simply becoming open—vulnerable—to God's compelling presence as She or He or It moves through our lives in each moment. Over the years, more through feminism than through the church, I would learn that prayer is an expressed yearning for God, whether silent or spoken, sung or danced, walked or even ridden on a horse.

I was yearning for someone to help me realize these truths about prayer and mutuality and creative spirituality. I was not looking primarily for someone to have sex with, but rather someone who could help me realize the spiritual foundation of my sexual yearning. I needed someone I could lean on for this help, someone to talk honestly with, someone who would listen to me, someone who could understand what I was saying, someone to help me realize that I was neither crazy nor bad.

However, no parent, no teacher, no priest in my world understood much more than I did about this simultaneously sexual and spiritual yearning. And certainly no teacher, counselor, or priest could risk exploring it with me through candid conversation, or even prayer. The only paths such adults might have imagined were too precarious and frightening.

This was no one's fault—not my parents', nor my teachers', nor my priests' fault. Like mine, their senses of human goodness and decency had been shaped by a patriarchal, hetero/sexist Christianized culture in which women and girls had learned deep in our bodies and minds to do whatever we needed to do, emotionally and physically, to remain pure and "good"—to keep our legs together and not talk about sex. There was never a hint of connection made between sexual and spiritual yearning. To the contrary, sexuality and spirituality had been framed throughout Christian history as oppositional yearnings—one pulling us away from, the other toward, God.

Today, I understand this big disconnect—sexual from spiritual yearning—as the source of the most confusing relationships in my life—with the camp counselor in my mid-teens, the college professor in my late teens, and a gay or bisexual male priest in my mid-to-late twenties, whose relationship with me will be discussed more fully later. Each of these people was as much a prisoner of this pleasure-denying Christianized culture as I was.

In none of these instances of rejection in my life could any of these people help me, and in none could anyone else help us sort out what was happening. It may or may not be noteworthy that in none of these cases did anything "sexual" actually happen. Rather, each relationship was a site of deep yearning—in one of the relationships, with the young gay priest, a site of mutual yearning confounding us both. For me, in each case, my yearning was for God and for clarity about how this hunger for soulful connection with people who cared about me might illuminate my experiences of God.

These confusing relationships took place in the first three decades of my life, before I had much conceptual clarity about either sexuality or spirituality. The people to whom I was attached were conscientious, bright folks with the good emotionally protective sense to be scared of me—a young woman eager to be heard and taken seriously in my efforts to understand my hunger for spiritual and sexual connection, and needing guidance in figuring out what was, and was not, good or right in the realm of human relationships. I also needed solidarity—someone to affirm the yearning as a basic dimension of being a good, healthy, even holy person. I did not need "to have sex," I needed good friends.

Over the years, I've come to understand myself as bisexual. My sexuality has always had as much to do with my spirituality—yearning for mutuality and its root source—as with gender identity, either my own or my partner's, or with sexual pleasure, which, in a wonderfully mutual relationship, is a sacred pleasure. I'm often as in tune with my sexuality and spirituality—the same vulnerability or openness—when I'm riding a horse, listening to Beethoven, or gazing at the sea or the mountains or a sunset, as when I'm snuggling with my partner or at the altar during the Eucharist.

# Yearning for Justice

When did it occur to me that the yearning for God, the yearning for mutuality and good friendship and justice, were the same yearning? When did this notion first begin to take hold? When did I first consciously begin to care about social justice—making right, mutual relation—in the world and, moreover, understand it as driven by the Spirit?

When I was five or six, I learned something about racism, including my own participation, through the Bessie and Jeff incidents in Hendersonville, North Carolina. As a child of God, I felt ashamed of myself and of how white people, like Sheriff Keeling, acted.

In years to come, I had a chance to stand up for justice by taking Adlai Stevenson's part in the second grade debate, then several years later to grow through Miss Betty Smith's affirmation of me as a girl who dared to think my own thoughts about the state of the world, including my not-yet-very-clearly-formed critique of US colonialism, and of capitalism even before it became so fully global.

Sometime in the next years came my run-in with the bishop about desegregating the diocesan camp so that our youth commission—with its one Negro member—could meet there. We lost this battle, but I emerged knowing well that the one true God, the one whom Jesus loved, and the only God I cared about, was God of the prophets who cared about the poor and oppressed. God's message to the oppressors was to repent of our evil and join in the civil rights struggle for freedom.

Many threads were woven into my commitments to social justice at Randolph-Macon Woman's College, most memorably by specific teachers and mentors—Miss Mildred Hudgins of the campus YWCA, whose passion for racial justice was palpable and contagious; Dr. Shirley Strickland, who taught us about the social stratification of US society on interwoven foundations of race, class, and gender and who, I always suspected, was an early feminist in her heart of hearts; Dr. Mary Frances Thelen, who taught world religions and helped us understand that the Christianity most of us professed was *a* major religion, not *the* major religion, of the world; President William Quillian, whose presence and leadership reflected a commitment to justice, especially racial justice; and Dr. Edwin Penick, my faculty advisor in the religion department. Dr. Penick introduced us to historical and social criticism of the Bible and to the writings of theologians like Bonhoeffer, Paul Tillich, and civil rights leaders Martin Luther King and Malcolm X. We also read novels by such white Southern authors as Flannery O'Connor, Harper Lee, and Robert Penn Warren, whose works—though reflecting conflict and confusion regarding race—became springboards to our religion class's discussions of racial injustice and structures of social inequality.

My fellow students were white until my junior year, when one brave black girl from Atlanta entered the freshman class. A few of my friends stood out as our values and commitments were taking shape. I recall especially my freshman roommates, Embry Martin and Annabelle Corbin, both women I've kept up with over the years. I recall also my sister religion majors French Boyd and Jean Hill and my classmate Liz Colton who, with a number of "RM girls," as we referred to ourselves at the time, became well-known to the college administration as students who might be found on picket lines when racial justice was in dispute, as it often was in the mid-1960s in Lynchburg, Virginia. President Quillian stood consistently on the side of justice and encouraged Randolph-Macon students to put ourselves on the line whenever the Spirit nudged us to do so. Decades later, as we matured, several of my RMWC pals became close friends and inspirations in our shared struggles for justice in many forms.[28]

One college friend who became a dearly beloved sister-in-the-struggle in decades to come is Muffie Moroney from Houston who, alongside other brave Texas women, like her late friends and sister-activists Barbara Jordan and Ann Richards, has been a beacon for justice over the years. Through our shared participation in the movements for women's ordination in the Episcopal Church and justice for LGBT Christians and others, Muffie—a lawyer, activist, and Episcopal laywoman—and I have built a strong bond. "Tenacious" is the word that pops to mind when I think of Muffie Moroney, somebody you want on your side. Don't even think about promoting injustice if you're going to hang out with Muffie. I didn't know her very well at Randolph-Macon—she was two years ahead of me—but well enough not to have been surprised when she and I reconnected in the early 1970s, both activists in the church.

Over the years, I've heard Muffie speak truth to power again and again, inside and outside the church. She has labored in political campaigns for feminists in both the state of Texas and the Episcopal Church. She has been one of the Diocese of Texas's chief proponents for both women's ordination and LGBT rights. Muffie was also one of the most vocal opponents to Randolph-Macon Woman's College's decision about a decade ago to go co-ed. Muffie sounds fearless, but she's simply a sister of uncommon courage, a woman of integrity who speaks boldly in the presence of governors, bishops, and other institutional leaders who'd rather that she sit down and be quiet. But not Muffie. Years ago, she sent me a refrigerator magnet with a little gold-framed picture of a blond, blue-eyed Jesus in a white robe. The frame is adorned with flowers and it contains a caption: "Stop using Jesus as an excuse for being a narrow-minded bigoted asshole." I glance at it and can't help chuckling.

Not surprisingly, in a Southern women's college in the early 1960s, scant attention was paid to women's liberation even though, at our 1963 freshman year orientation, we read Betty Friedan's *The Feminine Mystique*,[29] one of the books that would over the next few years launch the women's movement. Beyond that one book, I don't recall a word being spoken publicly or in classes about "women's liberation." For us young, white, mostly Southern, Christian women in the mid-1960s, the paramount justice issue was race. We were in college just before the women's movement's second wave began to rise.[30]

Along with the racism in our lives, two particular events were astonishing to me during our college years, astonishing and terrible. They are etched forever on my mind. One was the assassination of President John F. Kennedy on November 22, 1963. Herr Baeppler, our German teacher, was called out of class early that afternoon and walked back in, speechless and pale. "President Kennedy has been shot. Class is dismissed." We hurried back to our dorm rooms to listen to the radio, which soon announced that the president had died. My roommate, Embry Martin, was sobbing. I don't recall my own response, other than being shocked and appalled. Like many of our generation, I had welcomed this presidency and been captivated by the first family's image of youth, vigor, and idealism. How could this have happened? Who could have done such a thing, and why? To this day, a large segment of the American public remains skeptical that we have found the answers to these questions.

The second mind-boggling event was Quaker peace activist Norman Morrison's self-immolation in front of the Pentagon on November

2, 1965. Mr. Morrison had taught Bible at East Mecklenburg High School in Charlotte while I was a student there in the early 1960s. The school yearbook from 1961 pictures Norman Morrison as advisor to the Serving Others Loyally Club. I have a vague memory of his meandering in the halls of the school, moving along softly, like an angel or a ghost. I hadn't known him personally but recalled, when he died, that he had seemed to me a gentle, unremarkable man. Like everyone else, I was stunned by his death and its global significance as a symbol of peace-activism in the context of the increasingly violent and unpopular Vietnam War. His death revealed Norman Morrison to have been a most remarkable human being. His widow said she believed he had given his life on the behalf of the children of the world, especially the children of Vietnam.[31] Today, there are several memorials to Norman Morrison in Hanoi, and he is often listed among civil rights martyrs and heroes in the United States.

Even on the idyllic campus of Randolph-Macon, we were not shielded entirely from the violence and systemic evils of our day and age. Many of us were grateful that we were being educated about life in the world beyond the red brick wall around the college. We had come to college to study history, sociology, religion, literature, economics, language, art, science, math, music, drama and, through these academic endeavors, to seek the truth about our society, our world, and our lives. We surely had not come to college to continue being protected from thinking critically and creatively about a world that has been, and is being, shaped by many cultures, classes, and colors.

On December 14, 1960, almost three years before my class entered Randolph-Macon Woman's College, two students—Rebecca Owen and Mary-Edith Bentley—both religion majors at the college, had been arrested and jailed for thirty days for sitting in at Patterson's, a segregated drug store in downtown Lynchburg. These women were heroes of mine and of many students who followed them in our justice efforts. No doubt because they had been vilified by many townspeople and affluent alumnae of the school, who were among the college's large donors, Mary-Edith and Rebecca remained largely unsung heroes at Randolph-Macon in the 1960s. Hardly anything was said publicly about these two women by the time my class entered in 1963.

Those of us who found out about Rebecca and Mary-Edith heard about their bold sit-in from several professors and staff members, including Mildred Hudgins, intrepid head of the campus YWCA, religion professors Thelen and Penick, and President Quillian. Each had supported the two students, and President Quillian had resisted calls from angry donors for the students to be expelled. The professors' ongoing support of these women, taking books to them in jail and letting them take their senior exams in their cells, was a primary reason I gravitated toward the religion department when it was time for me to choose a major. I was emboldened by this story and imagined myself linked with Rebecca and Mary-Edith in their courage, which was much greater than mine.

Through its infamous daily paper, the town of Lynchburg boasted a proudly racist heritage and commitment. We students were told, and it seemed to be true, that the *Lynchburg Daily News* published no good news about Negroes and nothing positive about the civil rights movement or its goal of integration. Ironically, in Lynchburg, Reverend Jerry Falwell of the Thomas Road Baptist Church, a little known preacher-man at the time, was scolding Christian activists—especially Randolph-Macon students—to shun the movement for racial justice. This man proclaimed that Christians should stay out of politics. In the next decade, Falwell became chief architect of the right-wing moral majority, a Christian fear-campaign that more or less picked up where the McCarthyism of the 1950s had left off.

Two summertime activities during college years also stand out in my memory. The first is a source of some embarrassment, because it's a snapshot of my race and class privilege and also suggests how relatively oblivious my family and I were, in the earlier part of my life, to questioning the roots and meanings of our privilege. I made my debut in Charlotte during the summer of 1964, following my freshman year. What was I thinking? I was thinking that my maternal grandmother, Nana, for whom I was named and whose first grandchild I was, really wanted to give the debut to me as a gift—either the debut or a trip to Europe. The way I was told about this choice, however, made clear that there really was no choice if I wanted Nana to be happy. So I agreed and was relieved that another handful of "debs" were friends from church who shared my feelings about the whole experience.

None of us had a well-formed critique at that point of the blatant classist, racist, and sexist underpinnings of the debutante tradition with its European roots and its Southern adaptation as a celebration of a plantation culture. So we made our debuts and, somewhere in my life, tucked away in the back of a closet, is a portrait of me as a debutante, dressed in a long white gown—trying my best not to look too much like the ugly duckling kid sister of Miss Scarlett. More truthfully, hoping to look as much like Julie Andrews as possible.

The title of this book is meant to suggest a tension common to many of us who have benefitted from social privilege of one, or many, forms—race privilege, class privilege, gender/sexual privilege, privileges of belonging to dominant religions or ethnic cultures. I am not using "privilege" here to convey a right or any benefit or possession that we have earned. In this context, "privilege" conveys an unearned benefit.[32] Inherited wealth is a classic example of economic privilege. Often we do not choose to be privileged; we are simply born into it. But often we do choose our privilege: we marry into privilege, or we strive to attach ourselves somehow—through appearance, connections, other forms of social manipulation—to position ourselves close to various kinds of social privilege. In making my debut in the summer of 1964, I was choosing a path of least resistance, going along with a classist, racist, sexist tradition that, even then, I could hardly bear.

One year later, in the summer of 1965, between sophomore and junior years, I worked with children in the Henry Street Settlement House on New York's Lower East Side. I remember hanging out the window of the car as we approached New York City, astonished by the tall buildings, the sheer verticality of the city. It was a good summer for me and my Randolph-Macon friend Lynn Hodge from Tennessee, both of us Southern girls who had come to New York more for an education in diversity and multicultural reality than to be all that helpful.

One of the Puerto Rican kids with whom we worked in summer school was a little hell-raiser named "Jesus." I have some memory of being embarrassed a couple of times when I had to scold Jesus for beating up on a smaller kid. It was the first time in my life I had spent much of each day in a bilingual situation, with Spanish spoken as much as English. I found it exhilarating. It made me want to study Spanish rather than the German and the French I had taken to meet language requirements at Randolph-Macon. Years later, I would study Spanish in several different contexts, in the United States and Nicaragua. Hoy hablo solamente un pocito!

Little question that the most consequential moment of the summer for me was a visit to the Union Theological Seminary on New York's Upper West Side where I browsed through application materials. Indeed, after graduating from college in 1967, I entered Union Theological Seminary in New York City. Despite the summer on Henry Street, arriving to live in New York City was a giant leap from having once thought that heading to Virginia to college was "going North."

Academically, I was well prepared for seminary, thanks to the quality of Randolph-Macon Woman's College's religion faculty. In the first semester, I was able to skip all introductory courses at Union and begin taking what interested me. I remember with special appreciation two courses—one on the prophet Jeremiah (taught by Hebrew Scripture scholar James Sanders) and another on the black church in the United States (taught by sociologist of religion C. Eric Lincoln). These courses, buoyed by critical thinking and enthusiasm for justice on parts of nearly everyone in the seminary, deepened my commitment to do my part—if I could figure out what it was.

I felt unsure and weak-kneed in trying to be part of the powerful collective push against racism and especially against the war in Vietnam, a movement that was surging in the late 1960s. While many of my male classmates were being scorned as "draft dodgers" by the Nixon and Johnson administrations, I was coming to know and admire them greatly as peace activists.

I was also enjoying simply being in New York City with its super-abundance of cultural opportunities. During that first year in seminary, I sat with a group of classmates at the back of Carnegie Hall to hear the duo that had become my favorite music makers by the late 1960s, Simon and Garfunkel. I played their albums every time I had a turn at the record player in the first floor lounge in the women's dorm at Union.

In relation to matters sexual, I found myself almost catatonic, having no idea who or what I was—gay (the term "lesbian" was too scary), straight, or perhaps bisexual, but way too confused to know or even to frame such questions. It was easier just to sit on these questions and not do anything. Once or twice, I ventured forth—most memorably, sleeping with one of my male student friends in the immediate aftermath of our watching a film of D. H. Lawrence's *The Fox*, a story about a lesbian couple in which a tree falls on one of the women and the other woman goes off with the male hero. Not too surprising that, in response to this tale, I should hop right into a guy's bed!

So confused was I about my vocation and sexuality that I spent Thanksgiving weekend in "Clark 8," the psychiatric unit of St. Luke's Hospital, located down the street from the seminary. In decades to come, Beverly Harrison—at the time, assistant dean for women students at Union—would chuckle about visiting me on Clark 8 and finding me busy at work on my Jeremiah paper and quite ready to return to the seminary, thank you.

I look upon that strange little episode in Clark 8 as a beginning of my adulthood. I was twenty-two, in chronological time. In *kairos*, I was probably both much younger, still naïve about most important matters, and much older than my years, because I had for so long been inquisitive and concerned about what makes us tick, ethically, spiritually, psychologically, as individuals and as a society. Being in Clark 8 flagged for me, and for people like Bev who could help me, the depth of my identity-quandary as a woman in a man's world and a patriarchal church that offered few vocational, relational, or sexual options to strong, independent-minded females with leadership aspirations.

Over the years, Bev noted that it was through experiencing her women students like me, who were struggling to figure out how to live and work in the ubiquitous presence of male domination and male privilege, that she would begin to realize the extent to which she herself had allowed the society to shape and define her. Bev insisted that it was chiefly through counseling and teaching her women students that she found her own voice.

Among women and men in liberal Protestant theological circles, Beverly Wildung Harrison is widely acclaimed as the mother of Christian feminist social ethics—she who gave the world scores of distinguished religious teachers, ministers, and leaders. Liberal Christian ethicist Reinhold Niebuhr, who taught at Union a generation before Beverly Harrison, has the larger name-recognition, while Beverly Harrison's legacy is celebrated by those Christian ethicists and religious leaders who profess a more radical, wholistic economic analysis based on a Marxian critique of capitalism. For example, Reinhold Niebuhr has been invoked by Barack Obama and other prominent Democrats, like the Clintons, to support even-handedness and liberal social policies such as freedom of speech, human rights, and economic justice. As political figures delve more deeply into the economic structure of our nation and world, Elizabeth Warren, Bernie Sanders, economists Robert Reich and Paul Krugman, and a more progressive Hillary Clinton would find in Beverly Harrison an ethical champion of their understandings of what holds the world together and, increasingly, is ripping it apart: advanced global capitalism and its economic, racial, gendered, and environmental effects.

Being at Union Theological Seminary off and on over a period of thirteen years was among the most important experiences of my life. It was unquestionably the most significant context of my vocational formation: my call, as a Christian feminist, to a ministry of liberation-based ecumenical and interfaith sensibilities. At Union, I learned well that the struggles for justice are foundational to all theology worth doing. Union was also where I met Beverly Harrison, who much like Betty Smith in earlier years, urged me in every way she could to celebrate the "me" I was discovering. Like Betty, Bev became my counselor, teacher, mentor, and later much, much more.

But in 1967, I wasn't quite ready personally, socially, or politically for the radicality of Union Theological Seminary. I delighted in my courses and did well. I was making good friends, mainly women, some who continue to be among my most cherished friends. I remained unclear about my sexual identity. By the end of the year, in the spring of 1968, I was ready to join in the anti-racist demonstrations at neighboring Columbia University. These demonstrations on Manhattan's Upper West Side effectively shut down not only the university but also most of its neighbor colleges and graduate schools, Union Seminary among them. In the late 1960s, students across the nation were rising up against racist practices and military alliances of universities.

Professor C. Eric Lincoln, who was teaching Sociology of Religion at Union, had helped us begin to understand the basis of the Columbia University demonstrations—the historical indifference of this major Ivy League university to the well-being of its closest neighbors, the black and brown people in Harlem. Along with hundreds of students, faculty, and staff from Union Seminary, Columbia University, Barnard College, Teacher's College, Julliard Conservatory, and the Jewish Theological Seminary of America—all located together on the western boundary of Harlem—I participated in the sits-in, was arrested, then released without charges.

When my father, who was distressed about this "riot," as it was being dubbed in the news, phoned Moultrie Moore, our priest in Charlotte, to tell him I'd been arrested at Columbia University, Mr. Moore's response was inspired: "Oh Bob, that's wonderful! I am proud of her!" His words both confused and comforted my dear parents.

The whole academic year 1967–68 was challenging and instructional, serving to validate every liberation hunch in my body and soul. A couple of years later, Union would become for me a launching pad into feminist liberation theologies and other theologies of liberation— black, womanist, *mujerista*, Native American, Latin American, African, Asian, queer, and environmental.

# David and Carter

In the spring of 1968, I returned to Charlotte where, during spring break, I had met and begun to fall in love with David Conolly, the young priest at St. Martin's, my home parish. David had recently arrived from his native Australia. Until I met him, I had assumed I would continue my studies at Union. Had I known that David was gay or bisexual, or that I myself might become more lesbian or bisexual, who knows what might have happened at this juncture? As it was, I remained in Charlotte for almost two years and worked at my home parish alongside David for the first half of this period.

It seemed to me that David and I had found something special with each other, and indeed we had. Although ours was an emotionally turbulent relationship, we each grew wiser and more tenacious because of the other's love and friendship. Because of our relationship—its depth and quality and even through its painful dynamics—each of us became stronger and clearer and a more vibrant priest in those parts of the world in which we would minister for the rest of our lives.

In 1968, I joined the staff of St. Martin's as a lay assistant, and I worked alongside David much of the time. During the spring and early summer of 1968, at Union in New York, and then with David in Charlotte, I was profoundly shaken by the assassinations of Martin Luther King Jr., in April, and Robert Kennedy in June. So was David, of course. In both cases, it felt as if, for a moment in history, evil was winning. With this social chaos as a backdrop, David and I were concluding that the struggles for justice and peace were essential to the love of God and that, whatever our ministries—his as priest, mine as question mark— each of us was increasingly committed to making justice efforts the centerpiece of our lives.

One of our most meaningful associations in our shared ministries was with the Black Cultural Association, which had been formed in North Carolina as an advocacy organization for racial justice-making— sit-ins, marches, educational and cultural events. Many in our parish were horrified by our political activism, which, they believed, had no business in the church. In this context—which we were learning is frequently the context of mainline Christian denominations like the Episcopal Church—David and I would help each other struggle with

ever-challenging questions about how to be both pastoral and prophetic in our ministries. One of the aspects of this man I most admired
and loved was that he believed, deep in his soul, that a good priest can,
and must, be both pastor and prophet, not one or the other.

I trust that this book is making clear how strongly I still hold to
this assumption, which I learned with my beloved friend David. We are
put here on earth by our Maker to be both healers and liberators. We
are not asked by God to choose between them except in particular situations. At those times, when we must choose—to speak prophetically,
for example, and let others offer pastoral care—we must not lose touch
with the Spirit who will, in some other moment or movement, require
that we be the pastor, the healer, the one who calms the storm, and that
we must someday let others speak God's prophetic word. We are not
put here by our Sophia Spirit to be only pastoral or prophetic as we
journey along. In many contexts, we can be both at once.

In the late 1960s, needing spiritual energy to be both pastor and
prophet, I was heartened by the music of Peter, Paul, and Mary ("If I
Had a Hammer"), Bob Dylan ("The Times, They Are A-Changin'"),
and many other folk singers. Their music simultaneously healed and liberated me. These artists emboldened me to work to be both pastorally
attentive to the teenagers with whom I was working in the parish—most
of them only six to eight years younger than me—and prophetically
alive to the justice work that needed to be done, especially in relation to
the civil rights movement in the wake of King's and Robert Kennedy's
assassinations and the dreadful War in Vietnam, which was increasingly
rupturing not only Vietnam but also our own nation. David and I were
interested in helping younger people make connections between their
own lives and the life of the larger world.

He and I enjoyed the "Rejoice Mass,"[33] an effort among some
eucharistic-centered Christians to contemporize liturgical music. We
were also fans of the Beatles who, by 1968, had evolved beyond their
British boy-band ambiance into a major cultural force for social change
and spiritual nourishment. To this day, Lennon's song "Imagine," Paul
McCartney's "Let It Be," and John and Yoko's "Give Peace a Chance" are
pieces in my ever-expanding sacred canon of music. In the late 1960s,
as I wrestled with matters of sexuality and spirituality, I was buoyed by
music as varied as folk singer Judy Collins's rendition of Joni Mitchell's

gentle, soulful "Both Sides Now" and stoned artist Grace Slick's halluci-
natory "White Rabbit."

A serious element in David's and my story was my growing interest
in the ordination of women priests which, in the late 1960s, was still
not permitted by the Episcopal Church. Because I had spent the year
at Union Seminary, I had met a few Episcopal women who wanted to
be ordained and I had begun to hear of others. I thought this was great,
though I had no sense of my own vocation to the priesthood.

David and the rector of the parish in which we both worked were
at the time opposed to women's ordination, an opinion that made no
sense whatsoever to me, given these men's passion for racial justice and
their commitments to liberal social movements in general. David and
Bart, the rector, would change their minds over the next couple of
years, yet this same split between advocating for justice and refusing to
support the ordination of women was prominent among many Episcopalians in the 1970s. This remains the case today among otherwise
open-minded, even progressive, Roman Catholics like Pope Francis, an
inspirational world leader on matters of economic justice and fairness,
yet stuck in traditional patriarchal structures of oppression and conde-
scension to women.

The church is different, we women would be told, as the movement
for women's ordination took off in the early 1970s. The ordination of
women is not about "justice," we would hear, but rather about the "natural order" of the sexes, in which man is naturally the head of woman
in the church, and about God's revelation of Himself in Jesus, a Jewish
male, thereby establishing maleness (not Jewishness, you will notice) as
essential to priesthood. People who made such claims evidently did not
realize the extent to which, trying to be faithful Christians, they had
fallen into a deeply misogynist psychosocial and spiritual pit.

David was the first man I ever really loved. A deep spiritual yearning
for mutuality drew me to him, a yearning to be close to someone, a man
in this case, who would affirm me in my strength and whose own gifts
I could affirm wholeheartedly. Our relationship would be built on our
shared passion for justice, which was emerging as the direction my life
journey would take—someday as priest, theologian, and teacher. And
although David and I would not become lovers or partners in life, we
became, for a while, each other's best friend, counselor, and confidant

in our shared commitment to keep justice at the center of our spiritual vocations and our lives.

David did not tell me about his sexual history, and he gave mixed messages about what he needed or wanted from me. At the time, his ambivalence hurt me, because I loved him and sensed that it was a mutual love between us. Because I too was rather unclear about my own sexuality and also because I had been socialized to let the man take the lead in a relationship, I waited for David to say or do something. It was a stressful, anguished personal stretch in my life and, I would later learn, in David's too.

Yet our shared pain and inability to communicate what was happening between us set in motion the series of events in my life that led me to Philadelphia to be ordained a priest. For David, it sparked a way of being that helped make him an articulate advocate for justice, including both women's ordination and gay rights, in the Australian church, as well as a prophetic and pastorally gifted parish priest and a diocesan voice of courage over a period of five decades.

# Surprising Myself

After David left the United States to return to Australia in 1969, I worked in a Head Start program in Charlotte and, a year later, returned to Union, having been away from the seminary for two years. Movements for change were shaking the seminary. The war resistance was mounting and, thanks to the emerging women's liberation movement, several consciousness-raising groups were being formed. Along with going into therapy to sort out my relationship with David, I joined a women's consciousness-raising group and began a personal journey, which, in feminist terms, would be both personal and political.[34]

This was a moment of serious spiritual, intellectual, and emotional growth, which took place primarily in my women's consciousness-raising group, and with the help of mentors at Union—professors Daniel Day Williams, Tom Driver, Bev Harrison, and vocational counselor Sidney Skirvin. I also had an excellent experience in psychotherapy with a young pastoral counselor. Following the defeat of women's ordination to the priesthood at the Houston Triennial Convention in 1970, my therapist encouraged me to join the struggle for Episcopal women priests although I still did not think I personally would seek ordination.

In the fall of 1971, a year after my return to Union and two years since we had been in touch, David stunned me with a phone call, in which he asked me to come to Australia to try out our relationship. I could hardly believe it. To the chagrin of my consciousness-raising group and my therapist, I was ecstatic. I said yes and began to plan this trip. I would leave Union Seminary, the women's ordination struggle, my friends and teachers, my women's group, and my therapist and fly to the other side of the planet to try to build a good relationship with a man with whom I had experienced a traumatic emotional connection. But I had loved this gifted priest and wonderful man, and I still did. I got my passport and visa and became increasingly excited about the possibility of making a life with David in Australia.

But to my own surprise . . . about two weeks before my flight, after much intense conversation and debate with my therapist, my women's group, my mentor Bev Harrison, and my parents, I made myself phone David to tell him that I had changed my mind and would not be coming after all. I said that I had decided to seek ordination to the priesthood here in the United States.

I was as startled as David must have been when I heard these words pop out of my mouth. Little did I imagine in that moment that I would be joining a movement of bold women, and some male allies, to disrupt the rule of the Father over His church. No longer children, we would become fully grown daughters, participants in the ongoing incarnation of God, as we had been all along, of course, but less aware.

# Part Two

## Incarnation

Depart from evil, and do good; seek peace, and pursue it.

—Psalm 34:14

With what can we compare the realm of God,
or what parable shall we use for it?
It is like a mustard seed, which, when sown upon
the ground,
is the smallest of all the seeds on earth;
yet when it is sown, it grows up
and becomes the greatest of all shrubs,
and puts forth large branches,
so that the birds of the air can make nests in its shade.

—Mark 4:30–32

# The Son

**Do I love Jesus?** Yes, with a full and grateful heart, and a curious, critical mind. And what I learn from Jesus is that our spiritual vitality is in the ongoingness of God's incarnation, with us now and forever—not in one person, even Jesus. In one story, or parable, after another, Jesus tried to tell his disciples and followers that, like the mustard seed, his life and work on this planet—and theirs—would "grow up" and "put forth large branches." We are born into this earth to be like the mustard seed, to "god" (verb), to be like Jesus, in that sense to follow him, making God incarnate through our lives in our own generations and cultures, doing what we can as well as we can. We are not here to do it perfectly or do it all. Neither was Jesus.

In ways partial and imperfect, my life has been wrapped around images and stories of a human Jesus—a man once much older than me, today much younger—a working man, maybe single, maybe partnered, we don't know. We don't know much about him historically, but we do know Jesus was a well-versed Jew who, because he was rooted and grounded in the love of God, was determined to teach and embody an ethic of neighbor-love as the most important "call" we humans share, along with our love of God. More than anyone, Tom F. Driver, my doctoral advisor and a wonderfully creative, justice-minded theological professor at Union, accompanied me in exploring the whats, whys, and wherefores of Jesus of Nazareth whom the early church designated as "the Christ."

So how and why did earlier Christians turn this human brother, Jesus of Nazareth, into Jesus Christ and, several centuries later, into God Himself—God the Son? And what on earth does this have to do with us today?

Early church fathers transformed a *ben a'dam* (Hebrew for "son of man" or "human one," meaning a person like us) into not only the "Son of God" but—with greater theological consequences—"God the Son," the incarnation of God, the second "person" of the Trinity. This process of turning the human Jesus into a divine person set the stage, historically and theologically, upon which generations of Christians would be taught that we are worshipping God when we worship Jesus.

The transformation of Jesus into God lifts him out of our common humanity and tucks him away, concealed behind thick clouds of Greek philosophy. Over time, it becomes increasingly difficult for the rest of us humans to remember him as one of us, simply a brother from Nazareth who spent a good bit of time preaching and teaching near the Sea of Galilee.

The following section, on how the early church turned Jesus into God, is an overview of Christology—the study of in what sense Jesus is Christ. It's a heady study that can be tedious even for professional theologians. I urge you to give it a go if you wish; you might find bits and pieces to savor! Or you can skip the next few pages and pick up on page 77.

# Spinning Back into Strange Worlds of Symbols and Meaning

We must trek back in time to understand how the name of Jesus became significant for countless people throughout the world, crossing cultures and reflecting different, sometimes competing, understandings of who this man was and why he matters. How was one human being turned into not only the Son of God, but also God the Son, a divine "person" of the Christian Trinity?

During his life, Jesus was an itinerant teacher and spiritual leader, rather traditional in his observance of Judaism, though bold in his insistence that neither Jewish nor Roman law should take precedence over God's requirement that we love God and our neighbors as ourselves. Jesus's followers seemed on the whole to be commoners, working men and women who became devoted to the man and his message about loving God and neighbor, serving those in need, and being willing to contravene both religious and state laws in order to practice and spread the love of God. Over several years, Jesus—both his message and the groundswell of his following—was experienced increasingly as a threat to the established order by both religious and secular leaders of the day. For this reason, Jesus was arrested, tortured, and executed by the Roman state, a fate shared by many of his disciples, then and now.

To his early followers, Jesus was a friend and a compelling spiritual teacher. As they grew to know him over several years, they came to believe that he had a special relationship to God, like a son to a father. As a son of a Father God, he was worthy of deep respect. Some of his followers spoke to, and of, Jesus as their spiritual "lord" and "master," much as people today refer to their "spiritual teachers" and "gurus" and "mentors." Such terms did not signify that Jesus was "divine" or anything other than a fully human brother with a vibrant connection to God and evidently a special gift to teach, lead, and inspire. To his friends and disciples, Jesus was seen to be a remarkable man, perhaps even the Christ of God—the Jewish Messiah prophesied by Isaiah. Indeed his disciple Peter said to Jesus, "You are the Messiah" (Matt. 16:16). Peter did not mean that Jesus was God, but rather that he was the Jewish Messiah. To have identified Jesus as God would have been unthinkable, unimaginable, and blasphemous to Peter and to all good Jews, including Jesus himself.[35]

Over the next several hundred years, Christian leaders would debate who Jesus really was. Was he simply a human being, a special son of God, perhaps even God's Christ, the Messiah, as his early followers had believed, and as the Christian Scriptures suggest? Or was Jesus also divine, which is implied in the Fourth Gospel, but more symbolically and mystically than literally?

This question of who Jesus was seemed important to church leaders in the first several centuries of Christianity for this reason: If Jesus was simply a human being—someone like the rest of us, but with an exceptionally strong sense of his, and our, connection to God—then a church being built on his legacy would be primarily committed to remembering Jesus's moral and spiritual authority. We would remember him as teacher and prophet, a most significant leader and perhaps even as our Christ and Lord, but we would not understand Jesus to be God any more than we understand ourselves to be God. Nor would we understand Jesus's death on the cross as anything other than a horrible way to die at the hands of a frightened and violent Roman state, responding to the power of Jesus's ministry and to the growing crowds who were paying more attention to Jesus's message than to the rules and customs of either traditional Judaism or the Roman state.

If the early Christian church had remembered Jesus in this way—simply as a human being with a special relationship to God, a relationship that we ourselves could share—Christianity might well have become a prophetic, countercultural movement of bold witnesses to God's love for everyone and every creature. As it did evolve historically, however, the spiritual force of this radical social movement was muted and marginalized when the church turned Jesus into God.

Here is why: the early Christian leaders knew that if Jesus were remembered as not only fully human but also fully divine, the church being built in his name would be primarily devoted to celebrating Jesus Christ as not only Lord and Savior, but as God Himself in human form. Jesus's extraordinary and unique identity as a divine man would raise Christianity above all other religious traditions—including Judaism and Roman paganism. Referring to Jesus Christ as our divine Lord and Savior would indeed signal the supremacy of Jesus Christ and his church over the whole world.

At least as important, Jesus's death on the cross would be not simply a public execution of a human being by the state. The crucifixion of Jesus would be the willing self-sacrifice of a divine man at the hands of a frightened, hostile world, a torturous event in which the divine Son would hand himself over to death in faith that his divine Father was somehow still in charge. Indeed, to early Christians—those who lived a generation or two after Jesus—God's victory over death, and Jesus's divinity, became apparent in the Resurrection.

In centuries to come, Christian theologians would propose several different understandings of "atonement," or how humanity and God are reconciled through Jesus. But questions about atonement were not part of the early christological debates. Of course, the several doctrines of atonement that later took shape in the teachings of such theologians as Anselm (eleventh century CE) and Abelard (twelfth century CE) had roots in the assumption that Jesus of Nazareth had some sort of special relationship to God, an assumption that has undergirded Christian theologies from the beginning, including the christological debates of the fourth century CE.[36]

During the first five or six centuries of the church, theologians debated how Jesus was related to God, how the Son was related to the Father. Some, perhaps most famously the popular priest Arius of Alexandria, Egypt (fourth century CE), taught that the Son was subordinate to the Father; others, like Alexander, Arius's bishop and superior, insisted that Father and Son were co-equal in every way. This controversy led to the Council of Nicaea (325 CE), which condemned Arius's position.

Some, like Nestorius, Bishop of Constantinople (fifth century CE), taught that Jesus was a creature, a fully human being; others, like Cyril of Alexandria, held that Jesus was fully divine. The tensions between these perspectives led to the Council of Ephesus (431 CE) to officially resolve the matter of Jesus's divinity, and to the Council of Chalcedon (433 CE) to articulate in what sense Jesus was both fully human and fully divine.[37]

Struggling with different, not directly christological, questions, Christian theologians like Pelagius (fourth/fifth centuries CE) stressed the saving power of humanity's free will and good works while others, most famously, Augustine, bishop of Hippo (fourth/fifth centuries CE), held that faith in the Trinitarian God was paramount.

By and large, these early church leaders—almost always bishops and priests—were trying to correct theological perspectives which, they believed, had gone too far. The theological problems raised by these churchmen (and men they were, of course) got officially solved in Councils like Nicaea, Ephesus, and Chalcedon, groups called together specifically to resolve questions about Jesus and God that probably never occurred to Jesus, his disciples, or the first generations of Christian women and men.

I suspect that most Christian readers of this book might identify with the first generations' desire to follow Jesus by doing God's will, period, rather than spend much time debating Christology. A big caveat, however, is that both then and now, theological questions, including discussions about Jesus, had social and political motives and consequences.

In 325 CE, the Roman emperor Constantine converted to Christianity, thereby drawing the church close to the empire for the first time—and, in so doing, jeopardizing the church's identity as a countercultural spiritual movement. This event, sometimes called "the Constantinian settlement," would be the first time in its three-hundred-year history that the church would make peace with the state and even, perhaps, become the state's official religion. It was even possible that secular leaders—emperors, kings, rulers—would be granted special religious favors, to the point perhaps of being elevated to divine stature. As James Carroll discusses in *Constantine's Sword*, the coming together of church and state would bless horrible theological mistakes, such as anti-Semitism, and crusades against Islam and alien religious cultures, to be undertaken under the auspices of a secular authority sanctified by God.[38]

Bishops and other theologians of the church in fourth century Rome were understandably concerned about the possibility of the state co-opting the church and manipulating spiritual authority. They were eager that Christians be able to maintain spiritual autonomy over which Rome would have no authority. Insisting on the divinity of Jesus Christ became an ideological tool in establishing the church's spiritual authority over the Roman state. Upholding the divinity of the human Jesus gave the church a stronger theological basis upon which to claim spiritual authority over all Christians—and to maintain some distance from the empire.

In the wake of the Constantinian Settlement of 325 CE, the theological question for Christian leaders became not whether Jesus was divine, but rather how, or in what sense. Church leaders were determined to reconcile theologically the human and the divine in Jesus of Nazareth. It was essential to the establishment of Christian identity that people come to believe that the human being who had become "Jesus Christ"—Jesus the Savior—was more than simply a good person, more than a prophet, more than an inspired leader. Jesus Christ was in fact God—the one and only God over all creation.

It's important to emphasize here something we've already noted: The questions with which Christians had begun wrestling immediately following Jesus's death had not been abstract, philosophical ones. The first Christians wanted and needed to know whether Jesus was the Son of God or simply a human being, one of them, a "ben a'dam," Son of Man. Furthermore, was he the Jewish Messiah, the Christ prophesied by Isaiah? These questions were born in the daily spiritualities of early Christians, not in academic debate, and not primarily in reaction to a political agenda. The early believers yearned to understand not whether Jesus had been human—of course he had been human—but rather how he had been related to God. As followers of this man, the first Christians had wanted to be related to God in the same way that Jesus had been. This was an honest human desire—to better understand Jesus's relationship to God—so that they, as Christians, could aspire to a similar connection. Their spiritual quest was probably much like ours today.

But this early Christian yearning to follow the man Jesus was co-opted in the fourth century by church leaders' determination to carve out a special spiritual identity for Christians among pagans in the Roman Empire, a desire to strengthen Christian confidence and community in the context of a world populated by unbelievers, and an effort to strengthen the hand of the church in the context of the Roman Empire. It was for these reasons that the church councils that produced the creeds of the church in the fourth century concluded that Jesus was not only the Son of God, but also God the Son.

According to these creeds, Jesus was truly divine, "true God from true God," second "person" of the Trinity. Jesus not only lived on earth as a human being—Jesus of Nazareth—but he also lives on eternally as God, both prior to his incarnation (his life on earth) and following his death, resurrection, and ascension. During the Roman Empire and over the next two millenia, right down to the present, these faith-claims would provide the foundation for Christianity's ascendancy not only as a great and noble religion but, moreover, in the assessment of many of its proponents, the one and only true religion in the world.

The Christology that emerged at this time—that Jesus had been "fully human and fully divine"—has been explicitly sustained over the years through the historic creeds of the "one holy catholic church," a term that referred to all Christian churches, everywhere, in the fourth century. The word "catholic" means "universal." Obviously, in the creeds, the word "catholic" did not refer to what would much later become the Roman Catholic Church. Indeed, the christological debates and the creeds they produced took place seven hundred before the "one holy catholic church" divided into Eastern ("Orthodox") and Western ("Roman Catholic") traditions (1054 CE) and more than a thousand years before the Protestant Reformation of the sixteenth century CE. Arguably the most famous creed of all—the Nicene—still occupies a central place in most celebrations of the Mass, or Eucharist, or Holy Communion, in Roman Catholic, Eastern Orthodox, and Anglican/ Episcopal churches throughout the world:

> We believe in one Lord, Jesus Christ,
> the only Son of God, eternally begotten of the Father,
> God from God, Light from Light, true God from true God,
> begotten, not made, of one Being with the Father.
> Through him all things were made.
> For us and for our salvation he came down from heaven:
> by the power of the Holy Spirit
> he became incarnate from the Virgin Mary,
> and was made man.[39]

This christological affirmation baffles or bores many faithful Christians and often contributes to their alienation from Christian worship and the institutional church. Where in such obscure assents, folks wonder, is there even a glimpse of the simple brother from Nazareth who taught love of God and neighbor?

Classical Christology was framed seventeen hundred years ago by churchmen under the influence of Greek philosophy. As noted, these men were trying to strengthen the church's identity in a secular society. Their Christology and creeds took philosophical and linguistic shape in an esoteric field of speculation about "essences" and "substances" and "persons," images and language that make little sense to most of us today.[40]

But we should be clear that the problem today is not that the Nicene Creed, excerpted above, is necessarily false or wrong—because, honestly, who can tell? The problem with creeds like the Nicene is that, in a philosophy that belongs to ancient Greece, the theology buried therein offers little help to people today who are genuinely trying to connect with a living Spirit. We cannot honestly, much less enthusiastically, affirm our faith in "essences" and abstract "persons." We are much better able to connect with the power of Jesus through stories of a human brother with a clear and straightforward message of love, compassion, and respect for God, other humans, and all creation.

There is no question that Jesus of Nazareth's life took on great spiritual momentum and significance very early, making his relationship to God a matter of pressing interest to Christians in all times and places, including our own. And if Jesus really was "God from God" and "Light from Light"—something I have come to imagine in the latter part of my life—perhaps it is in the sense that all of us are, or can be. Perhaps all who love neighbor as self, all who participate in struggles for justice and compassion, all such creatures embody "God from God," "Light from Light," "true God from true God." Perhaps all such creatures are "of one Being with" the Mother-Father-Creator-Spirit-God. This possibility—that we are all daughters and sons of God, all sisters and brothers of Jesus, and all spirited God-bearers to the world—is what part three of this book will be raising up, when we consider the Holy Spirit.

Meanwhile, in the realm of Christology, both in its origins and in our contemporary discussions, what has interested me most over the years was sparked by a question put to our systematic theology class at Union Seminary by Christopher Morse in 1970.

A graduate student and tutor at the time, Dr. Morse later became an esteemed, much beloved professor at Union. The question he asked our class to consider became the standard by which I would forever measure the value of every theological statement about Jesus, God, humanity, and the world. The most important theological question, Christopher Morse proposed, is never simply "What?" but "So what?"

What difference did it make, and does it make, that Jesus of Nazareth was born, lived, and died at the hands of a hostile state and was experienced by his early followers as in some way risen from the dead? So what? That is the question.

As a young and theologically more conventional girl, I had gotten hooked by the creed's implicit doctrine of Jesus's being "fully human and fully divine." This had fascinated me in my early teens when I was going to church almost daily, making a regular confession, and having intense discussions with my best friends about our devotion to God the Father and God the Son. Through college and the social movements of the 1960s, as I grew more convinced that justice and compassion are the incarnation of God's life, my interest in classical Christology continued as an academic study that I would pursue at Union Seminary in the late 1960s and throughout the 1970s.

In the course of the 1970s, however, an ever-deepening interest in justice-love as the core of the Sacred—not merely a byproduct— produced an answer to my "so what?" question about Jesus. The reason Jesus mattered so much to me then, I realized as I was setting off on my vocational and professional journey, is that Jesus taught and embodied God's passion for justice. For that reason, as I pursued my studies at Union, my interest shifted away from Jesus as a divine man, a supernatural figure of interest largely to philosophical theologians and defenders of Christian orthodoxy.

I became more interested in the life of Jesus of Nazareth, the human being: a brother whose way of atoning, being at one with God, becomes for us a "moral influence." The moral influence theory of atonement, which stresses our actively loving one another—rather than Jesus's sacrifice of himself to God, or God's requirement of a payment for the sins of the world—is associated with the life and work of French Christian philosopher Peter Abelard (twelfth century), who was himself accused of heretical thinking by the ecclesiastical authorities of his day.

That Jesus was male was not much of a problem for me by the late 1970s because, by the time I began teaching, preaching, leading worship, and writing theology, I had concluded that Jesus had been fully human, no more—and no less—divine at the core of his being than you and I. This realization of Jesus's full humanity, together with his passion for neighbor-love at the heart of his own life, excited me tremendously and became the wellspring of my vocational energies as a Christian priest, teacher, and theologian at the dawn of my ministry.

Though never a theological doctrine that I could take seriously as an adult, the importance of the maleness of Jesus would be raised publicly as a challenge to women seeking to be ordained priests. We would learn that, to many church fathers ancient and contemporary, Jesus's gender was essential to his being Christ (what I would much later refer to as his christic power)—and to his being the Son of God as well as God the Son. Only a Son would do, we daughters would hear again and again during the 1970s. And these men were serious. It was an old message, ancient as the church itself, and familiar to most (perhaps all) Christian women from our experiences as girl children in the family of God the Father. The eternally strong bond between Father and Son signaled unmistakably that sons were closer than daughters to God.

# Re-imaging "Incarnation": Christic Power

In response to this theological nonsense, a central theme in my teachings over the course of my professional work, spanning about fifty years, has been that the daughters of God need to come out of hiding, shake off our complacency, and metaphorically step out of the tomb, risen together as fully human beings, alive with sacred—christic—power, called together to incarnate an ever-rising God.

We have been misled by the traditional Christian assumption that the doctrine of "the Incarnation" refers specifically, and solely, to Jesus as the Christ, to God becoming flesh in Jesus of Nazareth. For most of my life, and all of my adult life, I have believed that God is incarnate in all creation insofar as we love one another, participate in healing and liberating our sisters and brothers, and extend compassion to our neighbors and kindness to the whole inhabited earth. The emphasis here is on *all creation*—humankind and creaturekind. God incarnate is in the love between us, our yearnings for mutuality, the spiritual sparks that fly between and among us, making each of us who we are at our best, and each of us, in that moment, an image of God incarnate, Christ, bearer of christic power. This power belongs to none of us, and to all of us.

In this more inclusive sense of incarnation, part two is shaped around what I have discerned as images of incarnation—times and places, moments and movements, people and creatures of many kinds, through whom I have encountered the body of Christ, or "christic power," a term I often use for God's taking shape among us.[41] Each of these images, beginning with the Philadelphia ordination of women priests in the Episcopal Church, is, like a grain of sand, the tiniest representation of the wellspring of all joy and struggle. The biblical quotes signal a connection between these modern images of incarnation and the story of Jesus's remarkable participation in the ongoing incarnation of God.

## IMAGE ONE

## The Philadelphia ordination

"You are my daughters, with you I am well pleased."

MARK 1:11 (ADAPTED)

God's pleasure was in the eleven who stepped forward and the three men who ordained us, but even more, She delighted in the deep crack inflicted by this ordination in the structure of a patriarchal church that had bent over backwards to keep women down and out of sacramental leadership.

I refer here to the sacrament of the Eucharist or Holy Communion, the sacrament of baptism, and sacramental blessings including the granting of absolution or pardon from sin. Over the years, the Anglican/Episcopal church had fiercely resisted women's sacramental leadership because the church has always taught that a "sacrament" is an "outward and visible sign of an inward and spiritual grace." A "spiritual grace" is a gift in which God gives Himself to us (male language intentional) through bread and wine, water, assurance of forgiveness. If women cannot represent God like men can, then women cannot be sacramental ministers. This theological—theo-illogical—reasoning continues to dominate the doctrine, discipline, and worship of Roman Catholic and Eastern Orthodox churches.[42]

The problem with the women "irregularly" ordained in Philadelphia, we often heard, was that we were too political. Not spiritual enough. We were seeking attention, power, fame, personal fulfillment, whatever; we were not seeking to be faithful to God. Otherwise, why would we have been so disruptive of the good order of the church we claimed to love? And in the months following the ordination, why were we so defiant of our bishops' pleas with us to stop upsetting good faithful Christian people by officiating at Holy Communion? In their eyes, we were eleven angry women, joined the following year by four more, women bound and determined to have our own way, even if we tore the Episcopal Church apart.

Between my decision in 1971 to seek ordination to the priesthood and the actual ordination of eleven of us on July 29, 1974, in the Episcopal Church of the Advocate in North Philadelphia, there was a great deal of movement—in seminaries, parishes, and living rooms throughout the nation, as Episcopalians talked about ordaining women. During these years, increasing numbers of theologically educated women were finding each other and gaining skills in community organizing, coming to realize that this action was exactly what it would take to convince the church to ordain and eventually accept women priests.

Our chief mentor in this process was the Reverend Suzanne (Sue) Hiatt, who had been ordained a deacon in 1971, six years after her graduations from both the Episcopal Theological School in Cambridge, Massachusetts, and the school of social work at Boston University. At Boston University, Sue had learned various community organizing skills to complement her theological training in the Bible, church history, theology, and pastoral counseling. In 1970, Sue had been hired by Bishop Robert DeWitt of the Diocese of Pennsylvania to put her social work skills to use, organizing wealthy white suburban Philadelphians to participate in the struggles for racial and economic justice. Bishop DeWitt knew that Sue agreed that such commitment and struggle is at the very heart of God.

After deciding to seek ordination rather than fly to Australia to join my beloved David, a decision that shocked me more than anyone, I got down to the business of involving myself more fully in the movement for women's ordination. Momentum toward this goal had begun to grow following the defeat of the proposal to ordain women priests by the 1970 General Convention of the Episcopal Church in Houston. I hadn't attended this convention, but one of the women who had been there returned to Union Seminary with a report of one of the deputies declaring on the convention floor that "God could no more ordain a woman than He could a cow." The months and years ahead were going to be strange ones, in which we women would find ourselves alternately astonished and estranged, angry and amused, hurt and healed by the sheer force of a Spirit who had little patience with that kind of ignorance passing itself off for faith.

Between 1971 and 1974, the movement for the ordination of women priests grew in strength and enthusiasm. So however did the movement of our opponents who ranged from conservative biblical evangelicals, holding onto their literal and patriarchal interpretation of the Bible; to traditional Anglo-Catholics, for whom the maleness of Christ was essential to ordained priesthood; to those Episcopalians who had no particular theological objection to women priests but just didn't think it was in good taste—like admitting women to the Harvard Club, in the words of a prominent male priest. Many Anglo-Catholics saw no reason not to ordain women. They just thought that Episcopalians shouldn't go running off to do something so offensive to Roman Catholics.

The force of fear in our lives is fierce, so it should have come as no surprise to us that, despite our best efforts to organize the voting deputies and bishops in the years leading up to the 1973 General Convention, the opponents to women priests won. Their victory, by a larger margin than in 1970, signaled to us that the time had come for women to move ahead, with those bishop allies who were ready to join us, and figure out how to proceed with the ordination of women priests— despite the General Convention's vote.

And so we did, some of us believing that we would be deposed, kicked out of the priesthood and the possibility of ever working in the church, others of us imagining that we would find places in the church to exercise our ministries. But all eleven of the women ordained in July, 1974, were confident that this was *kairos*, a major spiritual moment in which we had an opportunity to turn ourselves over to the love and care of God and let Her carry us along.

This is what we believed, we and the bishops and several thousand others who gathered for the Philadelphia ordination in July, 1974, and the Washington ordination in September, 1975: that the Spirit who yearns for us to make justice-love in the world had moved us to stand together.

Were we correct in our shared sensibility? Were we actually seeing one another, the world, the church, and ourselves through the eyes of God? Or were we, as our adversaries charged, a bunch of self-serving women out to stir up trouble in the church? Those who realize the toll of patriarchal Christian theologies on the lives of women and girls, as well as the lives of men, boys, and the entire creation, cannot remain neutral or indifferent without helping to strengthen the fabric of a male-centered tradition woven largely by men to secure their power over women, children, less powerful men, and the whole earth.

The primary significance for me of the movement for women's ordination, and the Philadelphia ordination, was in discovering the sacred power of collective action taken by women with male allies. Looking back, I especially celebrate our shared embodiment of God's power to heal the broken hearts of women and girls throughout the world, especially in Christian churches. I also celebrate our daring to come together in the Philadelphia ordination so that we could get on with our lives and ministries, as priests, with greater confidence in God, one another, and ourselves. It would take a long time for most of us to realize it, but in the Philadelphia and Washington ordinations and in the months and years that followed, my sisters and I came into our own as daughters and—as we matured spiritually—sisters of God.

The Philadelphia ordination, our launch into spiritual adulthood, took place less than two weeks before the resignation of President Richard Nixon on August 9, 1974, the culmination of the Watergate scandal. The ordination bumped the beleaguered Nixon, H. R. Haldeman, John Ehrlichman, and their fellow culprits out of the headlines for about a week, as media flashed images of women in long white robes serving communion to people who knelt in front of us while male priests and bishops scowled. The irony of the coincidental timing of these events—Watergate and women priests—was not lost on us. We didn't exactly see ourselves representing righteousness versus the wickedness of "Tricky Dick" Nixon, though some of our friends were quick to make this comparison. We certainly knew ourselves to be as complicated, morally and spiritually, as any of our adversaries either in the church or in the larger society, but we did indeed imagine, and hope, that God was doing some major house-cleaning—sweeping out the dust and rubble of an all-male priesthood and an errant, destructive presidency—to clear the air for some fresh starts.

There's a joke that when bishops gather around to consecrate a brother bishop by laying their hands on his head, they are actually removing his spine. When Bishops DeWitt, Welles, Corrigan, and Barrett laid their hands on our heads in the "irregular" ordinations, they were infusing us with a Spirit to keep our courage to be the priests, prophets, daughters, and sisters of a God who loves the world She has made with a relentless passion for justice.

## IMAGE TWO

## A priest forever

"Do you love me? . . . Feed my sheep."

JOHN 21:17

My first book was a story about my path to the Philadelphia ordination. No doubt one of the least read parts of *A Priest Forever* but probably one of the most prescient, was the Appendix:

> The identification of the priest with Christ is a doctrine perpetuated in order to maintain Priesthood as a caste: arrogant and closed, both to new kinds of members and to new theology. Any church doctrine built, maintained and employed to facilitate exclusion and separation rather than inclusion and unity is a doctrine unworthy of the name Jesus Christ. Perhaps a time will come when women and men, clergy and laity, can agree that, sacramentally speaking, all people are symbolic, representative, even iconographic, of Christ in his priestly sacrifice and otherwise.[43]

This was written in 1975, early in our ministries as new priests. Notice the insistence here on the inclusivity of all people, not just a special group (ordained people), in whatever we believe most represents Jesus Christ in the world. In other words, like Jesus, the ordained priest is not set above her brothers and sisters but rather is a sister or brother among them—and, in fact, these sisters and brothers are themselves as much like Jesus as she is. There is no one special son—or daughter. We are all daughters and sons of God, very much in the memory and spirit of Jesus.

One of my primary theological mentors and activist companions from the mid-1970s until her death in 2003 was the remarkable German theologian Dorothee Soelle, whom I met in Beverly Harrison's apartment in 1976. Dorothee had come to Union Seminary as a distinguished visiting professor. She and Bev were visiting when I stopped by to meet Dorothee.

Bev knew already that Dorothee and I were kindred theological spirits and thought we should meet each other. Those who knew Bev can well imagine her arranging this introduction, because Bev was a networker, always introducing folks to people who, she believed, they should know. Bev and I had both been energized and excited by Dorothee's early books, especially *Christ the Representative* (1967). Bev knew Dorothee as a new colleague at Union Seminary whose vision for social transformation she shared, and Bev knew me as a student increasingly alive with theological questions and passions very close to Dorothee's and her own. Moreover, through participation in the same women's consciousness-raising group at Union Seminary, Bev and I had begun to count on each other's love and support as women seeking to change the male-dominated ethos of the seminary, to chip away at the patriarchal character of the church, and to participate in the struggles for justice in the world.

When I rang the bell, Bev and Dorothee came to the door together. Bev immediately introduced Dorothee and me and remarked that, by way of introducing Dorothee to my work, she had loaned Dorothee my book *A Priest Forever*, which Dorothee had just finished. Before I could say anything but "hi," and before either Bev or Dorothee said anything else, Dorothee looked me in the eye, shook her head in a gesture of weary disbelief, and said, "I must ask you why any justice-loving woman would want to be a priest!"

I don't recall exactly what I said, but I'm sure I muttered some words about working for justice in the church. Although I was shocked, I was neither frightened nor offended by this encounter. I was fascinated by Dorothee Soelle, her audacity, and the wisdom implicit in her question, which even then—about two years after my ordination—I recognized.

Why indeed would any justice-loving woman want to be a priest? This question has lingered with me over the decades, sometimes dragging me down, sometimes challenging me to bear ever more hearty witness to the compatibility of organized religion and the various movements for justice. Still, I must say that I have often wondered, especially in the last decade or two, whether I might have been able to be more fully involved in justice work had I never thought about being ordained, because there is an inherent conservatism in institutional religion. An ordained priest or minister of any Christian church is a representative of this conservatism, regardless of our personal spiritual beliefs and political commitments.

By "conservatism," I mean a pull toward preserving whatever is good from the past, the tradition, and the community's life together. Regardless of what she may think of this community and regardless of how the community may regard her, an ordained person represents the church community for whom she goes forth and to whom she returns. This "representative" role is powerful and can be a forceful element in any struggle—whether for solace in grief, or for encouragement in the struggles for racial, gender, or environmental justice. As such, the communitarian basis of ordained Christian ministry, and of all religious leadership, can be a huge asset in the struggles for justice.

Of course, the same communal foundation is often a powerful force to thwart and inhibit justice of all kinds. Two flagrant historical examples in the United States were the roles of Christianity in efforts to tame or exterminate Native "savages" and the mainline churches' parts in securing slavery. More recent examples would be the silence of Christian leaders in the United States about Israel's extraordinarily inhospitable and violent treatment of the Palestinians; the opposition of many Christian churches to comprehensive immigration legislation; Christian leaders' complicity in constructing the draconian system of criminal injustice in our nation; Christian leaders' support for limiting women's reproductive choices; the churches' frantic efforts to block marriage equality; and Christianity's generally weak, toothless response to the savaging of planet earth.

A truly reprehensible contemporary example of the Christian church's complicity in evil and injustice has been the silence on the parts of many prominent Christian leaders in response to the powerful gun lobby in this nation. Murder and suicide by gun violence are not fundamentally about mental illness or background checks, although we as a society need to attend compassionately to our mentally ill neighbors, families, and friends; and we certainly need background checks for gun sales. The fundamental problem posed by gun violence in the United States, however, is the link between the proliferation of guns in this nation and the powerful moneyed interests represented by the National Rifle Association and their friends in Congress and state legislatures. In the context of this flagrant abuse of violent, deadly power, Christians choosing to stand quietly on the sidelines, or to look the other way, amounts to our ongoing participation in the crucifixion of innocent women, men, and children, each of them, like Jesus, a daughter or son of God; each, a representative of Jesus, hanging on a cross.

The NRA is one of the golden calves to which we as a nation are collectively bowing down. Through the story of Moses smashing the idols (Exod. 32:19–20), we can see that God's angry response is to crush the idols—the guns, the NRA, the Congress, the Supreme Court, as well as those who worship them with our silence or apathy.

So why in the midst of such social evils as gun violence, racist immigration policies, and the radically sexist foundations of the Christian church, would anyone who cares about justice want to be a priest? Why would anyone who cares about justice want to be alive on planet earth? My answer to both questions is that the problems of evil and injustice always lead us to moral challenges, which in turn raise serious ethical and theological questions. These pressing questions and challenges give serious meaning to our lives. They wake us up and spark our passion for justice and compassion and human well-being and creature-care. More than anything else, these questions and challenges are what led me to Beverly Harrison.

## IMAGE THREE

### With Bev, alive on planet earth

The Spirit of God is upon us,
because She has anointed us
to bring good news to the poor.
She has sent us to proclaim release to the captives
and recovery of sight to the blind,
to let the oppressed go free,
to proclaim the year of Her favor.

LUKE 4:18–19, ADAPTED

Each of us can name a few people without whom we would not be who we are at our best, folks who have shaped our hearts and minds and souls and, in some cases, touched and held our bodies tenderly, bringing us to life in ways we never imagined possible. From the perspective of Christian spirituality, these people lead us more fully into the realm of Spirit in which we ourselves, and they with us, become incarnate God-bearers in the world. They call us forth to live as sisters and brothers of Jesus, women and men who share Jesus's christic power to heal a broken creation and liberate oppressed and battered people. Beverly Wildung Harrison was such a person in my life. In many ways picking up for me spiritually where Betty Smith had left off, Bev Harrison showed me exactly who and what Jesus had been all about in his time and place. He had urged his friends and followers to embrace the sacred power they shared with him—to "pick up their beds and walk"—rather than fritter their lives away.

Bev and I met in September, 1967, when I arrived at Union Seminary fresh from Randolph-Macon Woman's College. Earlier in the summer Beverly Jean Wildung had married a fellow campus minister, James Harrison, and they were living in an apartment in Greenwich Village. Jim was working on his doctorate in clinical psychology at New York University and Bev was working as an assistant for women students in the Dean of Students office at Union. She was also teaching at Union while she worked on her own doctorate in Christian ethics.

From our first meeting in Bev's office that fall, she and I had clicked, we acknowledged years later. Each of us had recognized the other's integrity and a vibrant life-force in the other—and we had tapped this force in each other in transformative ways. The early shape of our relationship was of teacher and mentor to student, each admiring and learning from the other. When we were in the same women's consciousness-raising group in the 1970s, along with other Union students and staff, we began to share more deeply aspects of our lives as women, and we were drawn together more intimately as friends and sisters in the struggle against sexism in church and society. This strong sense of community was present not only for Bev and me but for all the women in the consciousness-raising groups that were springing up in the seminary and throughout the nation, as the women's liberation movement took off.

In the years that followed, Bev—a Presbyterian laywoman—became a mentor to a number of Union's women seminarians who were seeking ordination in the Episcopal Church. Like Sue Hiatt's work with us as a strategist, Bev's analysis of the structure of the Episcopal Church and of how change might be brought about strengthened us. The women's ordination movement was a less sentimental and a tougher movement because of Sue Hiatt, and because we had among our allies some other sharp feminist analysts like Beverly Harrison and feminist theologian Nelle Morton who was teaching at Drew Theological School.[44] During the mid-1970s, I grew close to Bev and Jim Harrison as friends with whom I would spend occasional weekends, along with other Union students, at the Harrison's getaway home up the Hudson River, about an hour north of Manhattan. Toward the end of the decade, as I was working on my own dissertation in theology, Bev was not only one of my academic advisors but, as importantly, one of the chief inspirations in my project on "mutual relation," which I was coming to believe is at the heart of all that is sacred. Upon its completion in the spring of 1980, I dedicated the thesis "to Bev, because we can count on so few to go this hard way with us." The dedication was an early testimony to Bev's own devotion to the mutuality she and I had tapped together. Over the years, we would each learn, more and more, to trust the power of God acting in history as the radical power of mutual relation—whether between friends and lovers, or between nations, races, cultures, religions, and even species.

In May 1980, I graduated from Union. Several months later, soon after Bev's decision to leave her marriage, a decision long in coming, she and I took our first vacation together in a little cottage near Cape Cod—and launched a special relationship that would span another thirty-two years, until Bev's death in North Carolina on December 15, 2012. Bev's and my relationship would be an ongoing source of wonder and delight, healing and empowerment. Our relationship would also be scarred, though never shattered, by our respective and interactive battles with addiction.

The energizing power of our relationship, grounded from the outset in mutuality and wrapped in immense gratitude and regret, is present throughout this book. Our shared joy and the value of our professional endeavors were interwoven and strengthened tremendously by each other's work. Neither Bev nor I could have become ourselves at our best without the other's supportive love. We informed each other's intellectual work and professional contributions and we helped each other engage other people, beginning with our families and closest friends, in the context of a world and church that did not, and does not, do justice to strong women. Our core spiritual beliefs grew together over three decades, seasoning her work in social ethics and mine in theology. We believed that our alliance strengthened each of our contributions to the larger world of feminist liberation ethics and theologies and, even as our relationship became in ways more challenging over the years, we were never happier or more confident than when we were working together as ethicist and theologian. We gave each other spiritual encouragement, psychological stamina, and physical support to persevere in what was for us a shared mission on planet earth.

## IMAGE FOUR

## Coming out

No one after lighting a lamp puts it under a bushel basket,
but on the lampstand, and it gives light to all in the house.

MATTHEW 5:15

Before Bev and I became partners and a year before I completed my doctorate in theology at Union, I decided it was time for me to "come out" as lesbian.

The Stonewall riots had occurred in New York's Greenwich Village in 1969, thereby sparking the gay liberation movement in the United States. Several years later, the American Psychological and Psychiatric Associations officially removed the long-standing stigma of homosexuality as a psychological disorder or psychiatric disease. With this impetus, many gay men and lesbians had begun to demand that our relationships be assessed and affirmed on the same basis as heterosexual relationships. In response, several large mainline Protestant churches in the United States, including the Episcopal Church, had begun to study human sexuality.

It was no time for lesbian women and gay men to stay tucked quietly away if we believed we could come out without damaging ourselves or others. Because quite a few male priests and laymen and at least one Episcopal woman priest had recently come out, it seemed to me the right thing to do—to stand in solidarity with these brothers and especially my sister priest, Ellen Barrett, who as a lesbian woman had put herself out there, alone, shortly before her ordination in 1977.

Furthermore, I had joined the faculty of the Episcopal Divinity School in 1975 and, from the outset, had felt duplicitous, sometimes almost voyeuristic, listening to students share their own struggles with questions about their sexual orientation and identity. How could I not at least acknowledge that I myself was no stranger to these questions?

So I made a strategic decision in the spring of 1979 to publish two essays in separate religious journals during the month of June. In each, I would come out—but in two different ways. In one essay, the text of a talk I had given in 1977 at the Episcopal Church of the Redeemer in Chestnut Hill, Massachusetts, I would affirm myself as "bisexual"—someone attracted to both genders (*The Witness*, June, 1979). In the other, I would say that I was choosing to name myself "lesbian" in order to take a clear public stand—and also because I assumed at the time that I would more likely bond sexually with women than men in the course of my life, given the shape of our sexist world and most heterosexual relationships in it (*Christianity and Crisis*, June, 1979). With these two articles, I was purposely articulating an important sexual tension that I believed then and now is a deeply human ambivalence, common to many.

So I came out in the summer of 1979. Before publishing the articles, I told four people to whom I felt I had some responsibility, since I knew they would have to share whatever reaction might ensue: Mary Ann and Bob Heyward, my parents; Harvey Guthrie, dean of the Episcopal Divinity School, where I was employed; and Paul Moore, bishop of New York, where I was canonically resident. My parents were a bit shaken but not distressed and not really surprised. Both responded as I knew they would: "We love you, regardless." Harvey Guthrie and Paul Moore were marvelous, offering to support me in every way they could. Bishop Moore even wrote a letter to my parents, identifying himself as the father of an "out" lesbian—his eldest daughter, Honor—thereby allying himself with Bob and Mary Ann Heyward, who treasured that letter and admired Paul Moore until his dying day decades later. Moore himself came out as a gay or bisexual man late in his life.

As it turned out, the fallout from my coming out was minimal, provoking little surprise. The people most agitated were those still reeling from the Philadelphia ordination, including several women in my mother's book club, who had decided long ago that, in me, my poor mama had wound up with a disturbed and difficult daughter. That my mother would always be a fierce defender of her kids was taken for granted by these nice Christian ladies as a sign of mother-love and loyalty. Over the years, Mama would tell me about these same ladies' opinions about most everything she brought up for discussion—including my first book *A Priest Forever* (1976) and Alice Walker's *The Color Purple* (1982). I watched from a distance as this small band of conservative Christian women chose to trivialize and dismiss Mama's ever-expanding spirit of inclusivity, and I also watched my mother grow in stature with God and woman-kind as she seemed to give not a whit. "They were superficial girls in high school," Mama said, "and they haven't changed a bit." Happily, she had a couple of devoted friends in this book club who hung in there with her, as ally and advocate. It turned out that one of them also had a gay son and lesbian daughter and had been afraid to tell anyone, even Mama. Several years before she died, this woman asked my mother for forgiveness. "Bill and I should have let you and Bob know that you weren't alone. We should have stood with you."

Following this second "coming out," fifteen years after the debutante ball, I continued to teach, preach, and write as a Christian feminist liberation theologian. This naming of my "sexual identity"—a more accurate term in my life, I would come to believe, than either "orientation" or "preference"—was an important grounding of my vocation as priest and theologian in the intimate convergence of sexuality and spirituality. This was not only my experience, but also that of many students and colleagues in theology and ethics who have discussed, lectured on, and written about this connection over the last four decades.

Church historians point out that a strong link between sex and spirit is evident in the testimonies of Christian saints, mystics, and theologians over the two millennia. Increasingly over the past four decades, Christian feminist and womanist theologians have insisted that sexuality plays a primary and central role in any honest theology of incarnation. Otherwise, the human body is only a shell—whether Jesus's body, our bodies, or the collective body of Christ, made incarnate whenever we love one another, sexually and otherwise.

Love is a sexual energy, not necessarily involving or leading to genital sex, in fact seldom involving or leading to sex, but nonetheless the same energy, the same love, the same God, that generates mutuality. In other words, God who is Love is also sexual energy. This was the theme of a book I wrote at the end of the 1980s, in which I suggested an identity between God and "the erotic" (*Touching Our Strength: The Erotic as Power and the Love of God*, 1989).

## IMAGE FIVE

## The question of marriage

Where you go, I will go;
where you lodge, I will lodge,
your people shall be my people,
and your God my God.

Ruth 1:16b

"Marriage equality" has come officially to the United States of America, thanks to a razor-thin, 5–4, vote in the Supreme Court (Obergefell v. Hodges, June 26, 2015). It's important to recognize that the legalization of same-sex marriage is the result not simply of five justice-affirming jurists. Their opinion was a culmination of the collective movement of several generations of LGBTQ activists, scholars, lawyers, doctors, ministers, teachers, parents, children, and others across all professions and religions. Marriage equality has become a reality because men, women, girls, and boys throughout this nation had the audacity and courage to challenge the misogyny and homophobia woven together into the fabric of our dominant religious and civil traditions over not just a few generations but hundreds of years.

Legal marriage between persons of the same sex or gender is a huge victory for justice-loving people everywhere who notice the connections between, on the one hand, sexual justice, fairness, and equality and, on the other, civil rights and human rights for all people around the world, regardless of religion or culture.

While I wholeheartedly support marriage equality, I have misgivings about marriage as a cultural institution that lifts the "couple" above all other relational patterns in terms of social and economic privilege. As a social institution, civil marriage doesn't do justice to single people or those who live in other arrangements. "Couple-dom" has never seemed to me to warrant a place of privilege in society, but rather should be celebrated as one, not the only, constructive, creative relational commitment we can make in the course of our lives. Moreover, marriage is a historically sexist institution, constructed to disempower women under the guise of legal protection, which arguably it is—in a social order founded on male entitlement.

As a gendered construct, marriage makes it more difficult for women to develop their own lives and easier for men to develop theirs. As a social structure in modern as well as older societies, marriage is an economic and social container designed to protect and control women and children. In his 2004 book, *Same Sex Marriage?*, Christian ethicist Marvin M. Ellison has done a fine job assessing, from a Christian feminist liberation perspective, the pros and cons of marriage as a social and theological institution.

Of course, Christianity and other major patriarchal religions in the world have held up marriage as a sacred covenant between a man and a woman. Unfortunately, these religions have done little to critique the sexist basis of patriarchal institutions in general, including marriage, in which the male is assumed to be head of family and household. It is not enough to decide, on our own, case by case, that we just don't agree with this and don't intend to live this way, not when the patriarchal underpinnings of the religion itself, in this case Christianity, remain fundamentally unchallenged.

We should be clear that Christianity does remain fundamentally unchallenged and unchanged as long as God is assumed to be a "Father"—not a Mother—and as long as salvation is linked inextricably to a central relationship between a Father and a Son. This continues to be the case throughout most of the Christian church, except in small pockets of feminist and womanist resistance, including this book. A patriarchal understanding of Christianity underlies the church's obsession with marriage and monogamy as the only moral way for men and women—or persons of the same sex—to live as partners.

By the time Bev and I became partners in 1980, we had decided separately not to have children, and neither of us viewed sexual monogamy—a form of "coupling"—as necessary to a loving, creative partnership. For most of the previous decade, Bev and I had been clear in our writings, our professional relationships with colleagues, and our personal relationships with friends that we harbored strong misgivings about marriage and monogamy. I seriously doubt Bev and I would have married had it been a legal option in the 1980s. But who knows? Despite the patriarchal shape of marriage as an institution, most of us—Bev and I were no exceptions—experience a strong social and psychological lure to publicly celebrate our lives, loves, and commitments. We found ways to celebrate our relationship among friends and family every chance we could and we both experienced strong support from loved ones.

From the outset, like most couples in love, neither Bev nor I had a speck of desire to be anything other than monogamous, and neither of us was basically "polyamorous"—wanting multiple partners, much less imagining that our relationship needed a polyamorous foundation or challenge. At the same time, we did not want to box ourselves or each other into being a couple, which we both viewed as an unnecessarily closed relational system, in both sexual and non-sexual ways. We wanted to be open to a future we could not imagine, and we were confident in the depth and quality of our relationship. Our shared position on relational monogamy—that we would not impose it on our relationship—was well-considered and faithful, but perhaps also foolish. I sometimes wonder.

We knew that our relationship was rooted and grounded in a trustworthy mutual love that did not rest upon a monogamous expectation. We were right about the quality of our connection. We also knew that our relationship, along with that of many other same-sex couples, was indeed shaping the emerging politics—and theology and ethics—of the LGBTQ struggle, including the movement toward marriage equality. Bev and I knew well, and we were grateful, that our relationship was playing a role in the historic struggle for sexual and gender justice. We wanted to model relational openness and freedom, rather than a closed or coupled system. We understood that our life together had a place in the larger context of a political, spiritual, and moral effort to which we were both fully committed. We knew that, whether we liked it or not, our relationship was something of an open book among other feminist theologians and ethicists. Mostly, we accepted this and were grateful for the support of our ever-expanding community of friends and colleagues whom we also were trying to encourage and support in every way we could.

In suggesting that, even so, our choice to be non-monogamous might have been foolish, let me be clear I'm referring specifically to Bev's and my relationship, not to sexual non-monogamy or polyamory as a possibly good and faithful choice for others. As a matter of fact, throughout our life together, Bev and I had many sexually non-monogamous friends. We knew of several non-coupled partnerships—among lesbians and gay men—including several triads of committed partners that were unquestionably devoted and deeply moral relationships.

In a heterosexist social order, which is historically a resource of patriarchy, the choice to be non-monogamous is largely available only to people who are not in heterosexual relationships because only heterosexual relationships carry enough social power to be regulated. Now that marriage equality is more fully a reality, the choice among lesbians and gay men to be non-monogamous, to live for example in triads rather than couples, will become a less socially acceptable option even among gay men and lesbians. Tighter regulation is a price those on the outside pay whenever they are admitted to any institution, such as marriage.

In gaining marriage equality, we lesbians and gay men have been admitted to the heterosexist, patriarchal institution of marriage. Only time will tell if, and how, the institution of marriage will be transformed in significant ways by openly homosexual and bisexual bondings. As some of marriage equality's most ardent foes have asked anxiously, will we now see triads of people asking to be married?

Let me tell you a story. I have a dear and wise friend named Jim, a brother priest, who had a gay son, Jon. For a number of years, Jon lived with two life companions, Eddie and Greg, in Miami. In the early 1990s, Eddie was diagnosed with AIDS. During his illness, Greg and Jon nursed him and were with Eddie when he died. Before long, Jon got sick. As Jon became terminally ill, Greg asked Jon's father, my priest friend Jim, to come down from the North Carolina mountains to be with them in Florida. Jim spent the summer of 1997 with Jon and Greg and was with them when Jon died in September. Not long afterward, Greg became ill and, in Jim's words, "died tragically, alone, in a rat-infested apartment" in Atlanta. Following Greg's death, Jim and his wife Annette brought Greg's ashes to their home in Balsam Grove, North Carolina, where they laid Greg's ashes next to Eddie's and Jon's. Upon hearing this story, a bishop acknowledged that it's a powerful testimony to the strength of God working through people who love one another. "However," the bishop said, "it's not the way we do things in the church."

Monogamy is how we do relationships in the church. But is it always the best way, ethically and psychologically? Most ethicists, pastors, priests, rabbis, and other spiritual and religious teachers have believed that it is. Moreover, for a couple of millennia, both Jewish and Christian religions have taught that monogamous marriage is, by definition, between a man and a woman.

Bev and I did not assume that marriage must be between a man and a woman, and we did not assume that a healthy, happy primary relationship is necessarily monogamous.

In the wake of a loved one's death, it is easy to ask "what if?" questions. What if Bev and I had made a decision to be monogamous? Were we foolish not to do this? Might we have loved each other better? Might we have been better able to care for each other in the real world of the social, political, and personal challenges that can strengthen or fray the fabric of any relationship? In this real world of ours, Bev's and my relationship was both buoyed and battered by events in the world and by the dynamics of addiction that each of us had carried into our love and work. Would being married, or coupled as partners in a monogamous relationship, have helped or hindered us in our life together?

As it was, Bev and I both did the best we could in relation to each other and, to be sure, in Ntozake Shange's language, we "loved each other fiercely."[45]


## IMAGE SIX

## Global struggle against capitalist spirituality and christo-fascism

No one can serve two masters. . . . You cannot serve God and wealth.

MATTHEW 6:24

But woe to you who are rich, for you have received your consolation.
Woe to you who are full now, for you will be hungry.
Woe to you who are laughing now, for you will mourn and weep.

LUKE 6:24–25

The 1980s were socially and spiritually a dreadful, debilitating decade in at least the short-term history of our nation and planet. All US presidents, like other global figures, are larger than life caricatures of particular values and events for which they have stood. They become symbols. People like my own mother, who voted against Ronald Reagan twice, still referred to him as a "nice man," just a lousy president. I have no idea whether Ronald Reagan was a nice man—a good dad, for example—and neither did my mother. But let's give him the benefit of a doubt and assume he was. What we do know, for a fact, is that Ronald Reagan was a Hollywood actor who found his voice in the presidency of the United States, and—despite perhaps being a nice guy personally— became a symbol of the selfishness and greed in which global capitalism must be drenched in order to maximize profit, its chief motive.

With a handsome, cowboy-ish, "aw shucks" style, Reagan presented himself as a father figure to those who believed that the emphases on social justice and economic fairness of the 1960s and 1970s had gotten out of hand and needed to be reined in. In this spirit, many Americans believed that Ronald Reagan represented the antithesis of his predecessor Jimmy Carter. A common perception among the people was that where Carter was weak—remember the hostages in Iran—Reagan was strong. In truth, where Carter's style was patient and reflective, Reagan's was brash; he tended to punish first and ask questions later, as in the case of the fired air traffic controllers. Carter asked the whole nation to share the load of helping the poor, and Reagan told the poor to help themselves, becoming our own modern-day Marie Antoinette, who is said to have quipped about the poor, "Let them eat cake!"

Ronald Reagan proudly represented the rise of what Beverly Harrison would name "capitalist spirituality"—linking Christian faith with financial gain—and Beverly Harrison represented the antithesis of Ronald Reagan and everything he stood for. Like her friend and colleague Dorothee Soelle, Bev sometimes referred to the Reagan administration as "christo-fascist"—and so did I.

In coining the term "christo-fascist," Soelle suggested that fascism was creeping into the United States as it had fifty years earlier in Germany and Italy. Bev and Dorothee also sensed that, even more in the United States than in Germany, a nascent fascism would have the blessing of many Christians because the United States tended then and now to be more religious than Germany.

Soelle saw "christo-fascism" in the unbridled capitalism being raised up as God's own economy by the Reagan administration. Remember that

Dorothee Soelle was a German who knew, firsthand, fascism's wicked
ways and was determined to struggle against even a tendency toward
fascism wherever it might stretch its death-dealing tentacles. Remember
also that Beverly Harrison was a highly regarded economic ethicist who
understood advanced global capitalism as a basically immoral system
that lends itself to our worst, most selfish, human instincts. Bev assessed
the worship of wealth over human well-being, the spiritual basis of Rea-
ganomics, as the essence of "capitalist spirituality." She understood well,
and opposed with every breath in her body, the politics and spirituality
of advanced global capitalism which she, like her colleague Dorothee,
believed was indeed conducive to the rising of christo-fascism among us.[46]

It can be argued that it's better not to risk alienating allies by using
inflammatory words like "fascist" and "christo-fascist" to describe current trends. Some may not find the term "fascist" helpful except as a
reference to Hitler, Mussolini, and their followers then and now. I agree
that we ought to use such strong, historically based language thought-
fully and sparingly. But this language can be an effective tool in making
a point ethically or theologically. Dorothee and Bev's critique of global
capitalism in general, and Ronald Reagan's administration in particular,
as providing a breeding ground for "christo-fascism" was, in my opinion, right on the mark.

Were they with us today, I have no doubt that Dorothee and Bev
would both use strong language—no doubt controversial—in their
theological and ethical assessments of the capitalism, tribalism, racism,
and sexism rampant in the world, especially their European and North
American contexts and most particularly following the Brexit vote in
the UK; the election of Donald Trump to the presidency here in the
United States; and other nativist movements around the world that are
hostile to people of different religions, languages, cultures, and customs;
and resistant also to forging global economic partnerships and securing
protections of the earth's water, air, and other natural resources.

These factions draw strength, of course, from a significant numbers of white Christians—in the United States and globally—who
tilt fascist in their hatred of black and brown people, Muslims, Jews,
gays, abortion providers, and feminists, as well as in their belief that
God has a preference for them and their faith. Their christo-fascism
becomes especially death-dealing through easy access to powerful

guns. The young white supremacist shooter of the nine African Americans at Mother Emanuel AME Church in Charleston, South Carolina, in June, 2015, is a horrifying example of contemporary fascism in its especially deadly, racist garb.

Seeds of the same fascist movement among us were strewn in the Reagan administration's high-profile war on drugs, which constituted a broad-sweeping assault on the African American urban poor beginning in the early 1980s.[47] The war on drugs and what it set in motion—the incarceration of vast numbers of poor people of color—was, and is, not precisely analogous to Hitler's campaign in the 1930s to purge Germany of "impurities"—Jews, homosexuals, gypsies. Yet in each case, the national government purposely generated hateful propaganda, based on lies, against certain groups, and followed up with violent action against these groups in order to eliminate them. In Germany, it was Jews, homosexuals, and others deemed dangerous and expendable. Since the early 1980s in the United States, it has been poor people, especially the urban poor who are largely black and brown people, being harassed, arrested, and incarcerated on drug charges. Comparable drug offenses in predominantly white suburban middle-class communities have generally been downplayed and often unacknowledged, underscoring a misperception among the white majority that people of color are the serious "drug dealers" in our midst.

In Germany, people were exterminated. In the United States, people have been locked in cages and forgotten or—as evidenced by events unfolding among us more recently—shot on sight by law enforcement officers or community patrols. While "Black Lives Matter" is not a response to an officially fascist state, it certainly signals resistance to deeply disturbing currents in a nation that boasts of being the land of the free and the home of the brave.

As feminist Christians and liberation theologians, Bev, Dorothee, and others drew devastating connections between the gilded spirituality of the Reagan administration's worship of capital and the more extreme, xenophobic spirituality of Hitler's hatred of Jews whose very existence was deemed economically and spiritually threatening to everything truly German: white, right, pure, blond, Aryan.

Christo-fascism, capitalist spirituality, the world according to Ronald Reagan and Margaret Thatcher and the neocons: This was the social and political backdrop against which feminist liberation theologies were being shaped in the 1980s and 1990s. Bev and I found ourselves among the shapers and the shaped—through teaching, preaching, speaking, demonstrating, workshops, reading, writing, and through collaboration with other feminist and liberation theologians, including womanist, *mujerista*, black, Native American, and Asian American theological companions in the United States and also sister and brother theologians, pastors, and ethicists from around the world, from such nations as the Philippines, South Korea, China, New Zealand, Australia, South Africa, Kenya, Britain, Italy, Switzerland, Germany, Peru, Argentina, Nicaragua, Guatemala, Canada, and Mexico.

## IMAGE SEVEN

## Mutual relation and making connections

Follow me.

MARK 1:17

If anyone will not welcome you or listen to your words,
shake off the dust from your feet as you leave that house or town.

MATTHEW 10:14

In 1973, seven years before Bev and I became partners, I read Mary Daly's *Beyond God the Father*, the book that probably more than any other placed feminism near the center of liberal Christian theological education and sparked a movement in Christian feminism. Over the next several decades, feminism would come into its own as a spiritual and political force to be reckoned with. Not only God the Father but also God the Son would be interrogated by several generations of women scholars and activists, pastors and priests. The centrality of the Son—Jesus Christ as Son of God and God the Son—was fascinating to me as a student of Christian theology, a recently ordained priest, and a young feminist theologian. Together with the centrality of Jesus Christ in every facet of Christian life, especially worship, the ubiquitous presence of evil in the world had become a compelling theological interest to me.

Writing a doctoral thesis in the late 1970s gave me a chance to try to link these two special interests: the pervasiveness of Jesus Christ and the haunting presence of evil in the world. I chose to focus my research on the Holocaust, which had been met by the silence of most Christian churches in Europe and elsewhere. In response to this historical fact—the presence of evil and the silent response from those who teach and preach the saving power of Jesus Christ—I asked, "To what extent are we responsible for our own redemption in history—and for the redemption of God?" In other words, since God does not step in supernaturally to "save" people from evils like the Holocaust, isn't it up to us to step in? Don't we, in Nikos Kazantzakis's words, become not only the saviors of one another, but also "the saviors of God"?[48]

Furthermore, are we not incarnating God when we step in to save one another from evil? When we love the world, our sisters and brothers, enough to do our best to save the world from evil, are we not "the body of Jesus Christ"? Didn't Jesus of Nazareth tell us to live this way, to join him in this mission to save, heal, liberate, and love our neighbors as ourselves?

In my thesis, I proposed that when we live this way, God is in fact "our power for creating right, or mutual, relation"—in which we position ourselves neither above nor beneath others but rather alongside one another as "friends," brothers and sisters. In this sense, God is a sacred power or energy that we embody and share whenever we genuinely love anyone—any person, any creature, the earth itself, and its Creator God. And whenever we really love, we call forth the best in those whom we love, urging them to "go and do likewise" much as Jesus urged his disciples.

The failure of most Christian churches to respond to the evil of the Holocaust exemplifies the enormity of the moral and spiritual challenge we humans face: to look away and act as if we don't notice evil or to do something. In my thesis, published as *The Redemption of God: A Theology of Mutual Relation* (1982), I urge us to do something—pick up our beds and walk into the world, acting together, incarnating a God who is our power for making mutual—just, loving—relationships in history.

Much of the rest of my life as priest and theologian would be spent trying to demonstrate and articulate in different situations the extent to which, like Jesus and in his Spirit, we participate in liberating God as

well as each other whenever we are most mutually engaged in life, helping love and justice, or justice-love, roll down like waters. The oppressive character of the 1980s in the United States was a wake-up call to
feminists and other liberation theologians to "make the connections,"
in Bev's words,[49] between the various structures of injustice—racism,
economic exploitation, sexism—in the US and elsewhere. The poor
of the world were being increasingly targeted by violence in order to
secure the foundations of capitalism, through which wealth would be
generated for the rich. Those in power insisted that this wealth would
"trickle down" to the bottom rungs of society. Unfortunately, this did
not happen in the 1980s, and it does not happen today.

Contrary to the rhetorical manipulation of conservative politicians, like Ronald Reagan in 1980 and Donald Trump in 2016, greed
does not generate generosity. This was the pastoral and ethical warning
of El Salvador's Archbishop Oscar Romero, gunned down in 1980 as
he celebrated Mass in the cathedral in San Salvador. It is the same message Pope Francis is sending to the church and world today. Greed does
not generate generosity. Global capitalist goals are incompatible with
Christian faith.

Yet throughout the 1980s, fueled by the political power of conservative Christians, the Reagan administration did everything in its
power to subvert the socialist government in Nicaragua that had been
established in 1979 by the Sandinista revolutionaries upon their ouster
of the dictator Anastasio Somoza, a reliable and repressive ally of the
United States. Having traveled to Nicaragua in 1983 with Witness for
Peace, I returned in September 1984 with a group of students from the
Episcopal Divinity School. Our mission was to learn some Spanish and
as much as possible about the Christian "base communities" in which
Latin American liberation theology was taking root. [50]

The basic tenets of all Christian liberation theologies are that God
lives among the poor and at the margins of society; that Jesus came, and
continues to come, as an advocate for the poor and oppressed; and that
the church must decide which side it's on. Do we stand with the oppres-
sor or with the oppressed? Does our Jesus Christ proclaim, "'Peace,
peace,' when there is no peace" (Jer. 6:14)? Or do we follow a Jesus
who leads the struggle for liberation from injustice in every situation of
social oppression?

Our month in Nicaragua opened our eyes to the stunning contrast between the base community churches we met there and most of our home churches in the United States. The differences were stark and clear between their respective experiences and understandings of Jesus. In Nicaragua, we were introduced to Jesus as the hope of the poor, a liberator of people from poverty and despair. Whereas back home, most of our experiences had been in middle-class white parish churches in which Jesus, as the Son of God and God the Son, reigns without much ethical content, sort of a fill-in-the-blank Jesus Christ who is whatever comforts us. Moreover, we were shocked to see for ourselves the toll our nation's violence was exacting against the people with whom we worshipped in Managua, meeting family members of sons and daughters killed by the US-sponsored *contra* and breaking bread with worshippers who had almost nothing else to eat during the economic boycott being waged by our homeland against these people.

Some images from my trip with students to Nicaragua in September, 1984, have stayed with me: A boy, his face expressionless, kneeling in the road playing with bullet shells. A member of our group who'd been bitten by a dog receiving a series of rabies shots for which, in Nicaragua's socialist society, there was no fee. A group of mourners outside a church, waving their arms together, shouting, "Presente!" (meaning "Be present!" or "She/he is present!") This was their way of both inviting the deceased into their midst and announcing that, in fact, the dead one is here, alive in our midst! A meal of tostados and queso with several Nicaraguan women, sitting together on a dirt floor in a one-room home, listening to the women discuss God's love of the poor—and God's forgiveness of their American foes who "do not know what they are doing."

How could these people not hate us? we wondered. Again and again we heard from people that we *gringas* were not perceived as the enemy, but rather our government was, and we were urged by our hosts to return to the United States and do everything in our power to change our government's hostile attitude and violent assaults against Nicaragua's poor.

Back home, the Episcopal Divinity School was developing a first-rate program in Feminist Liberation Theology and deriving much of its impetus and content from Latin American liberation theology as well as from black, feminist, and womanist theologies in the US. In fact, throughout the United States, Canada, Western Europe—and, increasingly during the 1980s, throughout the world—feminist liberation theologies were shaped not only to challenge male supremacy but also to make connections among the various interactive structures of oppression based on variables such as gender, sexuality, race, culture, ethnicity, class, religion, age, and ability.

One of the liveliest groups in my life at the time was the "Liberation Group" that met in my apartment for breakfast every week. Largely composed of EDS students and faculty, with some students from Harvard Divinity School in the mix, we met to discuss current events and how we might organize to impact them. In 1983, for example, members of the Liberation Group protested regularly against the launching of the Trident submarine war machines from Groton, Connecticut, and we often participated in demonstrations in downtown Boston against the Reagan administration's on-going assaults on the people of Chile, Nicaragua, El Salvador, and Guatemala. We knew well that Ronald Reagan's ostensibly "anti-communist" motives were a cover for his determination to prop up dictators throughout Latin America who would be loyal to the global capitalist interests of the United States.

During the 1980s and 1990s, some of the most valuable lessons of my life came through my professional relationships, work, and friendships with a number of African American, Latina, and Asian women colleagues who challenged me, along with other liberal, well-meaning white women, to examine our racist assumptions. Through these challenges and relationships, we white feminists learned the difference between "intention" and "impact." Few of us intend to be racist or sexist or in any way unjust in our actions. Yet because we white women bring our white privilege into everything we do, we are often liable, regardless of our intention, to say or do something that is demeaning, hurtful, or otherwise unacceptable to our sisters and brothers of color.

Let me give an example. In the mid-1980s I could not understand why African American lesbian Christians were, on the whole, unwilling to "come out," as quite a few white lesbians had done by then. I didn't understand until several of my black sisters, both lesbian and straight, pointed out how much more an African American woman who is known to be a lesbian has to lose in a white, racist, sexist, and homophobic church and society. What seemed obvious as soon as I stopped to think about it had not occurred to me. My white privilege had shielded my consciousness from realizing what it means to be white, or black, in this society. I had to stop and think about this.[51] Three decades later this is still the case. Although I am much better tuned to detecting racism, my own and others, I still have to stop and think about the impact of what I say and do in relation especially to matters of race and class.

In the 1990s, the lingering colonialism of the Western world, especially of Europe and the United States, would expand and deepen the context of liberation theologies. Postcolonial theologies would begin to spring up in the 1990s and 2000s, in which theologians like Kwok Pui-lan from Hong Kong and Christopher Duraisingh from India would challenge and stretch not only traditional Christian assumptions about God, Christ, and church but also Western liberation and feminist theologians' sensibilities. Even among those of us who take pride in painting outside the lines and thinking outside the box, we Western Christians tend to be more linear and bipolar than many of our Asian colleagues in our thinking about history, good and evil, sexual identity, economics, and other fertile ethical and theological issues.[52]

Still, throughout the 1980s and 1990s, Bev and I were immersed in teaching, preaching, leading workshops, and writing feminist liberation theology and ethics. There is no question that the collective global effort among women, liberation, and later postcolonial theologians and ethicists generated Bev's and my primary professional, political, and spiritual energies and greatly enhanced our love and respect for each other.

With our feminist, womanist, and other colleagues in these liberation movements, Bev as an ethicist and I as a theologian aimed to be clear in our work that God is a force for generating mutuality—making justice-love—wherever there is oppression, injustice, poverty, or violence. In a racist situation, God is always an anti-racist activist. In a sexist situation, Jesus is always an advocate for justice for women. When the earth is being stripped of her resources, the Spirit of Life always fights for the earth's well-being and is never on the side of corporate greed.

The Body of Jesus Christ—the incarnation of Jesus's christic spirit—catches us off balance both because She takes two distinct, unmistakable forms that appear to be very different in human history and because She is always on the move. About the time we think we see the sacred Body of Jesus Christ, He is somewhere else—and He is "She." She is both Victim and Liberator. We see Her hanging on the gallows, a Jewish girl in Auschwitz, and then we see Him in the Allied forces arriving to liberate the camps.

We see His vulnerable Body as the family left homeless while Israeli tanks bulldoze their home; then we notice Her as the peace movement of Palestinians and Israelis, Jews and Muslims and Christians, struggling to restore Palestinians to their rightful homeland, living in peace with Israeli neighbors. We see Her present in and among human and other creatures who are beaten, starved, or violated by people with the social, physical, economic, or political power to harm others, and we know that He is always those who come to liberate the oppressed and heal their broken bodies and spirits.

Throughout human history—long, long before Jesus of Nazareth was born—God's christic Body, which is Her transformative Spirit, has appeared time and again to bring hope to the downtrodden and to cast down the mighty from their thrones. She comes in many guises, many languages, bearing many names, through many religions and none at all. And everywhere He, She, They, appear—in past, present, future—a more fully mutual relation is being generated, God is on the move, and those who participate in this sacred work are godding, making God incarnate, yet again.

Both as Victim and as Liberator, Jesus's body—the body of Christ—is beautiful to those who see through the eyes of God, beautiful and precious and yet also broken. And although the body of Christ is ultimately stronger than death, it is usually difficult for us to notice this, and hard for us to believe it, because our eyes are so weakly tuned to see the Spirit working Her mystery and magic where there is even one small candle shining in the dark, one small heart pounding fiercely for justice, one grandpa telling his granddaughter a story about Jesus or Aung San Suu Kyi or Rosa Parks, Oscar Romero or Wangari Maathai, Barack Obama or Eleanor Roosevelt, Pauli Murray or Jane Goodall or any other liberator-healer of the people and creatures of the earth.

## IMAGE EIGHT

### Newborns

Let the little children come to me; do not stop them;
for it is to such as these that the kingdom of God belongs.

MARK 10:14

With the troubles in the world, so much violence and shame, such suffering and heartbreak, it's no surprise that we're drawn to babies of all species, including human infants. Although babies don't really have "pure hearts," we project purity and holiness onto them. Romantics like Wordsworth even imagine them "trailing clouds of glory" behind them as they arrive, small emissaries from heaven. They are images of innocence. When Jesus suggested that children are especially close to God, I expect he was referring not to their innocence but to their vulnerability—that is, their openness. Children, certainly babies, are more open to receiving and learning how to give and share the love of God.

As we grow, we shed much of our spiritual openness to love and be loved and, with it, if we are maturing morally, we also shed our selfishness. What I'm suggesting here is that, in the most moral situations, there are gains and losses in growing up: On the one hand, we lose our limitless capacity to touch and be touched by those who love us well. Outgrowing this radical vulnerability, or sense of openness to everyone and everything, is a real loss. On the other hand, this happens as we begin to develop capacities to discern good and evil; our consciences begin to take shape; we notice the difference between ourselves and others. We cultivate abilities to reason and seek knowledge. We incur experiences of evil, greed, and fear—which often dull our abilities to love one another and which can diminish our capacities to believe that a loving God is real, not simply a fantasy concocted by wishful and irrational people.

Though I decided in my thirties not to have children, and though my professional work has been largely with adults, I've always treasured babies and children as bearers of vulnerability, spontaneity, imagination, and possibility. Each time a baby of any species arrives among my family or friends, it is to me a source of great wonder, brimming with originality and hope. There are quite a few babies whose young lives I could lift up. I have chosen to focus here on the four whom, over the years, I have known most intimately.[53]

My sister Ann and her husband Bruce gave birth to Rob in 1984—a week after our father Bob's death—and their baby girl Isabel came along in 1988. Almost two decades later, in 2005, my brother Robbie and his wife Betsy brought their infant daughter Kate home from China. This was more than a decade after my spiritual friends Jan and Steve brought their infant daughter Katie Chun home from China. Katie would become a "goddess daughter" to me.

Shortly after Katie Chun's arrival in the United States, Jan and Steve held a "naming" ceremony for their infant daughter. Alongside a Jewish rabbi, a Buddhist teacher, a Unitarian minister, and several other spiritual leaders, I joined in this ceremony as a Christian priest. Together, we represented a whole world of blessing and possibility. This moment of blessing helped me remember my most ardent desire for all babies, all children—that each may be loved.

As children, many of us Christians sang, "Jesus loves the little children, all the children of the world, red and yellow, black and white, they are precious in his sight. Jesus loves the little children of the world." From a more universalist perspective, this little song is about the healing, liberating energies of God—the root of justice-love, compassion, courage, and kindness—touching all babies, children, and adults through the power of human love, human advocacy, and human struggle for our well-being and happiness.

The arrivals of these four particular babies—Rob, Isabel, Katie Chun, and little Kate—drew my attention to their future. It was as if these little ones had arrived with bright tags bearing messages like, "Here I am!" and "The future is ours!" and "Let's go!" Holding each in my arms, I would find myself spilling over with determination to redouble my efforts in building a justice-loving world, welcoming to this child and to other children, everywhere. To be true to these children, I had to be true to the vocation that I believe all humans share—to make God incarnate, to embody justice-love, to practice neighbor-love, to fight against oppression, to struggle for healing and peace.

And, of course, I believed that these babies, like all children, regardless of their parents' religious beliefs, came to earth just like Jesus did—to help make God incarnate, once again. Like the young Jesus, these babies could begin to learn—with help and encouragement—how to love God, their friends, their enemies, and the world. In each case, it would take a lifetime of adventure and misadventure, filled with joys and sorrows, victories and failures, gains and losses, and—if each of these babies were lucky—bundles of love from families and communities of many kinds, until each child found his, or her, voice and vocation. With enough encouragement, each of these babies would have opportunities, like Jesus, to bring light and love into the world regardless of how they might later frame their spiritualities.

But let me not overly idealize childhood. It is seldom easy, though some children, like these four, have greater chances for smoother passages into adulthood than many others in this society and elsewhere. As Caucasian Americans, Rob and Isabel came into this world with white privilege. Rob, Isabel, little Kate, and Katie Chun were all raised as children with a goodly amount of class privilege in the world's most affluent democracy. Rob and Isabel were born to parents in their thirties who had little money but enterprising determination to pool resources for their kids. Though later divorced, their parents have remained friends. The two Kates were born in China and adopted from Chinese orphanages when they were only months old, in both cases by parents in their late forties who cherished them before they ever saw them except in small photos. None of these four children has ever been seriously thwarted by economic need.

But the older three—Rob, Isabel, and Katie Chun—have struggled, each in his or her own way, with relational and vocational issues and with questions about how to live responsible, kind, and happy lives in a world that doesn't make it easy for anyone, especially kids who ask hard questions of themselves or others. Young Kate is still a child who has not yet hit the wall of adolescence. The other three have, and I imagine that, like young people throughout the world, each could tell stories of pain and fear, loss and disappointment, as well as tales of gratitude and gladness.

Fast forward to 2015: Rob is in his early thirties, Isabel in her late twenties, my little niece Kate is becoming a teenager, and goddess daughter Katie is in her early twenties. The two older ones, Rob and Isabel, are mindful that they have benefitted from their race and class privilege; in this context, they make only modest claims about their personal achievements. Both have also learned from the school of hard knocks, and these lessons have not been lost on them. Each has managed to construct young adulthoods in which they cherish friends and family, care deeply about human well-being and the struggles for social justice, and each is seeking to carve out a professional niche that will contribute to the common good.

Rob has become a father to a boy whom he cherishes. He and the boy's mother did not marry and are no longer together, but each is doing their best at parenting. Rob has recently completed his doctorate and is beginning his work as a full-time psychotherapist. At twenty-seven, Isabel is seeking vocational clarity. A woman of considerable courage and deep beauty, she has a knack for understanding and empathizing with human anxiety and a passion for animal well-being. Little Kate is a bright-eyed, inquisitive child whose love of life and all things beautiful—especially animals and art—is a source of wonder and delight to everyone in her life. And Katie Chun, my goddess daughter, continues to bless the world around her with a compelling, thoughtful reverence for creatures of all kinds and for the earth.

The most beautiful thing about these four young people is that each is immensely kind. More than anything else, their kindness will provide the surest foundation of their love and work, in everything they do, whatever it is, wherever they go, and with whomever.

Though I taught adults in seminary, my sense of what makes a good teacher or good priest is quite similar to what makes a good parent in relation to babies and children and a good person in relation to our companions and friends. We are here on this earth, all of us, whatever our vocation or profession, to help light the spark in others, to call forth whoever the person is at her best, to notice that special "place" in the other and tap it so that he can live with greater confidence. That is exactly what Jesus did, as I read the story of his travels and ministry. He brought out the best in people and sent them on their way to do the same for others. That's what it means, to live as God incarnate.

This is my prayer for each of the young ones, the four named and many others: May you bring out the best in others—and allow others to do the same for you. Light sparks! Bless the world! Encourage us all! As my sister Ann is fond of saying to her children, "Remember who you are."

## IMAGE NINE

## Travels to far off places, seeds of hope

I will pour out my Spirit upon all flesh,
and your sons and your daughters shall prophesy,
and your young shall see visions,
and your elders shall dream dreams.

Acts 2:17, adapted

One of the adventures Bev and I shared in the 1980s and 1990s was traveling to places across the United States and elsewhere in the world to learn and teach whatever we could about feminist and other liberation theologies. Together, we went to California, Colorado, New Mexico, Texas, Georgia, North Carolina, Minnesota, Illinois, Indiana, and all up and down the East Coast, as well as to Canada and Mexico. We journeyed together to England, Germany, Switzerland, Italy, Australia, and New Zealand, and separately to the Netherlands, Belgium, Norway, Sweden, South Korea, South Africa, Brazil, Nicaragua, and Honduras. On every trip, our deepest hope was that we and others might together god—bring God to life, help make Her incarnate, in whatever the situation. I believed that this was the basis of our shared vocation, and Bev also insisted that the basis for all theology and spirituality would always be rooted in actual human struggles for right, or mutual, relation. We both realized that good works and liberating faith move in a spiral, each generating the other, as on and on they go.

Perhaps our most intriguing trip was to Cuba in 1985, as part of a team of liberation theologians from the United States who were invited to join our Cuban colleagues at the Protestant Evangelical Seminary in Matanzas. We participated in a dialogue about liberation theology which, we witnessed, was alive and well in Cuba, a country absurdly and tragically defamed during the second half of the twentieth century by our own nation's Cold War paranoia. In our treatment of Cuba, the legacy of Senator Joseph McCarthy lived on beyond his destructive reign in the early 1950s.

Nonetheless, over several decades, Cuba had managed well—remarkably, in providing health care, housing, food, and education to everyone, though not as well in its refusal to guarantee personal freedoms of speech, religion, and association, which we in the United States have always valued.

In Christian liberation theologies, there are two great goods. One is the common good—the health and happiness of the whole body of Christ, which includes health care, food, housing, and education for all people of all tribes and religions. These shared social provisions constitute a great good and are always an ethical goal for Christians. The other great good is the relative freedom of individuals to speak, write, worship, and build associations with whomever we please, much as the Constitution of the United States and its Bill of Rights promises. Individual freedom is, thus, an equally great good. But our rights as individuals cannot stand on their own apart from the common good. Each must be measured and balanced by the other: common good and individual freedom.

Over the course of my lifetime, the most morally compelling leaders of the United States have kept both goals in view—to provide food and housing, health care and education, for everyone while safeguarding freedoms of speech, religion, association, and movement. It is not always an easy balance. Even the great Franklin Delano Roosevelt, who championed both social justice and individual freedom, came up woefully short on the latter by authorizing the imprisonment of Japanese Americans during World War II.

I am not a historian, but it seems to me that the United States, at least during my lifetime, has tended to err more on one side—giving greater weight to individual freedom than to social justice. The Supreme Court's absurd interpretation of the Second Amendment is a case in point. The framers of the United States Constitution surely did not intend to lift an individual's "right to bear arms" above the nation's duty to protect the lives of innocent children, women, and men from gun violence. I am sure beyond a doubt that neither Thomas Heyward nor Ann Hutchinson, two of my ancestors among our nation's "founders," could have imagined a disturbed man walking into a school room with an automatic rifle and mowing down twenty six-year-olds or into a church and shooting to death nine people with whom he had been praying for an hour. The Supreme Court's Heller decision (2008), I suspect, is among its least legally sustainable or socially responsible. Its promotion of an individual "right" at the expense of our common well-being is legally unbalanced and poses a threat to the general safety and well-being of our society.

It is sometimes easier to see the strengths and weaknesses of our own nation when we find ourselves in other cultures. Traveling around Cuba, sometimes with a guide, often on our own, we United States citizens witnessed for ourselves an impressive array of health care and educational facilities. We met people in Matanzas and Havana, as well as in the countryside, who were proud of their county and its leader, whom they affectionately called "Fidel." Even so, many of the same people were critical of Fidel Castro's rigid adherence to communist principles, sometimes at the expense of certain freedoms that many Cubans cherished, including the freedom to worship as they pleased.

Our US delegation of visitors was urged to consider the duress under which the new Cuban government had been formed in 1959, following the demise of Fulgencio Batista, an economic puppet of the United States and a brutal demagogue to his own people. Our Cuban hosts, who were Christian liberation theologians, told us that Castro's well-known violent purge of conservative, pro-Batista, religious leaders in the early 1960s had been deemed necessary by Fidel to protect his young, fragile revolutionary government. We expressed skepticism about this, some of us recalling images of conservative religious leaders being shot by a firing squad in the early 1960s. Castro's forces were "excessive," our hosts admitted, but the young ruler and his comrades did what embattled governments too often do in similar circumstances—execute, or otherwise rid themselves of, those whom they believe, rightly or wrongly, are trying to subvert them.

Although we white privileged citizens of the United States don't often think of our nation as conducting mass slaughters of its foes, we most certainly have done horrific violence to Native and African Americans, often in great numbers. Think of the Trail of Tears. The Middle Passage. The lynchings and beatings of African Americans. We had to admit that the United States has its own stories of men and women executed because they were politically radical or because they were experienced as threatening to the established order. Think of John Brown. Think of Nicola Sacco and Bartolomeo Vanzetti. Think of Ethel and Julius Rosenberg. Like the genocide of Native Americans and the brutal legacy of slavery, the executions of individuals—guilty or innocent—at least in part because they are political dissidents who threaten the established order are not cases we like to remember, nor do they illustrate our nation at its best.

Leaving Cuba, our group felt privileged to get a glimpse of yet another beautiful, broken body of Christ, battered by global capitalism and its primary ally, the United States of America, as well as by some of Fidel's own excesses and brutal policies. We left Cuba grateful for the experience, ashamed of our country's treatment of this small island nation to our south, and recommitted to doing whatever we could with our best resources and talents—teaching, preaching, writing, speaking, organizing, and voting—on behalf of One whose Body is being broken every day in countless ways by our collective fear and greed. As I was writing this book in the summer of 2015, the Obama administration officially opened the US embassy in Havana—for the first time in half a century—and our nations signaled a desire to build a mutually empowering relationship.

Boldern is an Evangelical Protestant retreat center near Zurich, Switzerland, which provided a different forum for learning and teaching for Bev and me over a couple of decades, beginning in the late 1980s. Our sister liberation theologian, Reinhild Traitler, Christian feminist and creative organizer, put together a number of conferences that brought women scholars, ministers, and activists from all over the world to do liberation theology. Dorothee Soelle came in from her home in Hamburg, Germany, and her teaching post in New York City to help lead some of these conferences. So did Eva Renate Schmidt, German feminist psychotherapist and educator who travelled from her home outside Milan, Italy. With these sister-feminists and others, Bev and I went to Boldern several times over the years, working as ethicist and theologian in dialogue with women and men from all over Europe.

Among the brilliant reflections of liberation theology in action at Boldern were the extraordinary, exquisite pieces of clothing and other forms of art being woven, painted, and sculpted by Christian women in their daily lives. These artists told us that their creations were ways of giving shape to their faith as fluid, colorful, connective, and evocative rather than as drab, systematic, and boring. Bev and I were invited to try on new colors and shapes of cloth to see if these new, women-inspired and women-woven garments might generate inspiration to our voices on behalf of justice for all women everywhere. Each of us bought several garments, which we treasured, reminders of this beautiful Body of Women, this whimsical, colorful body of Christ, too often broken—but also creative, resilient, inviting.

On the other side of our planet home, Bev and I had a wonderful stay in Australia and New Zealand in 1997, where we joined other women in leading workshops in feminist liberation theology and ethics. Susan Adams, a prominent Anglican priest and feminist leader in Auckland, and Angela Moloney, a Dominican sister and a founder of the Sophia center for women's spirituality in Adelaide, South Australia—both of whom became lasting friends—called together groups of women to meet with Bev and me. This engagement with bright, talented women all over the world was a source of ongoing inspiration, energy, and intellectual stimulation for us.

The Sophia center continues to provide creative liturgical settings for women who are seeking woman-affirming spaces in which to worship Sophia, the Wisdom of God. In addition to the eloquence and integrity of the many women we met at the Sophia center, I have in my mind's eye an image of the exquisite Moreton Bay fig tree which, like a giant mushroom, provides a huge canopy under which the Sophia center is tucked. Nearby is a cemetery in which the remains of the Dominican sisters are interred, each marked with a simple white headstone. Having returned several times over the years to visit Angela Moloney and her colleagues at the Sophia center, I find myself remembering the Dominican sisters, those who have passed, those still with us now, some who have been teachers, some psychotherapists, some hospice workers, artists, administrators. These sisters are linked by a common thread—their love of their Sophia-Spirit-God whom they have experienced most fully through their friendships with each other and their work together on behalf of women and children.

In New Zealand, Susan Adams is a spirited woman priest, married to an equally spirited Methodist minister, John Salmon. The two are a formidable justice-making team, not easily turned back by those who counsel patience with injustice. Like Muffie Moroney, the Texas lawyer and Episcopal laywoman, and like Bev, Susan is not someone you want to tangle with if you're not committed 100 percent to justice for women now, not later, and not just for women—but also justice for Mauri people, African American, Latinas, LGBTQ women and men, and poor and marginalized communities. One of my favorite photos is of Susan,

Bev, and my mother, Mary Ann, standing arm in arm outside Susan and John's Auckland apartment in 1997. I smile at the image of my mother's face in that moment, radiating such joy, a budding feminist herself at age eighty-two.

Back home in the United States, Bev and I went twice to Ghost Ranch, not long ago the desert home to Georgia O'Keefe, and currently a retreat center of the Presbyterian Church USA. The desert is an iconic place of wilderness, so each retreat at Ghost Ranch becomes an opportunity to reflect on what matters most. Moreover, it is hard not to notice the Sacred in the desert—in the bones and sticks lying beside a dried-up creek bed or in clouds hanging like white puffy drapes over a nearby mesa. You wonder about the relational stories in the bones. You try to imagine what once happened here. You think you see shapes of Native peoples in the cloud formations. Walking about in the desert, climbing to the top of the mesas, is a bit like smoking dope or dropping acid, which I did once, in the early 1970s—your mind stretches beyond its normal range of vision and imagination, and your heart opens to every creature who has walked this way, and you know we are moving together through history, in our different species and alien cultures, as one beautiful, broken body.

In 2006, Bev was invited to Mexico City for the publication in Spanish of her first book, *Our Right to Choose: A New Ethic of Abortion* (Beacon: 1983). She and I were hosted by the Mexican chapter of Catholics for Choice at this celebration of the movement for women's reproductive choices and health in Mexico and throughout Latin America. As we participated via headphones and translators, we were reminded on this occasion that reproductive freedom is not simply a "First World rich white women's issue," as we are told repeatedly by rich white men and their spokespeople in the First World. Much as we had in the Philadelphia and Washington ordinations and other events in which women have stood up to be taken seriously, we experienced the Sacred energy among women struggling for the integrity of their bodies, their lives, and their choices.

To her dying day, Beverly Harrison believed that women's campaign for our reproductive freedom was, and is, a struggle for the most basic human rights in the world: the right to produce, or not to produce, children—and an accompanying right to health-care provisions for safe birth control, safe pregnancy, safe abortion, safe neonatal care, and safe birthing, as well as health care for mothers, infants, and children who are born. Bev believed that reproductive freedom would be the hardest right in the world for us to secure and that it would take generations of social turbulence, political maneuverings, and legal battles beyond the 1973 Roe v. Wade decision of the US Supreme Court. She would not be surprised in the least today to see that, while LGBTQ rights appear to be on their way to victory in the West, abortion rights continue to be hotly contested and are being set back in many of our more conservative states.

Why is this? I can hear Beverly Harrison speaking through me here: Half of the LGBTQ population are men. Abortion is a woman's issue about women's bodies, women's blood, women's babies, women's lives, women's choices. Of course abortion rights are harder to secure than marriage equality. One hundred percent of those who need abortions and reproductive freedom are women. Now look at the composition of Congress and Parliaments and executive and judicial branches of governments in the United States and elsewhere. How many women do we see? Of course, not all women are pro-choice. Many are not. But Bev always maintained that, if women were fairly represented among lawmakers, judges, and heads of state, the right to safe, legal, medical abortion would be secure.[54]

Why is marriage equality less controversial today than reproductive freedom in the United States? Folks may argue it's because weddings—unlike abortions—are upbeat and joyful and make a positive public impression. There may be some truth to this, but Bev would argue that the bottom line is that men don't get pregnant. Back in the 1980s, I heard both feminist philosopher Mary Daly and African American lawyer Florence Kennedy quip, "If men could get pregnant, abortion would be a sacrament." Amen—and it would also be legal in every state and nation in the world.

One of the dearest and most memorable trips of my life was in 1986 with my mother and brother two years after my father's death. I had been visiting Bev's and my friend Bridget Rees, a bold activist in the Anglican Church in England, Palestine-Israel, and South Africa. Bridget and I had been traveling together in the UK, spending time with other Christian feminists and activists. On this visit in 1986, Bridget and I had been attending a feminist theological conference at the cathedral in Canterbury. My mother and Robbie had decided to fly over to meet me in London for a family excursion into the city and countryside and to go on from there to Germany to visit Dorothee Soelle and her family. It was a sweet time and became an occasion for us to get to know each other better as friends with much in common, not simply as parent and child or as siblings. It was also a moment in which my mother was beginning to enjoy painting, a talent she had tapped following our father's death in 1984. So Mary Ann had her camera and an eye peeled for inviting landscapes and images.

One evening while we were there, Robbie ordered chocolate mousse in a small French restaurant in London and the waiter brought an entire large fishbowl-size vat to the table and set it before him with just a small spoon! To this day, Robbie and I have no idea what this was about. In any case, the three of us laughed as Robbie dug his spoon into the giant bowl. Later that same night, we shared a moment that transcended time and space for me: sitting on the top row of one of London's oldest theaters, enjoying the original cast performance of *Les Miserables*, to this day my all-time favorite musical.[55] In the last scene, when Colm Wilkinson's Jean Valjean sings that "to love another person is to see the face of God," everything good in the world was validated for me in that moment. Such was the power of that revolutionary story—and the power of music—giving voice and sound to images of christic power throughout our life together on this planet.

## IMAGE TEN

## Approaching the wilderness (1984): grieving, grateful, tired

And the Spirit immediately drove him out into the wilderness.
He was in the wilderness forty days, tempted by Satan . . .

MARK 1:12–13a

My father had been forced to retire in 1975, nine years before his death, when he was diagnosed with multiple myeloma. During the last decade of his life, he would take strolls through the neighborhood or along the beach with his miniature dachshund. He began making butter mints and peanut brittle, which he'd take to neighbors and friends, who would often ask for more, and more would appear at the next holiday or birthday. During those last years, Daddy told me that quitting work and slowing down was the best thing he'd ever done in relation to everything he cared most about, beginning with my mother, his children, and his dog. Walking along a South Carolina beach the summer before he died, Daddy said to me, "Baby, we gotta slow down if we're gonna smell the roses."

My father died several months later, on September 24, 1984, a week before the birth of his first grandchild, Rob, who was named after him. Daddy's death was the most significant personal loss in my life to that point. This loss, followed so closely by Rob's birth, moved me to the edge of a wilderness which would become for me a place of spiritual reckoning for the rest of the decade and into the 1990s.

We are likely to downplay both the first thirty years of Jesus's life and, to a lesser degree, the significance of his time in the wilderness early in his public ministry. The first thirty years we know almost nothing about, other than that Jesus was born in humble circumstances and is presented as an inquisitive boy who loved learning. We also hear from authors of the New Testament that, upon his baptism by John, Jesus went into the wilderness. There he stayed for forty days, we are told. In the wilderness, he was tempted by Satan, or the devil—traditionally, a name for the negative energies that lure us away from God and keep us from loving our neighbors as ourselves. Jesus seems to have encountered the Satan in the form of several temptations, having to do with a lust for power, authority, and immortality. (Luke 4:1–13) Jesus refused to give in to the temptations, though we might assume that they resurfaced in the course of his ministry, and we can only imagine the demons with which he wrestled in the Garden of Gethsemane shortly before he turned himself over to the Roman authorities to be crucified.

The wilderness is a metaphor for a time or place of withdrawal from business as usual. It often refers to a period of reckoning with choices made and unmade and with questions about direction—where to go now? My wilderness experience happened somewhere in the middle, rather than at the beginning, of my adult life—and toward the end of my professional work. Something about how I was involved in the church, and therefore also the seminary, was getting in the way, not impeding the Spirit's calling me to justice-making, which I was doing gladly, but rather hindering the cultivation of a deep inner sense of peace or joy.

The "something" was a frenetic quality that pushed me ever faster to stay busy and full and productive. As I grew older, I would find I was also missing an experience of God's spaciousness, sometimes referred to by Christian mystics like Thomas Merton as an "emptiness"—the space and time in God as well as in ourselves that we can experience only inasmuch as we're not filling ourselves with activity, possessions, and food.

Throughout my life, the devil had been for me the strong pull to achieve, pressed down under layers of accomplishment. Much of my activity during these years—I'd like to think, most of it—was motivated by God-loving, justice-seeking commitments in the company of splendid colleagues and comrades. My life had not been wasted, my goals had not been wrong, I had often walked willingly in the Spirit. It had been a wonderful life and, I trust, a source of happiness for God, found whenever we love one another and participate in healing broken bodies and liberating oppressed people and creatures.

The spiritual problem, for me—what I am calling the devil or the demons in my life—had been the lure into being busy, so busy that I often had difficulty experiencing a genuinely mutual, sustainable relation with God or with God's creatures. Simply put, I was so busy doing more and more that I often missed noticing the beauty around me, within me, often right beside me, like the box turtle I had treasured as a child or like Bev sitting quietly on the couch beside me, working a crossword puzzle, in our little cottage on Deer Isle. Perhaps I had become a caricature of Martha in the story as Mary sits with Jesus while Martha moves around the house, busy doing important things but not taking time just to be (Luke 10:38–42).

Alcohol had been the devil's chief tool of manipulation in my adult life. Looking back, it seems to me that Daddy's death and Rob's birth issued a wake-up call for me to look honestly at the devil's cunning presence in my life. My experiences of grief in the wake of Daddy's death and gratitude for both his life and the birth of his grandson, my nephew Rob, in the fall of 1984, began to stir my energies for spiritual reckoning.

It took me a full year after my father's death to stop drinking. When I did, in the fall of 1985, I began to see that alcohol had become a chosen way of numbing my spiritual sensibilities so that I could keep going without getting tired, without hearing God's sighs in my own body and soul: "Slow down, look around, the ground you are standing on is holy, be at peace," She would whisper, and I often could not hear Her. To make matters a bit more complicated, alcohol was not the devil's only tool: Multiple addictive patterns had long conspired to dampen my spiritual energies and wear me down. Overeating, spending more money than I had, staying busy, had worked together to mute the healing voices and restorative tunes in my heart and body and soul.

I needed to slow down so that I could wake up to what had been happening in my life from the beginning, when the girl-child me gazed worshipfully at the turtle and knew she was being met by God. Throughout my life, the beautiful Sophia—the Wisdom of God—had been perched right beside me, like the bluebird my mother so loved, always within view—in reality, in memory, in imagination—whenever I took time to notice rather than rushing on by.

A central place of wilderness in my life, where much of my best spiritual work would occur, would be with Bev, at our little cottage on Deer Isle in Maine, which we had bought in the fall of 1985, about a month after I quit drinking and a year before Bev did. I can tell you about Bev's addiction, as well as my own, because she spoke so candidly about her alcoholism and was so proud to be in recovery.

For Bev and me, our little cottage, which we named Mud Flower,[56] became a place of healing and hope. Walks with our dogs along the causeway, meandering in the lupine field in which our little house sat, sitting on the deck together, taking the canoe out into Mud Cove, attending our favorite AA meeting in the tiny red schoolhouse in Sedgwick across Eggemoggin Reach, making splendid new friends, nearly all in recovery from addiction. These would be significant wilderness rituals for Bev and me as we began to struggle together with the demonic power of alcohol in our lives.

## IMAGE ELEVEN

## In the wilderness (1985–early 90s): demons of addiction and shame

O God, all my longing is known to you;
my sighing is not hidden from you.
My heart throbs, my strength fails me;
as for the light of my eyes—it also has gone from me.

PSALM 38:9–10, ADAPTED

Let me circle back here to explain how I came to understand myself as an alcoholic, and say something about the challenging role addiction played in Bev's and my relationship.

It's hard for most of us to realize how fundamentally our lives as individuals are constantly being formed, reformed, and deformed by the life of the world—by the planet and the people with whom we share it now and from whose lineage we have come, generation upon generation. The better part of wisdom is for us to simply assume that, like the earth itself and all its other inhabitants, we ourselves are being made and unmade, broken into pieces and patched back together, throughout our lives. We are products of history and culture as much as of particular genes, and our physiological and psychological "selves" are constantly being done, undone, burnt out, and fired up by the world in which we live. All of these many forces shape the contexts for the alcoholism and other addictions that Bev and I and countless other sisters and brothers have had to struggle with over the course of our lives.

On October 10, 1985, Robin Gorsline, a former student and remarkably honest friend, told me that he and many of my friends and former students were worried about my drinking so much. I recall being surprised that Robin would have the audacity—and courage—to say such a thing, but I also recall knowing immediately that he was right. "Okay," I said, "I'll try to stop drinking this weekend when Bev's out of town." I was living with Bev in New York at the time, during a sabbatical leave from my work at the Episcopal Divinity School. "It'll be easier when I'm alone," I added. Robin's response still moves me: "Carter, you've taught many of us so much about the power of mutuality and how we need each other's help, how we actually call each other to life. How can you possibly believe that you can begin to stop drinking alone?" I was stunned and, in my memory, silent.

That night I phoned a friend in New York City who, I knew, was a member of Alcoholic Anonymous. "Connie," I asked, "do you know if there's any AA meeting in New York anytime soon?" Connie chuckled! "Honey, there are hundreds every day! I'll pick you up at 8:30 tomorrow morning." That night I also had my last drink of alcohol, and I attended my first AA meeting with Connie on the morning of October 11, 1985, in the basement of a Catholic church on the corner of Amsterdam Avenue and 96th Street in Manhattan. By the christic power working through friends like Robin and Connie and Bev and other loved ones, I've been sober ever since.

The process of recovery is not easy for any addict. The challenges posed by addiction and the recovery processes are always deeply personal and take particular, unique shapes in each person's life. Bev and I were not exceptions. At the same time, we both understood that our battles with alcohol and other addictions were social and political, not simply personal, problems.

Historical processes unfolding during the Reagan administration and the decades that followed provided the backdrop against which Bev and I struggled together, each of us in her own private way, against demons of addiction that had been with us since childhood and adolescence. Early in our lives, little Beverly Jean Wildung in Minnesota in the 1930s and 1940s, and little Carter Heyward in North Carolina in the 1940s and 1950s, were beginning our growth into strong, passionate, intelligent girls in a world and church in which—especially in adolescence—there seemed to be no place for us as girls to feel good about ourselves.

In part one, I discussed the conundrum of girls in the kingdom of a Father God who has little use for stubborn daughters who want their own way and intend to make their own path. Despite having genuinely loving and remarkable parents, Bev and I had experienced ourselves as un-belonging in the world around us, so powerful are the social norms and expectations in which children grow. Sexism was in the air we breathed, as were other toxic social energies, like white racism. Had either Bev or I been sons, we still might have become alcoholics, and we might have always struggled with how best to make our minds and bodies fit in with the dominant society. But the kingdom of the fathers in mid-twentieth century America was structured economically, socially, and psychologically to support talented white boys who drank too much to degrees unthinkable in relation to young white girls trying to find spaces for ourselves in this world. The domain of white male social and economic privilege was also entirely out of reach for all children and adults of color in the 1940s and 1950s.

By the time Bev and I met in 1967, long before we became lovers and partners in 1980, she and I had already been confounded, though hardly undone, by the world and church in which we had grown up. There is no question that, in decades to come, one of the most precious gifts each of us brought to our partnership was to choose sobriety in the mid-1980s and to accompany each other on the path of recovery from alcoholism for the rest of our life together. There is also no question that our relationship suffered through our difficulties in reckoning with the pain, shame, and psycho-spiritual roots of our addictions. These roots were no doubt steeped in our childhood experiences of andro-centric, woman-fearing attitudes and expectations. Each of us was also confused by the other's particular ways of coping with these patterns of pain and shame, patterns exacerbated by our shared tendency to quietly withdraw from the other's attempts to engage.

In 1987, when I was about a year and a half sober—still early in recovery—I entered psychotherapy with a psychiatrist recommended by my primary care physician. My problem, as I experienced it, was emotional fatigue. I had become weary trying to figure out my best place in the world as a Christian priest, professor, theologian, and les-bian. I needed someone to help me make connections among the many various parts and pieces of my life in the world and church—including Bev's and my caring but complex relationship. My life seemed to me like a jigsaw puzzle—with many pieces and little time and space to put them together, beginning with the decision to stop drinking:

- My job: There was my full-time teaching at the Episcopal Divinity School, where I was helping develop the new program in Feminist Liberation Theology.

- My travels: I was speaking and preaching widely in the United States, Latin America, Canada, Europe, and elsewhere as a les-bian feminist Christian theologian and priest and as advocate for marginalized and oppressed people, especially those under attack by the US government, as in Nicaragua.

- My writing: I was writing essays, articles, and books, and enjoying it.
- My particular grief: My father had died a couple of years earlier.
- My shame: On a 1986 trip with my mother, brother, and several German friends to the former concentration camp at Neuengamme, near Hamburg, we had stood in silence amid small daisies growing everywhere there once had been ashes.
- My love for Bev, and our addictions: Bev and I were both in early recovery from alcoholism and were also struggling with other addictive patterns, each of us, and both of us together.

How did these pieces of my life fit together?

I was nearing the mid-point of my professional work as teacher, priest, and theologian and I didn't realize at the time what I see today: Until 1985, when I stopped drinking, I had used alcohol as a fuel to help keep me going, busy, and active. The alcohol had been numbing the effects of an over-busy life. When I drank, I didn't feel tired. Having given up alcohol, I was becoming tired to the bone. I felt like I was wearing out, and I was only in my early forties.

It was the exhaustion that propelled me into therapy in 1987 with a woman I have referred to in previous writing as "Elizabeth Farro" (*When Boundaries Betray Us*, 1993). It was a most unfortunate choice, but at the time I didn't know that what I really needed was simply to continue attending AA meetings. I also needed what Janet Surrey and Steve Bergman would call "spiritual friends" (*Buddha's Wife*, 2015) as I tried to put together the pieces of my life. I needed help making the connections between my body-self as an individual woman on planet earth and the life of the world constructed on patriarchal, androcentric values inherently hostile to strong women like me, Bev, and so many others.

I was too tired to see that a traditionally schooled, tightly boundaried psychiatrist was neither what I was looking for nor what I needed. A more intuitive therapist might have realized that, given my theological and ethical commitments to mutuality as the heart of my life's work and my faith, I would not—I could not and should not—settle for anything less than a fully mutual relationship with my helper. When I realized my therapist wanted to, but could not, meet me where I was, I regret not simply leaving the therapy. I stayed in therapy for eighteen months— about seventeen months too long. By the time I garnered the energy to leave, I felt beaten up by this strange, stressful relationship with an ambivalent psychiatrist.

Fortunately, along with Bev, several good friends emerged at this time. Each navigated some significant psycho-spiritual passages with me in depths the therapist could not. They met me in ways she could not by joining me in processes of mutual spiritual questing in which their journeys were as important as mine. The mutual inter-activeness provided the healing energy for me, and for each of these friends. Together, and only together, could we god.[57]

Janet Surrey and I met in 1987, not long after I began therapy with Elizabeth Farro. Jan was a clinical psychologist and psychotherapist, a founding member of the Stone Center at Wellesley College and a feminist Buddhist Jew. She and I had been appointed to serve on a mutual friend's doctoral committee in Boston University's School of Theology. Almost immediately, we realized we had much in common. We were both feminists on a spiritual quest who were interested in making connections between theology and psychology. We had lunch a week or so later. From that day forward, we have tried to talk regularly, every week or so. Jan has been a faithful spiritual companion as she and I seek to notice and appreciate the spiritual, relational energies connecting the various issues and events in our personal, professional, and political lives.

Meanwhile, Bev's and my relationship was growing stronger through our couple's therapy with an extraordinary woman, Bonnie Engelhardt, LICSW. Our work with Bonnie began in 1988 and continued off and on until my retirement from the Episcopal Divinity School and departure from Massachusetts in 2005. Bev and I both credited Bonnie for helping us figure out how to continue on as life-companions after we separated as a more traditional couple. With Bonnie's support and a sturdy network of friends and companions over three decades, Bev and I were able to weave a relational tapestry with threads of mutual courage, regret, and gratitude.

More than anything, Bonnie's great gift to each of us was that she saw, respected, and came to love each of us in our strengths and our foibles. She taught us not to fear our silent withdrawals and to feel more able to share our deep feelings of remorse. She would tease us gently about some of our nuttier addictive habits—like the time we went from store to store all over several western Boston suburbs with two friends, loading up on pints of Ben and Jerry's New York Super Fudge Chunk ice cream, making sure we had at least one pint each for the night, or like the time we spent money neither of us had to buy each other gorgeous coats, hand-woven by a friend in Maine. She would laugh out loud about Bev having to feed rotisserie chicken to the dogs and about my purchasing more and more books and tapes of conversational Spanish but not making time to study, listen, and learn.

Bonnie's non-judgmental spirit helped us deal with our fears of failing each other. Facing our shame as individuals and as a couple released our guilty emotional baggage and allowed us to more often express our real, and abiding, love for each other. She had us talk to each other about what we adored in the other, and also what bothered each of us. She had us write it down and send each other letters with this information. Bonnie also insisted that we talk to each other about what we most valued and loved in ourselves. Bonnie worked with us toward discovering how we could keep on in life together as beloved friends who simply couldn't live together. She helped us imagine ourselves as life-companions who might or might not be lovers, who might or might not have other lovers, but whose love for each other was secure and ongoing and faithful.

Bonnie Engelhardt helped us trust our relationship as a blessing to each other as well as to others. Thanks to Bonnie, Bev and I came to realize in our later years that our relationship was truly a body of Christ, beautiful and broken and strong.

## IMAGE TWELVE

### Leaving the wilderness (early to mid-1990s): with Angela, soul-friend

A friend loves at all times.

PROVERBS 17:17

My brother, Robbie, and I took another trip together, five years after our trip to Europe with our mother. In January 1991, we flew to

Melbourne, Australia, to visit David. We were watching the Australian Open when an image of US President George H. W. Bush flashed upon the big screen, announcing the beginning of "Desert Storm," the first US-led war against Iraq. The crowd around us grew quiet as all eyes turned to the screen. I remember the eerie hush. If Robbie and I could have imagined that this decision by Bush Sr. was setting in motion a series of events that would lead to his son's ill-advised, tragic decision twelve years later to invade Iraq, we'd have fallen to our knees and wept.

In Melbourne, I received an invitation from some of Australia's Anglican women to join them for a conversation on feminist theology at a monastery northwest of Sydney. Several of us flew up to Sydney and from there to Newcastle, where we were met at the airport by Sister Angela of the Community of Clare, whose monastery we would be visiting.

This was the beginning of a stunning relationship that would transform my spirituality and help me begin to emerge from the wilderness, a renewed person, in some ways reflecting the girl-child I had once been. Although Angela and I were never partnered, she accompanied me into new spiritual terrain much as Bev had been doing since our first meetings at Union Seminary in the late 1960s. They were very different women, and my relationships with each strengthened different dimensions of my life. Bev was so deeply and brilliantly justice-centered and grounded in this world. Angela was a renowned sculptor and a mystic who seemed to live always with one foot beyond the veil. In years to come, as they became friends, Bev would bring out Angela's justice commitments, and Angela would turn Bev into something of a mystic. I lived and breathed and found my spiritual moorings between these remarkable women while they were alive here on earth, and I still do.

With Angela, it began in a tree house which she and the other Franciscan sisters had built on the grounds of their monastery in Stroud, a town out in the bush of New South Wales. The tree house had been designed as a small guesthouse or a place for a nun to take a little retreat away from the other sisters. I was a guest in the tree house during my visit over several days. Angela would bring me tea and biscuits each afternoon after our feminist theology conversations with the other women who had come to the meeting. In the evening after services,

Angela would return to the tree house with me and our conversations would continue.

We were amazed by the similarities between us. We were women who loved God but not the God of patriarchal Christianity—yet whose lives ironically had been spent serving, more than we had wished, the God in whom we did not believe. We were women who had come from loving homes, with parents and siblings who cared for one another, yet we had experienced shame as girl children who did not fit into pre-scribed female roles.

We had each been in love with men earlier in our lives and, for different reasons, had given up those particular relationships in order to serve the patriarchal God. Angela had left a relationship with a man in order to enter the Anglican Order of the Poor Clares in Oxford, England, and I had chosen not to pursue my relationship with David but rather to seek ordination as a priest. Angela would later become a priest as well. We were both women-loving women, though Angela had not had a lesbian relationship. Still, her deep connection with the women in her religious order in many ways paralleled Bev's and my life-companionship as well as the several close women friends and colleagues, like Sue Hiatt, with whom I'd worked and lived over the years.

We were women whose ways of being ourselves had confounded people to whom we had turned for help. With another Anglican nun to whom she had turned for counsel, and by whom she had been turned away, Angela had encountered her own version of Elizabeth Farro. We were women who had wrestled throughout our lives with fears of being crazy. We knew better but still wondered, sometimes.

We were women who had been told that we were too angry to be good Christians, too needy of affirmation to be of much help to anyone else, and too out of the box to be good theologians. We were women who had been told by bishops who did not want to deal with us that we had "authority problems."

We were women tired to the bone who, until that moment, had not realized that we had a spiritual clone on the other side of planet earth! Meeting Angela was like encountering my own soul in a somewhat older, taller, more willowy, mind-bogglingly creative Australian artist and nun. Angela told me that being with me had drawn her into the depths of her own soul. Both of us were committed to a radically incarnate relational

Spirit who lives and breathes and takes shape constantly between and among us, whenever and wherever we are weaving relational mutuality, struggling genuinely to love one another. Angela spoke of Christians, Jews, Muslims, and people of other spiritual traditions—of European and aboriginal cultures in Australia—and of the wallaby, the eagle, and God's Spirit with the same respect.

In the 1970s, Angela had forged a spiritual friendship with Helen Joseph, a white South African anti-apartheid activist who had been sentenced to decades of house arrest at about the same time that African National Congress leader Nelson Mandela had been sent to Robbins Island. Though not in prison, Helen found herself isolated and under death threat from defenders of the racist apartheid system. Angela had heard about Helen and wrote her. Although they met only once—at an airport in Johannesburg with guards standing by—they offered each other new perspectives and new strength. An atheist, Helen found herself drawn to Angela's spirituality. For her part, Angela—at the time an enclosed contemplative nun, set apart from the world—found herself attracted to Helen's radical social activist spirit. Angela sculpted a small, smooth edged, wooden cross which she called a "holding cross." She sent it to her friend Helen with the assurance that, whenever Helen found herself afraid, she should hold the cross and know that someone was praying for her. Angela and her Franciscan sisters began to carve holding crosses for people all over the world and to sell them for a small sum to support their community.

At the heart of relationship with Angela was a shared experience of a Spirit that runs through everything, connecting all that is. This Spirit yearns to be noticed, while forever under attack by relentless powers of fear and greed that do not give up, even though they cannot ultimately bear up under the force of the Spirit that is God that is Love. My holding cross, once Angela's, is among the treasures in my life.

Another sculpture that represents the foundation of our shared faith is a three-foot tall image of an all-female Trinity, carved by Angela in 1994 from a single piece of Tasmanian pine that had been charred by fire on one side. This image of God sits in my study as a reminder of how Angela and I emerged from the wilderness together, and of why we both eventually wound up at Redbud Springs.

## IMAGE THIRTEEN

## Redbud Springs: mutuality in community

I lift up my eyes to the hills—from where will my help come?

PSALM 121:1

In May 1995, a decade after both of us quit drinking, Bev and I joined my extended family in the mountains of North Carolina to celebrate my mother's eightieth birthday. My siblings and I had rented a retreat house, in which about thirty of us gathered for a weekend to toast our mother's life. It was a festive, upbeat occasion, during which Mama seemed to realize how deeply cherished she was by family and several close friends who had come along.

Our second night there, I joined a handful of younger family members to take a guided night-hike through the woods and across several fields and, as I recall, at least one shallow stream, which we crossed on rocks. Our guide, a college student on the staff of the retreat center, was talking to us not so much about creatures and night-life as about the history of the center and the land we were walking on. He stressed that he had always regarded these mountains as sacred. The Appalachians are after all very ancient hills, sometimes said to be the oldest mountain range in the world.

At some point, I found myself hanging back, meandering, to enjoy the sounds of the hills—cicadas, twigs snapping under my boots, an occasional small out-of-sight creature scurrying away, my own breathing. What was happening? I wondered. I was thinking about the old hills, about the people and creatures who have lived in them over millennia, including my own family in the 1940s and 1950s. I was thinking about whether or not I might ever return to the mountains to live. Beyond these thoughts, I have only foggy memory of these several minutes as they passed, but I recall feeling energized and filled with something more active than hope, something more like expectation. A few minutes into this reverie, I realized the group had disappeared somewhere ahead. I knew better than to wander around in the mountains alone at night. So I scurried quickly along, sticking closely to the path and soon caught up.

Bev was in our room reading when I returned. She and I had not been partnered as a traditional couple for about five years, but we had long since committed ourselves to continuing on together as life companions. I told Bev that on the hike a few minutes earlier I had realized something. I had realized I needed to begin to return to the mountains of North Carolina and that I hoped to retire here someday with her and maybe others too, women who might want to join us. I asked Bev what she thought about this. Her immediate response was, "Let's do it."

Bev was still at least three or four years from retirement from Union Seminary, and I had a decade to go before I could retire at sixty. We thought it would be wonderful if other women wanted to join in such an adventure and move to North Carolina together to find land and build a women's community. We didn't have particular friends in mind, but we figured there might be some feminist theological colleagues who would be drawn to such a possibility.

During the next few months, a number of friends expressed interest in this effort and a year later, in the spring of 1996, several of us bought land together in western North Carolina. Within a few years, seven women had decided to move to North Carolina as soon as possible. We gathered regularly in our homes in Massachusetts and New York to lay plans for a small, intentional feminist community. We named it "Redbud Springs" after the small tree with the delicate pink flowers that blooms in the early southern spring and after the water that flows abundantly on the land we had found. Although none of us could live there full-time for the first several years, we began hosting occasional feminist theological programs and building projects, such as recruiting family and friends to help build a small barn for "Sugar," a twenty-eight-year-old mare I had bought—my first horse, a sweet, affectionate, whimsical creature whom I adored.

In Redbud Spring's first decade, eight women became full members, investing in the land and building new houses or renovating old ones. Our primary common links were that we were lesbian women and, even more importantly over the years, people with a passion for social justice. Over time, our numbers shifted. Two of the original eight left Redbud Springs to buy their own land on a nearby mountain. Within a few years, we had been joined by other women, including Sister Angela, who spent the last three years of her life with us, and also by a number of family and friends who moved to the neighboring town in order to be part of Redbud Springs' extended community.

More recently, we've been joined at Redbud Springs by several younger families—women, men, and kids—who share basic values and tasks on the land and have brought to Redbud Springs some youthful vigor, fresh ideas, and an abundance of talent in a range of endeavors, like writing, pottery, and woodworking; home-schooling on the basis of progressive values and educational philosophy; organic farming of fruit trees, vegetables, chickens, and bees; and teaching wilderness education. By the summer of 2015, including its "off-campus" community in town, Redbud Springs had become a community of twenty-five adults and six children.

Among the eight who formed the early group and are still living, our various projects include struggling for racial justice especially through the NAACP and Rise and Shine Freedom School (a local after-school tutoring program for children and teens); participation in movements for reproductive freedom, women's rights, and marriage equality in North Carolina; working with the Democratic Party; serving on various boards and staffs, including Free Rein Center for Therapeutic Riding; ministering in local churches and officiating at baptisms, weddings, funerals, and memorial services; spending time with elderly or sick friends and family; and sharing farm work, road work, and other land-management projects. We are also involved in ongoing ways with our children, grandchildren, nieces, nephews and, in several cases, parents who are still living.

For enjoyment and relaxation, we are interested in writing, travel, painting and pottery and other forms of art, photography, playing music, walking and hiking, swimming and tennis, yoga and shibashi, caring for and riding horses, tending to dogs and cats and koi fish, cooking and baking, movies and plays and concerts, and communicating through social media as well as old-fashioned letters and phone calls. We also spend ever more time going to primary care physicians, dentists, endodontists, audiologists, ophthalmologists, pulmonologists, oncologists, podiatrists, orthopedists, dermatologists, psychiatrists, physical and massage therapists, acupuncturists, other health-care providers, and health food stores as we do our best to keep on keeping on, one day at a time.

On a map of western North Carolina, Redbud Springs is located about twenty miles, closer to ten as the crow flies, from the yard in Hendersonville in which long ago the young girl in the baseball cap and pigtails was photographed gazing at the box turtle. My home's name at Redbud Springs is "Turtle Hill," for the small reptile who appears occasionally to remind us how we got here.

Carter as a kid with box turtle, Hendersonville, North Carolina, ca. 1950.

Carter as debutante, Charlotte, North Carolina, 1964.

Carter in Charlotte in 2017, with her brother Robbie Heyward, his wife Betsy Alexander, and their daughter Kate, one of the four young people Carter discusses in part 2. (*Photo by Albert Dulin*)

Carter Heyward and Sue Hiatt at the Episcopal Divinity School in the mid-1980s.

Carter Heyward and Beverly Harrison at their vacation home, Deer Isle, Maine, 1985.

Carter with Katie Geneva Cannon, speakers at the Stone Center, Wellesley College, Massachusetts, 1989.

Demostration with other religious leaders on behalf of Puerto Rican liberation movement, Central Park, New York City, late 1970s.

With The Rev. Li Tim Oi, ordained to the priesthood in Hong Kong in 1949, and The Rev. Mary D. Glasspool, at consecration of The Rt. Rev. Barbara C. Harris in Boston in 1989.

Shortly after her ordination as a priest, Carter co-officiates with a rabbi in a wedding of two friends in Tavern on the Green in Central Park, New York City.

Carter and her mother, Mary Ann Carter Heyward, on Mary Ann's eightieth birthday, Lake Toxaway, North Carolina, 1995.

Carter in Charlotte in 2017, with her sister Ann Heyward and Ann's daughter Isabel Drinkwater and son Rob Drinkwater, two of the young people Carter lifts up in part two. Rob is holding his son, Cooper Heyward Norris, and Ann's husband Robert Dulin is standing behind his wife. (*Photo by Albert Dulin*)

At the twentieth anniversary celebration of the Philadelphia Ordination, 1994.

*Right*: Hiking in North Carolina mountains, 1998.

*Below*: Carter and Bev hiking in Maine, 1995.

With Judith Plaskow, Emilie Townes, and Larry Rasmussen on a panel celebrating Beverly Harrison's retirement from Union Theological Seminary, in New York City, 1999.

Carter with Sister Angela, CC, and Beverly Harrison, with Bev's dog "Duffy," at Redbud Springs, near Brevard, North Carolina, 2000. (*Beverly Hall, photographer*)

With Sue Sasser and Beverly Harrison at Bev's seventieth birthday party, Redbud Springs, 2002.

Carter and Sue Sasser at Redbud Springs, 2003. (*Beverly Hall, photographer*)

*Above*: Carter with dogs Bailey and Pom in woods outside her home on Turtle Hill, summer 2016.

*Right*: At Redbud Springs, 2003. (*Beverly Hall, photographer*)

Carter riding Red, with baby Feather trotting alongside, 2003. (*Beverly Hall, photographer*)

Carter on Feather, Sue on Red, in North Carolina mountains, 2009.

With Tom Shaw, Gene Robinson, Muffie Moroney, and friends at Episcopal Church General Convention, Minneapolis, 2003.

The women of Redbud Springs celebrate Christmas 2005; *left to right*: Peg Hall, Gerry Azzata, Bev Harrison, Carter, Sue Sasser, Nancy Richards, Jennifer Rouse, Gerrie Kiley.

Celebrating ordination to diaconate of Gretchen Grimshaw. *Left to right*: Katherine Styles, Ann Franklin, Gretchen, and Carter in Jamaica Plains, Massachusetts, 2006.

Jan Surrey, Carter's friend and spiritual companion in exploring the meanings of "mutuality" over three decades, is pictured in 2000 with her husband and chief professional collaborator Steve Bergman (aka author Samuel Shem), also a dear friend of Carter's. Between them is Katie, Carter's "goddess daughter," and one of the four young people Carter lifts up in part two.

Carter and Red, at Redbud Springs, 2009. (*Photo by Albert Dulin*)

At Free Rein Center for Therapeutic Riding, Brevard, North Carolina, 2010.

Carter with David Conolly in Melbourne, Australia, 2010.

Sue, Carter, and Angela Moloney, OP, in South Australia, 2010.

Speaking at NAACP rally in Brevard, North Carolina, protesting bullying in schools, 2016.

Feather and Carter at Redbud Springs, 2015.

# Part Three

## SHE FLIES ON

I was fifteen years old when I understood how it is that things break down: people can't imagine someone else's point of view.

—Sonia Sotomayor, *My Beloved World*[58]

# The Spirit

A challenge in writing this third and final section of the book is that She does indeed fly on! Trying to speak any truth about God in Her ever-moving, swirling, transformative presence through stories that may convey some spiritual insight, I am hoping in these pages to illuminate a few intimations and glimpses of God's healing beauty and liberating power in motion. This task is the one before us now—mine to offer, yours to accept, reject, or shape to correspond to your life journey. For each of us—writer and reader—part three is likely to feel like we're riding waves, going up and down, over and under, sometimes moving along smooth and easy, sometimes tossed about in turbulence.

The sacred Spirit, God's eternal and ongoing energy, the Sophia Wisdom who has animated Jesus and all the saints, nudges us beyond a static Christianity and beyond patriarchal religion into non-dichotomous realms beyond ourselves, beyond national and religious boundaries, beyond political divides, beyond gender and racial identity, beyond species and human words, beyond life and death as it comes to us all. Now, is this "beyond-ness" pure madness, fantasy, the spiritual imagination cut loose of a seventy-one-year-old feminist theologian, or can it be also an expression of sacred Spirit, breaking through?

I lived the middle portion of my life doing my best to follow Jesus as brother and Christ. My childhood had moved in that direction, and the Philadelphia ordination had delivered me into the heart of such a vocation. A pale imitation of Jesus of Nazareth, as his life is reported to us, I spent the most public part of my life and ministry largely in communities of feminists and other activist-scholars and pastors, trying to discern the will of God and do it. In part two, I presented various images of incarnation that I experienced over about twenty years. These images were meant to demonstrate that following Jesus, embodying his christic Spirit, doing our best to make justice-love in the world, is messy business in which we do not always make good choices and we do not always win in our efforts to create a little more justice, compassion, and peace on earth. Still, we do what we can, which is what our brother from Nazareth did.

Unlike me, Jesus didn't live to an old age. He didn't enjoy a retirement. As Christians know, his public ministry was cut short on a wooden cross. I find myself wondering what Jesus's life as an old man would have looked like. What shapes would his life have taken had he lived another several decades? What if he had lived in some sort of relational community with several of his disciples or with a partner? Would he have married? Would he have partnered with a woman, maybe Mary Magdalene, as Dan Brown suggests?[59] Would he have partnered with a man, maybe John, "the disciple whom he loved" (John 19:26)? Was his vocation to a single and perhaps celibate way of being, or might he have had more than one intimate partner, sexually, emotionally, spiritually?

Would the spiritual movement Jesus generated have formed itself around him had he not been crucified and had his disciples and followers not experienced the presence and leadership of an ongoing, "resurrected" Jesus? These fanciful questions move us into realms of fiction, poetry, and prayer, where imagination can soar and open us to the workings of the Spirit among us.

Often cited by Christians as "the Holy Spirit," She is spiritual energy, the creative and liberating wellspring of the power to grow, to heal, to love. She is the ongoing and eternal source of all that is good. She is the Spirit that connected Jesus to God and connects God to all creatures.

In 1985, the Anglican Church affirmed its belief that the Spirit comes from "the Father" not "from the Father and the Son"[60] which is how the Roman Catholic and Anglican communions have historically understood the Spirit's origin. By contrast, the Eastern Orthodox Church, unlike the Roman Church, has always held that both the Son (Jesus) and the Holy Spirit come from the Father. Its 1985 theological affirmation places Anglicans officially closer to the Eastern Orthodox, and further from the Roman Catholic, understanding of how Father, Son, and Spirit are related. This distinction is important because it invites Christians to imagine that Jesus was a human being like the rest of us and that his sacred power—the Spirit—came to him, and lived through him, by the grace of God, much as the Spirit works in all creation and all beings.

If Jesus had become an elder sage in his community, we can imagine that much of what he did, or chose not to do, would have been inspired by God, holy spirited by the One to whose voice he was open, and whose work in the world he did his best to share. My own experience has been that, over the years, my understandings of myself and others, of the whole created earth and the Creator God—has become increasingly Spirit-based and less focused on Jesus. As a brother in the Spirit and an inspiration, Jesus will always be important to me and the Christian communities to whom I am connected, but Jesus is no more my God today than the turtle and the trees and my sister and brother humans who try to discern the will of God and do it. All of us are spirited by God, like Jesus—indeed, that's what Jesus's chief message to us was. It becomes our shared vocation to live, work, love, and do whatever we can in, and on behalf of, the Spirit who yearns for us "to do justice, and to love kindness, and to walk humbly with our God" (Mic. 6:8, adapted).

# Signs of the Spirit

But how do we know it's the Spirit of God and not some devious energy? How can we be sure it's the sacred source of our capacities to make jus-, tice and practice kindness, and not some twisted force that is weakening the possibility of our making right relation? How do we know it's not just our own personal desire or whim or hunch, something we are concocting, perhaps unaware, to benefit primarily ourselves? What distinguishes the Holy Spirit from other spirits, energies, and winds of various kinds that blow us about? How do we know we're being faithful to the Spirit of Justice-Love and not attaching ourselves to idols that can easily seduce us, such as people who insist upon our allegiance, faithfulness, or love on their own terms?

How do we know it's the Holy Spirit? The answer to this question is simple but not so easy to make incarnate in our daily lives. Jesus offers this guideline on how to distinguish between Spirit and idols, the true and the false. "A good tree cannot bear bad fruit, nor can a bad tree bear good fruit" (Matt. 7:18). "Thus you will know them by their fruits" (Matt 7:20). This means we often have to wait to see what happens over time. We have to be patient to discern what is being driven by the Holy Spirit and what is not. We often do not know beforehand what the Spirit is doing, and what She is not, even in our own lives. Maybe especially in our own lives.

I believe the last two decades of my life were moved by God's Spirit, powerfully at certain times and in specific places, by no means always or everywhere, and not always with my cooperation or awareness. In making this claim, I do not assume that I am anything other than a fully human creature, like you—which means also that I assume the Spirit has been at work in your life in particular ways. I ask you, dear reader: Do you also believe this is true? Do you imagine that She flies on between, among, and within us? If so, how do you know the Spirit when She is present? Let me suggest that the Spirit has several unmistakable features by which we can recognize her movement:

- She is the ongoing and eternal energy of radical mutuality, our power for generating mutual relation, or justice-love, as individuals and communities.

158

- She is the wellspring of compassion, kindness, and courage in all situations.

- We recognize Her by what She does—the actual justice-love that She makes in the world, Her embodied acts of courage, Her displays of kindness among us, Her offerings of compassion to us and through us.

- She is always moving on, never static, though She does from time to time hover like a mother hen over Her brood.

- She is never simply "mine" or "yours," never only "ours" or "theirs." She belongs to no one religion or spiritual tradition. She cannot be possessed. She belongs to all and She belongs to none.

- She transcends borders and boundaries, connecting us all, regardless of what we may wish or whether we are aware of Her.

- She is not bound by time or place and She is not confined to this world or this cosmos.

- She celebrates ambiguity, but She is never ambivalent about struggling for justice, extending compassion, or offering kindness.

- She understands well the difference between accepting, and resigning ourselves to, difficult circumstances.

- She carries us beyond the need to be "right"—and beyond any assumption that we can ever know it all.

- She impresses us with the need, always, to be kind and non-violent, even when angry, even when saying no, even when rejecting someone or something. Always be kind, if we can, and non-violent, if at all possible.

- In the lovely, lilting language of Canadian hymnist and Anglican Bishop Gordon Light, She flies on, lifting us up and carrying us forward together on Her wings.

# Beyond Us

She is never simply "like" us or solely "in our image."

One of my spiritual mentors in the last couple of decades has been my sister, Ann, seven years my junior, once a sweet little girl with long blonde hair and bright blue eyes with whom I shared a room when we were kids. Today a beautiful woman in her early sixties, Ann is more conservative than me in her Christian faith. We put the theological pieces together differently—God, Jesus, salvation, prayer—but, like many folks who share basic values and who care about each other, Ann and I arrive repeatedly on friendly, neighboring spiritual, moral, and political ground. Ann embodies and has shown me the transformative spiritual power of personal integrity, kindness, and patience. It's not just me, her sister, who is moved by Ann's spiritual energy, but people throughout our family and in her larger community. So if perhaps you, the reader, wonder where I get these notions about spiritual power—the Spirit moving among us—I can honestly say that, while I'm well-educated as a professional theologian and priest, many of the lessons I have learned come from people in my life like my sister, whose ways of incarnating God are contagious sources of wisdom, courage, and Spirit in my life.

The Spirit has no nationality and no religion. She spins and sparks globally and beyond without favorite people or cultures or species. She is too vast, too deep, too intelligent, too loving to live in one place only, though She lives with, in, and through each of our lives. The turmoil we are experiencing globally in these times reflects our collective and personal fear that we are coming apart. Our identities, the ways we have named ourselves and our God and have claimed certain spaces on this planet as our own, are breaking up. Like cell phones with poor reception, we often can't hear clearly or understand what is happening around us, or even recognize who we are in relation to the world around us.

In his poem "The Second Coming," William Butler Yeats described a world in which "things fall apart" and "the center cannot hold." Written in 1919 as a Christian allegorical description of Europe in the wake of the First World War, this poem has an eerily contemporary ring in its reflection of chaos and tribulation:

Turning and turning in the widening gyre
The falcon cannot hear the falconer;
Things fall apart; the centre cannot hold;
Mere anarchy is loosed upon the world,
The blood-dimmed tide is loosed, and everywhere
The ceremony of innocence is drowned;
The best lack all conviction, while the worst
Are full of passionate intensity.
Surely some revelation is at hand;
Surely the Second Coming is at hand.
The Second Coming! Hardly are those words out
When a vast image out of *Spiritus Mundi*
Troubles my sight: somewhere in sands of the desert
A shape with lion body and the head of a man,
A gaze blank and pitiless as the sun,
Is moving its slow thighs, while all about it
Reel shadows of the indignant desert birds.
The darkness drops again; but now I know
That twenty centuries of stony sleep
Were vexed to nightmare by a rocking cradle,
And what rough beast, its hour come round at last,
Slouches towards Bethlehem to be born?[61]

Yeats writes that the "Second Coming" must surely be at hand. This refers to a traditional Christian belief that Christ will return to earth in the wake of terrible global events, marked by instability in the context of dreadful war and violence. Is this horror as real and present today, in the early twenty-first century, as it was a hundred years ago? Is "mere anarchy" being "loosed upon the world" today?

I would say, yes. Our life together on planet earth is as "blood-dimmed" as ever. Because we are linked around the world by the greed of advanced capitalism; a terrible resurgence of violence and cruelty in the names of God; the ongoing, ubiquitous threat of nuclear war; and ominous promises of climate change and environmental devastation, the entire earth has become more volatile than ever in our history. Today there is no "centre"—no nation, no religion, no culture—that can hold the world together. This is our disruptive context, the global arena in which we are living and breathing together, and in which we are also dying together. This time and space of grief and hope, fear and love, confusion and compassion, provides the wider social and psychological, political and spiritual, context in which I am writing and you are reading this book.

In realms of Spirit, everything is up for grabs, or so it seems. In the West, Muslims, Jews, and Christians are tightening their grips on some of the most conservative, archaic understandings of these religious traditions—hence the spread throughout the world of the most radically fundamentalist interpretations of Christianity and the rise of medievalist Islamic groups like ISIS. If we are awake, we are likely to be unclear about what roles, if any, our religious or spiritual communities might creatively play at this time—and, as important, about the roles we might play in helping shape or reshape our religious and spiritual communities if we dare.

In this last part of the book, I reflect on movements of the Spirit who is shaking us up, tossing and tumbling us about, carrying us along. Through this shake-up, I am focusing on our life together in the United States because this is my home. Even here, I am often thrown off balance by God's Spirit as She spins and sparks and swirls among us.

As I finish proofing these pages, in the very same week, the nation in which I live and breathe *intends* to inaugurate Donald J. Trump to the Presidency. In my sleep and in my waking, I am haunted by the often startling difference between *intent* and *impact*.

Even so, She flies on, igniting our anger at the lies and greed, the violence and oppression; sharpening our minds, tools, and strategies to make justice-love throughout the land; and securing our confidence in Her ongoing power as the root of hope.

# Gun Madness

Propelling us beyond our national gun mania, She pleads with us to lay down our arms, to beat them into "plowshares" which, for us, might be to find ways of turning them into money for food, clothes, shelter, health care.

Consider our so-called "right to bear arms" which, according to the National Rifle Association—since 2008, with the Supreme Court's assent—may be interpreted as every American's constitutional right to buy, sell, keep, and carry into public places of our own choosing any firearms we choose, from the smallest handguns to the most powerful assault rifles. When interpreted through these lenses, the Second Amendment can hold us hostage to our fears and paranoia, fostering indifference, and even contempt, for the well-being of others and of our society as a whole.

Dorothy Samuels, a senior fellow at the Brennan Center for Justice, and a columnist for the *New York Times*, wrote,

> To grasp the audacity of what Scalia & Co. pulled off [in District of Columbia v. Heller, 2008], turn to the Second Amendment's text: "A well regulated Militia, being necessary to the security of a free State, the right of the people to keep and bear Arms, shall not be infringed." To find in that wording an individual right to possess a firearm untethered to any militia purpose, the majority performed an epic feat of jurisprudential magic: It made the pesky initial clause about the necessity of a "well regulated Militia" disappear. Poof! Gone. Scalia treated the clause as merely 'prefatory' and having no real operative effect—a view at odds with history, the fundamental rules of constitutional interpretation, and the settled legal consensus for many decades. . . .
>
> Then-justice John Paul Stevens correctly noted in his minority opinion, joined by Justice David Souter, Ruth Bader Ginsburg, and Stephen Breyer. "Neither the text of the Amendment nor the arguments advanced by its proponents evidenced the slightest interest in limiting any legislature's authority to regulate private civilian uses of firearms."[62]

Worldwide, many who know the gun culture in the United States view it as a morally bankrupt and crazed phenomenon. It is also among the most damaging social and political movements in our nation's history. From a progressive life-affirming perspective, the Supreme Court's two recent rulings on the public's right to bear arms (Heller v. District of Columbia in 2008 and McDonald v. Chicago in 2010) are among the most damning in its history, alongside Dred Scott (Dred Scott v. Sanford in 1857) and its Citizens United decision in 2010.

The court's Second Amendment rulings were certain to generate machismo, ego, and paranoia, on the one hand, and death and grief in large numbers, on the other. As Dorothy Samuels suggests, the court's interpretation of the Second Amendment in such a way as to make people imagine that we have a "right to bear arms" of any kind, in any number, and to carry them anywhere we wish, is the stuff of fiction, not of sound legal jurisprudence or historical precedence. The framers of the United States Constitution could in no way have imagined modern assault weapons, much less that these death-machines would find themselves in the hands of confused children or alienated citizens who shoot to kill.

The Spirit who yearns for our well-being and stirs us to create mutuality in every situation moves me to lament with every fiber of my being the gun madness in this country, and to resent and deplore the gun lobby's lock on Congress and a minority of the American public. Religious and spiritual leaders in this nation should be preaching and teaching forcefully against this wicked idolatry. Our gun madness is a vivid contemporary analog for the false idols that Moses smashed to the ground (Exod. 32:15–35).

If our nation is able to survive the violence that is being intensified by the Second Amendment idolatry—and it's not clear that we can—then surely, sooner or later, some wiser court will reverse the ruling, as with Dred Scott. That will still leave us with more guns than people in this nation—but a change in the ethos and politics of guns in America can lead to creative ways of imagining a new approach to the great numbers of guns in our society. Following Australia's lead, the United States government could launch a massive buy-back of powerful assault weapons and dispose of them. Of course, our nation is larger and more politically complex than Australia; steely determination, bipartisan cooperation, participation from responsible gun owners, and moral leadership of people across the religious spectrum will be required to gain the confidence of most Americans to help control guns and ammunition, and to help decrease the numbers of assault rifles and pistols in the hands of citizens. Most people on all sides of the gun debate acknowledge that there is no one solution to this major social problem: Too many people are shooting others and themselves. But we could perhaps begin to solve this problem if we, as society, could begin to understand it as a spiritual or moral imperative, not only a political challenge.

Making the morality and politics of this situation more daunting is another dreadful Supreme Court ruling, Citizens United, by which the justices swung open the doors to Big Money—corporate power—to virtually buy elections. The National Rifle Association, with its deep pockets, can more easily influence who will win elections and, therefore, who will appoint judges and justices who will bow to the same idols. We the people of the United States need to keep in mind that, in our nation, the president of the United States, with the US Senate's confirmation, appoints Supreme Court justices to their lifetime tenure. This fact underscores the importance of Presidential and Senatorial elections, and it requires us to pay attention to elections of Governors and state legislators, since most gun laws are forged at the state level.

# Mystery and Wonder

Even through these heartbreaking and daunting challenges, She flies on, carrying us beyond this time and space. Moving beyond what we can readily see and touch and know with our senses, She carries us into other realms of being in relation.

The last conversation Bev and I had, before her death from congestive heart failure on December 15, 2012, was over the evening news the night before, as the horrors of the Newtown, Connecticut, massacre unfolded—twenty children and six teachers dead by gun violence at the hands of a madman. Bev and I sat mostly in silence and disbelief—she sitting up in bed, me sitting close to her, holding hands, both of us shaking our heads. We were wrapped in a blanket of sadness, and anger, which came out an hour or so later as we snapped at each other over whether or not I would go to the store that night and buy a rotisserie chicken for Pom Pom, Bev's little dog.

"Pom doesn't need any chicken tonight," I insisted.

"But I want her to have some," Bev was adamant.

As it happened, the Spirit would be taking Bev away from the evil and madness in this world against which she had so long struggled as a Christian liberation ethicist, teacher, writer, activist, and feminist of faith. The very next day, Bev died peacefully, Pom Pom beside her on the bed. I was left dumbfounded and bereft, as folks are when loved ones die. Of course, I felt guilty for not having bought the chicken for Pom and, even more, for not having somehow known that my beloved companion had gone as far as she could in the life we shared here in this world. Like many couples, Bev and I had grown to assume that there would always be tomorrow to work out the wrinkles of the day before. But not so for us this time.

In days, weeks, and months to follow, Bev's spirit would join me on my morning walks with my standard poodle, Bailey, and Bev's little Pom, who had become my dog, too. Bev's and my connection has changed, terribly and sadly for me. I miss her deeply. But our relationship has not exactly dimmed, and it has most certainly not been spiritually diminished, in the years since Bev's death. The connection between us continues to be powerful and compelling.

Bev's spirit is active in my life, so active that she often speaks through me. Sometimes I hear her voice in my own, speaking in public, offering pithy analyses of the right-wing, woman-hating, racist political dynamics that have resurfaced in recent months. Bev wouldn't hesitate to call it as she saw it—for example, to lambast the current crop of North Carolina legislators for basing their religious beliefs about guns, abortion, gays, climate change, voting rights, and economic justice on what Bev called "Jurassic Park Theology." I can hear her now, and I see her winking at me as I type—because she knows these words are hers, too.

Many mornings, Bev talks with me on our walks with the dogs. When I say she "talks," I don't mean I actually hear Bev speaking, but rather that I know in my heart and mind and soul what Bev's spirit is saying to me. This is an example of knowing what we know, seeing what we see, hearing what we hear, through the mind and eyes and ears of God. This is Spirit-driven communication, trustworthy beyond a doubt—but only if we believe that the Spirit is alive and well and active among us, the relational energy that creates mutuality and compassion, kindness and truth, forgiveness and reconciliation and other graces of being. Otherwise, our religious imagination is simply a delusion.

Along with several other people and creatures who have died, Bev is a spiritual comrade who encourages me to persevere politically by pointing out that, on balance, the world is no worse now than ever, but also no better—and that in these times, as always, good people must speak out and do whatever we can to help move the struggles for justice and peace. These people—brave, smart, activist, faithful loved ones who have died—live on. I tell you, friends, that those whom we knew well while they were alive on earth are still available to empower us. Their presence can infuse us with Spirit, the energy to keep walking the path, and the wisdom to stop along the way to rest and play and be refreshed.

From among countless people and creatures who have passed on, the Spirit convenes a "heavenly council" to help me keep my balance. The members of the council whom I recognize are people, and also some creatures like my beloved horse Red, friends no longer here in their embodied ways of being themselves on this planet. Do these friends come to me because I evoke them? Or do they come forth because they know I need them? In any case, they come—together or individually—when I need or yearn to talk with them. They are friend, therapist, priest, and prophet all rolled up into one big beautiful spiritual resource that is eternal and ongoing. Along with Bev, my parents are on this council, as are Sister Angela, Sue Hiatt, Dorothee Soelle, Bob DeWitt, Bob Brown (one of my most courageous and wisest seminary professors), Betty Smith, and Red the horse, whom Angela sometimes rides to meet me.

Shortly after my father's death in 1984, I preached a homily on angels, in which I suggested that angels come in many forms, shifting shapes, leaping across and beyond creature-species. I do not believe that angels come primarily as individual representations of the people or creatures they once were. I believe angels touch our lives as currents of energy, or forces of memory, or living bodies of human and other creatures who do, in fact, represent more than just themselves. Angels convey the presence of the Spirit who connects us to those who have died or those from whom we are separate at this time, those who seem far away. By the power of the Spirit, angels come to us to lift us above this time and space and then place us emphatically back into the present moment, restored and ready to go on.

How do I reconcile my heavenly council, in which I am encountered by individuals who have died, with my sense of angels as streams of energy, largely non-individuated? Perhaps, as I age, I am so eager to stay connected with those who have died that my mind shapes the spiritual energy in such a way that I can see beloved ones as I remember them: Bev, Angela, Red, Dorothee . . . I can't pretend to know the answer to this question. Perhaps my heavenly council is a figment of my imagination? I recall that, years before her death, as we walked through snow in rural Maine, Angela said to me, "Don't ever forget that imagination is a window into God."

Whatever its spiritual root, my heavenly council is angelic and, for me, a primary source of God's love. I imagine there are tree spirits, rock spirits, turtle spirits and dinosaur spirits hovering near this heavenly council of mine. I occasionally wonder what they are doing or saying in their own languages.

Perhaps there are also spirits of those who have done great wrong but who have been somehow converted—turned around—and forgiven by the Spirit whose ways we cannot begin to comprehend or imagine. Once those who have done great evil have died, can their spirits be transformed? Can their spirits in some way make amends for the harm they did? We cannot know and probably cannot imagine an answer to these questions, but I believe it's important to wonder. It's an important spiritual exercise in getting beyond ourselves—to realize that these people too are our human siblings, even if their senses of our common humanity seem to have been lost. It's an important reminder that, regardless of our efforts to love, we ourselves participate in the perpetuation of evil every day, through our greed and fear, selfishness and ignorance, or simply by looking away from the violence being waged in our name.

I think here of Frederick Denison Maurice, a great Anglican theologian of mid-nineteenth-century England and one of my favorites. Maurice lost his teaching position at Kings College in London for his refusal to assent to the doctrine of eternal damnation, a refusal that was based on his belief in a loving God who would not condemn anyone for eternity. In reflecting on the spiritual fate of those who have done great evil, I am moving along the same theological track as F. D. Maurice.[63]

I assume my heavenly council is only a small representation of Spirit and that such resources are infinite in number, available to all who are catching intimations and glimpses of God. I cannot tell you how often the members of my council, sources of such spiritual energy, come to help me along, to encourage me, to strengthen my heart. Bob Brown and Dorothee Soelle are always near at hand to secure my resolve to struggle for social justice as central to my spiritual life. Sue Hiatt and Bob DeWitt are mentor-friends in relation to all matters of religion and spirituality. Betty Smith and Bev, my best teachers, remind me constantly to think outside the box—in Betty's words, "to dare to think [my] own thoughts in a world in which few do." Mary Ann and Bob, my parents, are everywhere, smiling and nodding their presence, spreading kindness, underscoring their love for me and my siblings, their grandchildren, and the world itself. Angela is my horse-loving buddy and spiritual companion always ready to push on beyond the boundaries that meet us at every turn. More than any other angels in my life, Angela and my father, Bob Heyward, attend Red and other creatures who have died and yet continue to live in me, and through my life.

# Family

She creates a welcoming space for all, reimagining "family," assuring us that everyone is worthy of justice-love, respect and care and dignity and basic human rights. She does not cast anyone out beyond the boundaries of Her family, which is the eternal realm of justice-love in this world and all others.

In 2006, my sister, Ann, found the son to whom she had given birth thirty-eight years earlier, when she was sixteen, and whom she had offered up for adoption. In months to come, Ann and her now-grown baby, together with the remarkable couple who had adopted him, became for a special moment in time, family. This discovery had several wonderful outcomes, including a strong, mutually respectful relationship between Ann and her newly found, eldest, son; a caring bond between the son's family and Ann's family; and a close, caring relationship between this son and her two younger children—Rob, in his early twenties, and Isabel, in her late teens at the time.

But the story also had a tragic dimension. Several years after his adoption, the young boy had been diagnosed with cystic fibrosis. For more than three decades, he and his adoptive family had known that he would have an early death. Ann and her family, of course, had known nothing about his disease. About seven months after Ann found the young man, he died.

At his funeral, his pastor publicly welcomed Ann and her family—Robert Dulin, Ann's husband (not the boy's birth-father), Ann's other children, and several others of us, including Bev and me. Affirming his belief that in God's house are many rooms, the pastor reflected with words to this effect: This wonderful family—shaped by birth, adoption, mutual extensions of generosity, and the coming together of a group of diverse individuals—is much like God's family, in which there is welcoming space for all.

I think of Alcoholics Anonymous, one of the great "family" networks on planet earth, crossing cultures, religions, national boundaries, races, genders, ages, abilities, and political affiliations. AA welcomes everyone with a desire to stop drinking, and from that welcome and generous spirit many twelve-step programs have been launched.

I think of my friend Delores, one of the world's great womanist and Christian theologians, whose husband died early, leaving her with four children. As her children grew up and her mother became ill, Delores left her professional work behind to return home to care for one adult child who had become chronically ill and an increasingly incapacitated mother. I will never forget Delores telling me, in 1983, about the terror she as a mother experienced every time her black son went out at night in New York City. "No mother of a black son can help but worry when her son is out of the house," she said. "Many white folks won't hesitate to shoot a black male walking down the street simply because they're scared of black men." This is the kind of worrying that many mothers know little about in our society. Through their candor and courage, many years ago, Delores and legions of other mothers of black children, together with black liberation and womanist theologians, were constructing compelling theological frameworks for the contemporary Black Lives Matter movement.

I think of Gerrie and Jenn, a lesbian couple, legally married in Massachusetts in 2004, living at Redbud Springs ever since. Now in her seventies, physically active and in otherwise good health, Gerrie has been going blind for about twenty years, and Jenn has been helping her wife continue to sustain a vibrant, fun-filled life even as she herself, like so many others, works two part-time jobs to help make ends meet. Jenn and Gerrie, proud parents and grandparents as well as caring daughters to Jenn's mother, continue to contribute as much as possible to the larger community through the NAACP, the American Association of University Women (AAUW), and other voluntary associations committed to building a just society.

Legions of people in the United States and elsewhere are choosing to build family with people who may or may not be their blood- or adopted-kin, but who are looking for family—women, men, and children in relationships with others in ways that empower them to become who they can be, at their best. In our generation and society, women have often taken the lead in these efforts. Redbud Springs is only one example. At the turn of this past century, the Greenfire community on the Maine coast, the Women's Theological Center in the Boston Theological Institute, and Holy Ground in Asheville, North Carolina, exemplified women's outreach to women around shared spiritual and political commitments to build more fully woman-affirming lives, families, and communities.

There are also many women and men in our society and world who are able and willing to build family with children and adults—sometimes their own kin, sometimes not—who are sick or suffering. I think of my beloved colleagues, Ann, a priest, and Elly, a nurse, who have provided tender care for two seriously disabled grandchildren even as they have continued to spend major periods of time working as parish minister, seminary development officer, prison chaplain, Christian allies to the Palestinian peace movement, and women struggling with their own health issues. I think of my dear friend Norene, who adopted her sister's abused child and years later became mom to another young girl in need of mothering. I think of Chris, one of Bev's most respected and cherished colleagues and former students who, with her husband, adopted several children who were terminally ill and needed a caring home in which to experience love, regardless of their diagnoses.

There are also folks who build family simply because they are moved to reach out beyond what is expected. BK is a Southern lesbian Christian sister with a ministry not only to the LGBTQ community throughout the US and other parts of the world, but also to her elder lesbian and feminist theological teachers and mentors, whom she chooses again and again to help. Without BK's active love and support, many senior lesbians and feminists in religion would not be able to navigate the increasingly challenging passages that come with age and infirmity. BK has chosen to create family not only with her partner, Devon, a feminist Jewish rabbi, but also with scores of sisters and brothers marginalized by generations of sexual, racial, and gender discrimination. She ministers with people both in person and online. Defying the limits of location, and an unusually able navigator of cyberspace, BK has ventured into "Second Life," an online virtual world, in which BK's minister-avatar works with those who, through their own avatars, seek her counsel.

Although I am aware that some question the politics and morality of international and cross-cultural adoptions, I also am mindful of how many couples and singles have adopted children, including at least two generations of Chinese baby girls, over the past several decades. My imagination soars as I try to imagine the many, varied life-journeys of these once-Chinese-babies-now-American-women. I once wondered if those who had been adopted by American feminists—as many had been in the 1980s, 1990s, and early 2000s—would return to China and help mount a feminist revolution! That was pure fantasy on my part because, as the goddess-mother of one such young woman and the aunt of another, I've watched both become full-fledged American young people with dreams and hopes and paths to explore like every other American kid. Although Chinese by birth, they are all-American girls and young women, at home in the United States of America, with all its promises and problems.

# Love—Wisdom and Folly

**In these stories and many others, She beckons us beyond conventional patterns of connection and emboldens us to create mutually empowering relationships as well as we can.**

When Bev and I parted as a couple back in 1990, we agreed that we would continue on in life as "companions" or "partners" or something other than a traditionally shaped couple. As I discussed in part two, we had never really been a conventional couple; all along, Bev and I had harbored misgivings about what we perceived as an unhealthy tightness and inwardness of most married couples. We perceived such couple-dom as often possessive and stifling of one or both partner's creative energies.

One of the challenges of the changing relational mores of our time has been finding language that suits us, whoever we are. Some women who have been living with other women, sexually or otherwise, for decades do not describe their relationship as "lesbian" or "gay." All along, some women-loving women have preferred to be called "gay" rather than "lesbian." Most lesbian feminists prefer the opposite and, at least in the midst of the feminist movement in the 1970s and 1980s, heard the word "gay" as referring primarily to men, not women.

From the time of the Stonewall uprising of 1969, which sparked the beginning of the modern gay movement, almost all openly gay men and lesbian women have distanced ourselves from the term "homosexual," hearing it as a medical and psychological term that had been used for almost a century to pathologize sexual non-conformists. Some have referred to those whom we love simply as "lovers," a term eschewed by others as too sexy, too narrowly focused on sex and a little too personal. Some have referred to those with whom they have made a long term commitment as partners, companions, significant others, or spouses. Even before marriage equality became widespread, some same-sex partners referred to one another as their husband or wife. Most of us have used different terms from time to time, depending on context and where we are in our lives.

Not long after we moved to North Carolina, someone—a sister priest, I was told—went to the bishop of Western North Carolina and told him that I had "two lovers."

This person apparently was aware that I had two life-companions, women with whom I was committed to spending my life, in community with them and other friends and colleagues. Whether I was lovers with either or both of my life-companions, the self-appointed reporter had no way of knowing. Neither did the bishop, who called me in to ask if it was true: "Do you have two lovers, Carter?"

I told the bishop that, as an unmarried woman, I had never professed to be monogamous. I said Bev and I had been together for over twenty years at that point as life-companions but that we had not been a couple in any traditional sense for over a decade. I said that, in the late 1990s, I had also become a life-companion to Sue. I told the bishop that, along with Bev and me, Sue had bought the land in the mountains and that the three of us had formed the core group of what would become Redbud Springs. Sue and Bev had been aware and had agreed to my being life-companions with each, and the three of us—Bev, Sue, and I—had set off as partners in the establishment and maintenance of Redbud Springs as a residential community for women and as a small center for feminist theological meetings.

Here is the gist of a small piece of dialogue between the bishop and me, in his office, in 2004. It's reconstructed on the basis of my memory—subjective and selective, but also instructive:

Bishop: "What you're describing makes sense to me and I see no problem with it, but you understand, I'm sure, Carter, that I can't simply say 'okay' to a priest who—at least some people think—has two lovers, even if their perceptions aren't accurate. You know that I couldn't affirm this if you were a male priest said to be sleeping with two women."

Me: "Well, Bob, how many unmarried male priests in this diocese have you asked about the numbers of women with whom they may be sleeping? Are you saying that no one of either gender, or any sexual identity, should ever have more than one sexual partner? Must everyone be monogamous? Do you assume that one size fits all?"

Bishop: "You know as well as I what the church has always taught, for better or worse, about marriage and sexuality. The relationships with the women, as you describe them, sound fine to me. But I'm not sure how I'd feel if you told me that both relationships are sexual at this time in your life. Regardless, in this case, it's a matter of perception—of how you, as a priest, are perceived by your sister and brother clergy."

The bishop and I parted friends. To this day, I admire this man for his integrity and his leadership on many issues, including an openness long before most bishops on the ordination of gay and lesbian priests. He retired a year after our conversation and his successor took the same position on my "two lovers." These two bishops are well-respected by Episcopalians across liberal-conservative lines. Our different perspectives represent what I believe to be the church's conservative overreach in realms of human sexuality and relationships. The church's always-begrudging position on sexuality is steeped historically in its radical failure to comprehend, or even try to comprehend, connections between our human experiences of sexuality and intimacy, friendship and commitment, faithfulness and family, and the Spirit's ongoing movement, crossing generations and transforming gender, as She soars, often taking comfort among us in our most compelling relationships.

Because I was retired and not employed by the church, there weren't many practical implications of these bishops' views of my relationships with Bev and Sue. There certainly would have been had I been seeking to work officially as a parish priest in the Episcopal Diocese of Western North Carolina, where Redbud Springs is located. But I wasn't. I had recently helped launch the Mountain Mission of St. Clare, a small Episcopal community that had emerged a year or two earlier in response to the local parish church's treatment of its LGBT members and friends. Because I had two life-companions, the bishops agreed with each other that I could not be the vicar (priest in charge) of St. Clare, but neither bishop made any effort to block my participation as a member—or, from time to time, as a priest—in the emerging mission, or as a priest in weddings, ordinations, memorial services, and other special services.

By the late 1990s, as the new project at Redbud Springs was taking off, Bev and I had been separated as a couple for six or seven years and had let go of the relational expectations that go with being a couple—such as spending most of our time together, sleeping or awake; doing most things together as a couple, like going to the movies, eating out, or even sharing a home, which we had done once before—our little Cape style summer cottage on Mud Cove in Deer Isle, Maine. And yet, even after we separated as a couple, and had let go of many of our couple expectations, we continued, like we always had, spending much of the best parts of our lives together, enjoying each other's company, and enlarging one another's senses of love, worth, and beauty.

Indeed, by the time we arrived in North Carolina in the late 1990s, Bev and I were devoted friends and life-companions who would continue to spend much of our time together, just the two of us—sharing meals and entertainment, vacationing and visiting each other's families as well as our friends and colleagues, taking professional trips and working together as ethicist and theologian, helping form the Mission of St. Clare, working politically, sharing the same house about half the time, and caring for and enjoying animal companions whom we shared on a daily basis and traveled with whenever we could.

The missing piece for us was the *intense primary focus* on each other that being a committed, monogamous couple often provides—for better and for worse. While we may have been spared some of the worse, more possessive, dynamics in such coupling, we also probably missed some of the better parts, especially that quality of special trust and unique bonding that can grow stronger and deeper between a couple when they are focused primarily on their own relationship so much of the time.

Officiating at weddings, both gay and straight, over the past several years, and speaking about marriage and commitment on each occasion, has reminded me what Bev and I had together, but also what we may have missed in our reluctance to take this step ourselves. Realizing what we may have missed sometimes makes me sad, but my gratitude for what we did not miss, what we were able to build together, makes my heart sing. Bev's and my relationship was strong and it was good, and I believe that, given who each of us was, the bond that Bev and I forged together may have been as fine and remarkable as it could possibly have been. Regardless of our intention not to be isolated or turned inward on our own relationship, our love was, over three decades, a primary relationship. There was never anyone more significant to either of us.

# "Fixing Busted Things"

Through it all, the Spirit brings new life. Surprising us, She stirs someone new into the deep wellsprings of the heart.

It was very good that Sue Sasser came along when she did and became, in many ways, the hub of Redbud Springs and of my life, including Bev's and my relationship. Not only has Sue been a life-companion to me in a variety of ways, she was also a devoted friend to Bev. Because Sue is a gifted, practical woman, who loves taking care of the land and all the life that is in it, and who knows more than most women of our generation about machines and how to "fix busted things," as she says, Sue is the one person most indispensable to the material functioning of our daily lives at Redbud Springs.

What's the matter with the water pump? You say a tree has fallen across the entrance to the property? Do we need to re-grade that part of the road? Who will bush-hog that pasture before it's as tall as the horses? What about the new TV screen—why isn't it working? And the old truck—how long can we keep it going? Can we thin out some of the trees to make some sunlight for the others? Oh dear, how are going to deal with the poison ivy without killing ourselves with toxic substances? What about the hornets' nest in the barn? What's our preparation plan for the upcoming storm? These are samples of questions that pop up at Redbud Springs and our small horse farm, often suddenly. Everybody who has ever visited our community, and certainly those of us who live here, think first of Sue whenever there is an issue or question about a building or a machine or about the land, the trees, the gravel roads.

Sue loves the first hint of spring—the redbud trees and the crocuses. She looks for the brilliant orange arrival of the flame azaleas in mid-May and the "blue ghosts" (bright blue fireflies) who haunt the woods around the streams later in the month. She delights in the first lady slippers, and is the bravest of all in rescuing the snapping turtle from the road or the copperhead from the garage. Sue is among the best with our horses and dogs. Like Angela and me, she also lost her heart to Red, the remarkable quarter horse who taught Sue and me both most of what we know about horses, how to care for them, how to ride them, how to love and lose and grieve for them.

Earlier in her life a member of Students for a Democratic Society (SDS), Sue is probably less politically radical today than I am, and we both are less radical, from a traditional leftist perspective, than quite a few younger folks and some good friends who are our contemporaries. Sue and I may have switched approaches from our youth: She may be more pragmatic and I more idealistic—although I'm aware of my own increasingly tenacious commitment to strategic thinking, and I delight in Sue's high-minded idealism that strives for a more fully just, kind, and sustainable world. Our combinations of idealism and pragmatic placed us firmly in Hillary Clinton's camp during the recent election cycle. Like Hillary, we also aspire to be progressives who get things done.

We discuss complicated and controversial environmental and economic issues like fracking and the Trans-Pacific Partnership (TPP), and we often help each other figure out what seems best. Neither of us likes fracking and both of us have serious misgivings about the TPP, but we agree that both of these contentious issues are more complicated than either their opponents or proponents admit. Sue and I usually wind up agreeing on most issues facing our world and nation, our state and local community. We are, for example, equally outraged by North Carolina's efforts, over the past few years, to turn the economic, environmental, and educational interests of our state over to the control of wealthy white men. Moreover, we are both distressed by the transparent, unapologetic racism embedded in so much of the anti-Obama rhetoric and behavior since the 2008 election.

Over the years, Bev, Sue, and I—with feminists, womanists, queer activists, and others working for justice—have come to realize that the mean-spiritedness worming its way more deeply into the soil of our society is a fear-based reaction to the breaking apart of the cultural, religious, and social mores that our generations grew up on in a world secured by white male supremacy. For this reason, Sue and I were not surprised by the emergence of Donald Trump in the summer of 2015, and Bev would not have been either. Still, like Bev, Sue and I had learned from our Republican and Democratic parents, and our communities of origin, a basic respect for human decency and kindness, qualities dramatically absent from the victorious presidential candidacy of Donald Trump. Through all of this madness, Bev is not spinning in her grave. She is helping stir the heavens on behalf of more justice-love and peace on earth.

It's from a spiritual perspective that Sue and I are most different, yet in a way similar. Sue describes herself as a non-militant atheist with little interest in religion or spirituality. She not only puts up with me, however; she is genuinely interested in what I think about the Spirit's movement in the world, and she never trivializes my spirituality. For example, when Bev died in 2012 and Red a year later, I felt on both occasions as if something in me had died. I told Sue that it felt to me as if God had died, again and again. Sue asked me to say more and she helped me clarify what I was trying to communicate. In these instances of enormous loss, I felt as if a life-energy—a bit of God—had gone out of me. It was a moment of deep grief in both cases, as it was also for Sue. For me, God had died, but She would live again in new ways, through me, through Sue, through our other human and animal friends, although it would take a long time for me to begin to experience more fully the living and joyful presence of God in my life. For Sue, these losses—like the losses of our mothers, Doris and Mary Ann, and our fathers, both named Bob—were onerous, grief-filled events from which we sadly have to move on, grateful to have loved and been loved by these special ones, whom we will carry forever in our hearts.

Sue and I often have a similar emotional or intellectual response to a situation—sad or joyful, empowering or frightening—but we have different ways of understanding and framing our experiences. I'm an idealistic theologian. Sue is a pragmatic materialist. Occasionally Sue speaks of her own values—honesty, kindness, responsibility, and faithfulness are some of the qualities she most values and, from time to time, names as "spiritual." For example, Sue will sometimes talk about the spiritual challenge of having to deal with someone who is dishonest, manipulative, or lacking in empathy.

Sue doubtlessly thinks I've gone around the bend sometimes, just as I occasionally find her approach to everything, including our relationships to each other and others, a little linear and over-rational. But I've often said of Sue that, whereas she's not spiritual—at least not in her own mind and experience—she's one of the most moral, ethical people I've ever known. Sue's honesty and integrity—her truthfulness about herself and the world—is beyond reproach. There's a wholeness to Sue. She's a woman in whom the pieces fit, so that the person you think you see is the person you see.

Sue also joins Bev and a few members of my family of origin in being among the most generous people I have ever known. Whether money, clothes, gifts, food, time, talents, or space for loving more people and creatures, these women's generosity reflects the Spirit in Her great abundance, showering us with whatever we may most need, whether or not we realize it. In terms of generosity, Sue is among the lively spiritual forces currently at work in the world around us.

In November, 2010, a few days after the nationwide elections that swept waves of anti-Obama politicians into office as a reaction to Obamacare, Sue and I flew over to Melbourne to visit David, my cherished friend, the man I had loved when he and I were so much younger. In the course of our visit, one of Sue's gifts to me was helping make time and space for David and me to be alone to reconstruct the narrative of our earlier relationship and what it had meant to each of us.

David and I concluded that, had we come along a bit later in life—perhaps in the late 1970s rather than a decade earlier—we might have been able to find some social support for us to try out our relationship, maybe by living together for a while, maybe by exploring to see if we might have been bisexual instead of predominantly gay or lesbian. As it actually transpired in the late 1960s, however, our relationship was doomed. We couldn't let ourselves risk naming, much less entering together, a realm of sexual ambivalence that frightened us both. And no one was around to help us, no friend or colleague with much awareness or wisdom about the ambivalence and fluidity of sexual identity. No one knew more than David and I about the mysteries and fluid dimensions of sexuality, and we knew so very little.

Fast forward forty years, to 2010, as David, Sue, and I found ourselves sitting at his kitchen table in Melbourne, laughing as we imagined David coming back to the United States with us. I could go to the bishop upon our return to North Carolina and report that I no longer had "two lovers." With David joining Sue and Bev, I now had three!

It was a great fantasy that we all enjoyed, and it was only that. Too much time had passed. David and I each had grown into lives that neither of us could even imagine dramatically altering, nor did we really want to. Each of us had lived a good life and we were both at peace, grateful and glad to be who we had become. To this day, David and I meet via Skype on a fairly regular basis and talk about things that matter to us—like the Spirit's moving to topple the world as we have known it and Her efforts to bring new life to people and creatures around the globe. She is, after all, flying on, healing broken community, liberating the oppressed, setting the captives free.

# Liberty and Justice for All

**As She moves along, the Spirit debunks our racist understandings of "liberty." . . . She helps us see more clearly that the other's freedom is as precious as our own, in every place and time, and that this is what it means—to love our neighbors as ourselves.**

Robert Dulin, my sister Ann's husband, has been a source of ongoing inspiration to me over these past years through his love of history in general, American history and Abraham Lincoln in particular. Robert's passion for what we can learn from our ancestors about fairness and justice has me thinking more about the historical roots of our contemporary political challenges.

Lincoln's second inaugural address is one of the wisest pieces of political rhetoric in history. It was also a profoundly spiritual offering to a divided nation tragically broken apart by the Civil War. This speech was given only a few months before Lincoln's assassination at the hands of a troubled Confederate zealot and Lincoln-hater. In his second inaugural, President Lincoln presented several difficult themes: The Civil War is hurting people on both sides. Both sides believe that God is on their side. Only one side can win. Morality (in Lincoln's view, God) is on the side of those struggling to put an end to the evil of slavery. The only way for the people to move forward together, regardless of which side they are on, is with "malice toward none, with charity toward all."

The power of Lincoln's words transcend time and space. He could just as easily have been addressing the people of the United States today. Lincoln's passion was for the whole nation, all the people, at a moment in which one side could not easily hear, or want to hear, or believe, the other. Barack Obama launched a similar effort with remarkable success in the months running up to his 2008 election and, for a short while, at the outset of his presidency early in 2009. Like Lincoln's foes, Obama's opponents hate him; like Lincoln and every other human leader who stands with unpopular segments of humanity—those, in any situation, who are poor, marginalized, oppressed—Obama's enemies seem bent upon destroying everything he stands for.

Obama had a fleeting moment to begin the processes of healing a nation that had been traumatized under another president's watch. He inherited the Great Recession as well as a raging mess in the Middle East that had been sparked by the ill-advised war in Iraq. In addition to the war and the recession, Obama inherited another challenge much like the one Abraham Lincoln had faced: the makings of serious civil strife, grounded in the historic tension between racism and "liberty," a conflict with roots that reach back into the origins of the United States of America.

Throughout our history as a nation, white people of European origin have assumed liberty as a God-given right to do pretty much as we please, without much regard for how that liberty has been built historically on the backs of people of other races: Native Americans, African Americans, Asian Americans, Latinos, and people of many mixed racial-ethnic cultures. This lifting up of the freedom of white lives and bodies at the expense of all others is the heartbeat of racism.

Racism has roots embedded in the history of our country, as does the peculiarly American obsession with raising liberty above all other social values. Whether in the language of personal freedom or states' rights, liberty too often becomes a code for granting my freedom a special privilege over everyone else's. When racism and liberty get twisted up together, the liberty of white Americans is lifted up by our public authorities above the freedom and dignity of people of color—and we become a contentious, combative, racist society. These two deep American roots—the evil of racism and white people's commitment to our own liberty—produced the American Civil War. These forces—ongoing racism and the raising up of liberty as an ideal—are again stirring a crisis in our society. Many white people are insisting on holding our own liberty, which we call a right, above the same rights of African Americans and Latinos. Through the racist vitriol of this past presidential campaign, it became increasingly clear to many voters that the drive to "make America great again" was more truthfully understood as an effort to make America *white* again.

In the context of our unabashedly racist history, the election in 2008 of an African American as president of the United States had been a stunning event. Barack Hussein Obama's election had signaled the dawning of a new possibility: that racism might actually be receding, and that liberty, along with justice, might actually become a reality for all, not some, Americans. But many of us—white progressives, at least—did not comprehend the fierceness of racism's insidious stranglehold on our nation. It appears that the 2016 election has tightened the death-grip of white supremacy on our nation. Racism will not let go this grip without further struggle, education, and spiritual transformation.

Looking back, I regard Barack Obama's presidency as both a miracle and a disappointment. On the positive side, Obama has managed some daunting achievements: the Lilly Ledbetter Act ending the great recession, saving our country from economic collapse; overseeing the creation of a stimulus bill that included major spending for education, infrastructure, clean energy, and anti-poverty initiatives; putting in place a national health insurance plan. The Affordable Care Act, or Obamacare, though incomplete and unwieldy (largely due to the GOP's resistance), was an important step toward universal health care; advocating and celebrating the Supreme Court's Obergefell v. Hodges 2015 ruling for marriage equality; pushing for comprehensive immigration and, when Congress failed to respond, using his executive power to propose a form of the DREAM Act for the children of immigrant parents; normalizing the United States' relationship with Cuba, something that should have happened fifty years earlier; drawing upon his executive power to put in motion regulations combatting climate change.

I was a critic of Obama, primarily his idealistic, even utopic, commitment to working on every initiative from a bipartisan perspective. In order to attempt to meet his critics halfway and to accommodate Republicans and less liberal Democrats in Congress, Obama was willing to back away from some of his most genuinely held convictions, such as his own strong preference to offer a "public option" as part of the Affordable Care Act. His desire for legislative compromise, such as the public option, was naïve and premature; it opened the door for the opposing party in Congress to begin blocking nearly all of his goals before he fully laid them out. While he had a chance to move legislation through a Democratic Congress during the first two years of his presidency, Obama often appeared more anxious about alienating his adversaries, with whom he hoped to compromise, than his friends, who were ready to join him from the outset in the work of justice.

Abraham Lincoln, Franklin Roosevelt, and Lyndon Johnson—three US presidents whose values and visions were close to Barack Obama's— did not hand over political power to non-cooperative opponents. Indeed,

as American historian Doris Kearns Goodwin points out,[64] Abraham
Lincoln was willing to share political power with his adversaries—but
only with those who were willing to work with him. Neither Lincoln,
Roosevelt, nor Johnson tried to "lead from behind" in relation to those
who most disagreed with them.

I suspect Obama's refusal to butt heads in the manner of some of
his greatest predecessors was steeped in a desire to bring opponents into
negotiation and compromise alongside a naiveté about what he was up
against as president of the United States. Obama was not a seasoned
politician. It didn't seem to dawn on him that the Republican leadership would seriously entertain only one primary goal: to make him a
one-term president, in the words of the Senate majority leader.

Barack Obama was a community organizer by trade and, from
much hearsay, an effective one. Certainly, his campaign strategies
reflected a brilliant organizational ability. But being president of the
United States requires more than a genuine commitment to hope and
change; more than a big heart and strong intellect; more than a beautiful vision of a just and loving society; more than remarkable oratory
skills and organizational ability. Obama had all of these gifts in abundance. Being president of the United States requires a willingness to
use a bully pulpit unapologetically and exploit the power and authority that comes with the presidency by staying a step ahead of, rather
than behind, the legislative curve. The largest demon that battered the
Obama presidency, however, was the hateful resistance of white racism.

Indeed, while folks like me can comment on Obama's weaknesses
and failures from the sidelines, a primary malevolent force we must
not overlook is that, unlike any of his predecessors, Obama has been
the target of a vicious, relentless racist campaign since the day he was
elected. More than any other single factor, this racism, and our failure as
a nation to address it, has sharpened the social and political divisions in
our society that were already present before the Obama presidency: different opinions about economic inequality, marriage equality, abortion
and women's reproductive choices, immigration, voting rights, public
education, health care, criminal justice and incarceration, capital punishment, the building up of our armed forces and military machinery,
the ubiquity of guns, and, if we are people of faith, how we understand
God. The pervasiveness of deep systemic and cultural racism, and the

violence that it engenders, have exacerbated every other major social, economic, environmental, sexual, and gender challenge facing us today. That is because all structures of injustice are interactive.

Racism colors every other issue. Everything that is not white—steeped in European history and cultures—is assumed by some members of the dominant race/ethnicity to be less good and less valuable. Because he is not white, President Obama has been viewed by many white Americans as less than a white man and, therefore, as unable to really be our president—hence, the birther charge by Trump and various white supremacists that Obama was born, or may have been born, in Kenya.

Several days after I finished the first draft of this book, a hate-filled twenty-one-year-old white supremacist walked into the historic Mother Emanuel AME Church in Charleston, South Carolina, and joined a small group of African Americans in prayer and Bible study. About an hour into this gathering, this morally depraved young man informed his black sisters and brothers that he was going to kill them. "You are raping our women and taking over our country," he stated before he shot nine of these people to death. One or two escaped death by playing dead, and the murderer chose to let one woman live so that she could tell people what he had done.

It's tempting to blame such a travesty on one rotten human being, bad parenting, mental illness, a particular set of circumstances in the shooter's case, sometimes even on the victims' behavior, rather than on the systemic racism that pervades our nation and the failure of our national and state leaders to curb gun violence by outlawing automatic weapons and limiting who can legally own any firearm. The rest of the civilized world looks at the United States of America as if we are insane, out of our collective mind. When it comes to guns, we are. Guns and racism are a particularly explosive mix.

# Empathy[65]

Even in our collective insanity, She carries us beyond despair, encouraging us to feel, think, and act, with one another, amidst our differences, especially amidst our differences. In this way, She offers us the radical spiritual gift of empathy, which is a deep and vibrant root of social change.

In the United States today, we need to make room for discussion and debate about equality, liberty, guns, and basic human rights. We need to come up with ways to explore these contentious questions together. We might begin in our religious associations, spiritual circles, community centers, schools, and colleges. We need to ask our religious, educational, and civic leaders to help us make ways beyond the despair that divides us by talking honestly together. In order to participate in this kind of civil discourse, we need to help each other learn to speak and, even more important in most contexts, to listen.

A prerequisite for such communication is *empathy*, a capacity to feel another's pain, an ability to imagine ourselves walking in someone else's shoes. Empathy is a spiritual capacity that can be cultivated. Most of us learn empathy by being around empathic people—parents and guardians, siblings and friends, teachers and mentors, coaches and bosses. We teach empathy by practicing it ourselves.

My brother, Robbie, and I talk by phone every week or two about the political lay of the land. We offer each other a shared sense of solidarity that helps each of us not to fall into despair or, in Bishop DeWitt's words, to keep our courage. I would say that this personal courage is a spiritual gift. Robbie would not use spiritual language. To Robbie, it's intelligent and kind, emblematic of human beings at our best—different perspectives on similar relational dynamics.

Robbie's primary way of sharing his courage is through empathy. He not only speaks candidly and consistently to his more conservative friends, many of them affluent white men—some of his tennis partners— in Charlotte, North Carolina. He also listens to them. According to my brother, these men—evidently arch-conservatives, mostly Christians and Jews—seem to hate Obama, Democrats, liberals on the Supreme Court, marriage equality, abortion and feminism, radical black people, illegal immigrants, socialists, terrorists, gun control advocates, big government and its regulations. Robbie tells them what he thinks about their views of God and the world, 90 percent of it antithetical to his views. But he also tries to understand why these men hold the views they do. He takes up for his friends when he speaks to me. He tells me what he values in them and, sometimes, a little about who they are. He tells me that he believes some of these men really do listen to him and, perhaps, are changing some of their opinions because he has taken the time to take them seriously. One way of understanding empathy is to "hear someone to speech," in the words of my late feminist theological sister Nelle Morton.[66]

I could not do what my brave and articulate brother does.[67] That sort of face-to-face verbal exchange with one's adversaries is Robbie's vocation, not mine. But there are things I can do, as a Christian feminist theologian, priest and educator. One such effort is to call for, and help implement, honest, empathic, dialogue in educational groups in which all participants come to learn from the others. In this fear-based, divided country, it is a moral responsibility of religious and spiritual leaders to empathically spark our courage, root our hope, and inspire us to love one another, moving collectively beyond despair.

We need empathy in order to consider the major role of racism in our life together. We need empathy to be able to understand our own, and others', resistance to talking about racism even in some of our most progressive organizations and communities. We need empathy in order to think together about the history and role of racism in our nation and world. Without empathy, we cannot make much headway toward providing basic human rights to everyone—especially those who need them most urgently: black and brown people, other racial/ethnic minority groups, and poor white people, throughout this nation and the larger world.

Once "the party of Lincoln"; later, the party of such esteemed leaders as Presidents Teddy Roosevelt and Dwight David Eisenhower, Senators Margaret Chase Smith of Maine and Edward Brooke of Massachusetts; the Republican Party has been more recently the political home of Senators Olympia Snowe of Maine and Lincoln Chafee of Rhode Island—progressive, thoughtful public servants. I recall my father's enthusiasm for "Ike" in the mid-twentieth century and many of my college friends' involvement with the Young Republicans in the 1960s. But in the 1964 elections, as the Republican Party shaped itself around a populist antagonism toward "the other" and a widespread fear of social change, the "Grand Old Party" began to slip away from its earlier allegiance to making justice for all. And now, a half-century later, large numbers of former Republicans, among them Democratic Senator Lincoln Chafee—moderate, reasonable people—want nothing to do with a party that presents itself as hostile to so much in the world.

It's important to remember that it was not Donald Trump who turned the Republican Party against the struggles for liberty and justice for all. Since the candidacy of Barry Goldwater in 1964, the GOP has increasingly presented itself as hostile or indifferent to poor people of all races and ethnicities and, in particular, to black and brown people; hostile or indifferent to undocumented workers and comprehensive immigration reform; hostile or indifferent to women's reproductive health and freedom, including access to safe medical abortion; hostile or indifferent to lesbians and gay men seeking marriage equality; hostile or indifferent to public education at every level and to public school teachers; hostile or indifferent to organized labor; hostile or indifferent to men and women who work for almost nothing and have no assurance of quality health care; hostile or indifferent to the environment; and shamelessly hostile to the first African American president in our nation's history—or simply indifferent to the hostilities expressed toward Obama by the "birthers" and other hate groups.

We could be asking our Republican siblings why they stay or why they have left, and listening to what they tell us. What might we learn from them, about their own values and experiences, and about ourselves? This learning could only be mutual and productive, however, in a context in which we liberals and progressives were also invited, and empowered, to speak about our values, our lives, and why we are whatever we are in the political realm: Democrats, or Socialists, or Greens, or Independents, or Republicans, or "no labels," or unaffiliated, or whoever and whatever we may be.

Indeed, we might ask many sibling[68] liberals why they are not interested in the Democratic Party any more. So far, the most compelling answer I've heard to this question—often from young people, including some of our young companions at Redbud Springs—is that we shouldn't rely so much on government to do what can be done more efficiently, more quickly, and less expensively by small groups of concerned people. Besides, they say correctly, all politics have been corrupted by Big Money. Why not just build our own lives without asking for much help from the government?

This "why do we need the government?" sentiment is also the Tea Party's more libertarian instinct, a motive theoretically distinct from its anti-Obama, anti-social justice, and Christian fundamentalist platforms. However, the current Republican and Tea Parties merge in their fiercely anti-federal government posturing and their antipathies toward people of color, women, poor people, and the LGBTQ communities. Adopting liberation sentiments when it suits them, Republicans like Rand Paul, Ted Cruz, Marco Rubio, Carly Fiorina, and Sarah Palin want to keep the government out of everyone's lives—except the reproductive lives of poor women and the relational lives and well-being of lesbian and gay men and our trans siblings.

Still, the libertarian, or small government, notion of building our own communities without much outside help is appealing as an old fashioned, romanticized, dream-like fantasy in which we might imagine ourselves recreating our great-great-grandparents' lives in rural America. But it is also naïve. It's one thing—and a good thing—for people to grow organic lettuce, raise chickens for eggs, build their own houses, tap water sources, share vehicles, and help each other as needs arise. But "living off the grid" entirely, or as much as possible, is feasible primarily in small rural communities.

In a world with an expanding population, in which several billion people live in crowded cities, and millions more in smaller cities and villages, a good, functional national, state, or local government shares some responsibility to make sure each of its citizens has access to nutritious food, safe housing, and public education in basic skills of communication, culture, history, and—we can hope—critical thinking. Moreover, a good government must make sure each person has access to health care and opportunities to work—and thereby contribute to the common good and be paid a living wage for this work. These social goods are the basic stuff of life. They should be human rights, available to all of us. They are not frills, not add-ons, not privileges that we earn or win.

The United States Constitution and the Bill of Rights rest on empathic assumptions, given voice a decade earlier in the Declaration of Independence in 1776. In this most basic of all American documents, Thomas Jefferson and his colleagues declared, on July 4, 1776, that all of us are "created equal" and that we are "endowed" with certain "inalienable rights." We are so endowed both by "the laws of nature" and by "nature's God" or the "Creator." Notice the compromise between the believers in God (theists like Benjamin Franklin and John Adams) and non-believers (the deist Thomas Jefferson himself). Among our endowments, these framers of the Declaration wrote, are "life, liberty, and the pursuit of happiness." They did not include "the pursuit of property" as an inalienable right, because they did not believe that the pursuit of property (which for many white men included black slaves at the time) was in fact a right, much less an inalienable one. [69]

With greater empathy, we could share more about our lives as Americans—those Natives among us who have been here for hundreds of years, those white and black Americans who arrived here on different kinds of ships more than two hundred years ago, those groups from Europe and Asia who have come more recently, and our contemporary immigrant populations from Mexico and other Latin countries as well as Africa, Asia, the Middle East, and Europe.

With empathic commitment, we could think together about our "inalienable rights." What are "inalienable rights"? Are they not implicit in our being "created equal"? Implicit to our "life, liberty, and the pursuit of happiness"? Do these rights not include food, shelter, education, health care, opportunities to work, and access to enough money—for most middle- and working-class Americans, earned wages—to live simply? With empathy, we could help each other realize that our inalienable rights are essential to our lives and to our being productive citizens. We could, I believe, help each other see that without shared rights to food and shelter, education and health care, our society cannot thrive, and many of us cannot survive. Without these rights, people cannot survive regardless of how much free speech, freedom of religion, or freedom of association they may have, and regardless of whatever rights to bear arms they may have. We might more fully comprehend that this was true of our nation in 1776, and it is still true today.

# Our Task

On wings of empathy, She flies on, urging us to keep working on building a justice-loving society.

As neighbors or fellow seekers, we need to think together about why access to food, for example, is a right common to all rather than a privilege accorded only to certain people on the basis of their race, gender, class, religion, or some other badge of privilege. If we were to agree that certain rights belong to us all, *how* might we assure one another of these rights? Human rights, after all, cost money: education, food, housing, health care, jobs, wages. None of these rights is inexpensive. So how might we find the resources to support our common well-being?

If "we the people"—regardless of our political affiliations or religious beliefs—could find ways, empathically, of having such discussions—beginning with sharing personal and community stories about race and class and gender—we might be on track to bridging our divisions. If we could begin to agree that human beings—all human beings—have some basic rights that are foundational to a decent society, we might generate opportunities for public political debate in which our differences could be shared and explained without hostility. Some of our debates would surely be about what these rights are. But many of the most intriguing questions would involve our figuring out together *how* to make sure everyone can eat nutritious food, not *whether* they should be able to; *how* to provide the best education possible for all of our children, not *whether* all children should be educated; *how* to provide a living wage for every worker, not *whether* every worker should be able to live on what she or he is able to earn at work.

If we could agree, empathically, on even a few basic rights that should be accorded everyone and not just some, a civil discourse might be possible, even energizing. I could imagine debates between Republicans, Democrats, Libertarians, and Socialists, if the question were not whether but rather how our government might most responsibly participate in making certain that health care is available to everyone. At issue would be not whether health care is a basic human right but rather how we could do it, how "we the people" could provide good, affordable health care for everyone in the United States of America. I suspect that, if we were to get down to these basics, we would discover that most Americans—Republicans and Independents as well as Democrats—might actually want a single-payer system. Many of our fellow citizens just don't want something called "socialized medicine," because scary ghosts of the Cold War continue to haunt this nation.

Out of ignorance, many Americans conflate "communism" and "socialism" whereas, in fact, these are distinct historical phenomena. "Communism" refers to a political system in which a strong federal government, representing the one and only political party in the nation, oversees the economic system and controls the wealth. The Soviet Union, China, and North Korea were the most notable examples of communism in the twentieth century, with smaller nations like Cuba also putting a Communist party in place. "Socialism" refers to a government's distribution of basic human resources for the well-being of all people. A "socialist" party can be incorporated into democracies as one among a number of parties. "Socialism" can also be loosely descriptive of social policies that are created as safety nets for the elderly, the sick, or the poor of any country. Medicare, Medicaid, and Social Security are primary examples of socialist policies in the United States.

Sweden is an example of a nation in which socialism has played a major role in the country's decision to provide universal health care to its citizens. Many European countries, as well as countries like Canada, Nicaragua, Australia, New Zealand, and South Africa have incorporated socialist policies, like universal health-care provisions, into their public life. Despite our anxieties about "socialism," the United States, through President Franklin Roosevelt's "New Deal" and, later, Lyndon Johnson's "Great Society" program, has crafted socialist principles into social welfare for older Americans by putting in place the universally popular programs of Social Security and Medicare. Senator Bernie Sanders refers to himself as a democratic socialist. In no way is Sanders "un-American" or unpatriotic, as his detractors insist. His prophetic voice not only has called us back to the "inalienable rights" in which our Founding Fathers and Mothers placed their faith, but also Sanders beckons us forward into becoming a nation that would be more fully a harbor of justice and liberty for all.

Is such a conversion to our deepest roots as a nation impossible for us to imagine? Does such radical empathy lie somewhere beyond our reach? Or are we being invited by the Spirit to join together in making history? Every significant social moment or movement I've had the honor of witnessing was thought to be impossible. I think immediately of the struggles leading to Brown v. Board of Education in 1954; the Montgomery Bus Boycott of 1954; the Civil Rights Act of 1964; the marches in Selma in 1965; the Voting Rights Act of 1965; the toppling of the Berlin Wall in 1989; the ending of apartheid in South Africa in 1994, followed soon by the celebration of Nelson Mandela as the country's new president, and South Africa's writing of a new, more radically just and democratic Constitution; the Stonewall Riots of 1969, which led eventually to the 2004 ruling of the Superior Court in Massachusetts, which in turn made marriage equality the law in that state. A decade later, on June 26, 2015, marriage equality became the law of the land.

Inside the churches, too, the Spirit turns the impossible on its head. Women are now Episcopal and Anglican priests all over the world. The presiding bishop of the Episcopal Church from 2006 to 2015 was a woman, Katharine Jefferts Schori, and an African American, Michael Curry, was installed on November 1, 2015, as her successor. Gay men and lesbians are being ordained, and they are marrying the people they love throughout much of Protestant Christianity in the northern and western parts of the world. As early as 2003, an openly gay man, Gene Robinson, was elected bishop of the Episcopal Diocese of New Hampshire. These breakthroughs would have been deemed impossible as recently as the turn of this present century. But the Spirit, the force of Love, She who generates justice with compassion, flies on.

If our leaders and the citizenry of the United States were to debate honestly our views on basic human rights, we might edge a little closer to a parliamentary system, in which many parties, not just two, could be serious political contenders. Is the Spirit calling us today beyond the polarization of our two parties into more nuanced divisions, choices, and affiliations? Many believe She is doing just that. I certainly believe the Spirit is pressing us to open our political system to multiple, diverse voices rather than just one or two loud, well-financed ones. She certainly is urging us to do whatever it takes to get rid of Citizens United and other excuses for turning our politics, our economy, and our lives over to Big Money.

Regardless of our political structure, the Spirit is warning us in the United States, and She is warning our siblings throughout the world: we must fight poverty and economic exploitation, racism, tribalisms, sexism, and heterosexism in all of their many cunning, violent, and hateful manifestations, beginning right here at home, wherever we are. We must clarify and affirm basic human rights—inalienable rights—for all humankind—and basic rights for all creature-kind as well to be treated with kindness and respect.

# Moral Bankruptcy of Big Money

She flies on, struggling to break the stranglehold of Big Money.

During the 2016 campaign, Bernie Sanders called for the overturn of Citizens United as a major step toward limiting the amount of money we can spend on candidates and political parties. There is a strong but elusive connection between Big Money, the resurgence of racism, our political divide, and the proliferation of guns in the United States. The connection is the fear and paranoia being financed by corporate power to scare the people of this nation. In fear, many citizens believe they need guns to protect themselves from people of other races, religions, cultures, and ethnicities, and from the United States government, which protects and defends these "aliens." The damning fact of the matter is that Big Money has made it easier for many of our fellow citizens to purchase guns than to vote for the people who stand against corporate power.

Corporate power has cleverly constructed a narrative about the United States of America in which "Big Government" (an argument heard most often during Democratic administrations) is constructed politically as "the enemy" (intent upon taking the money, property, liberty, and guns) of "the people" (working class and poor people, especially white rural folks). Of course, corporate power, owned and controlled by the financially elite, is motivated by the fear that the US government will radically redistribute its wealth via taxes and social services for the majority of citizens. This is Big Money's fear of "democratic socialism," a fear that is not unwarranted.

A fundamental spiritual question, however, is why so many rich people are afraid. Why does the possibility of sharing their wealth with poor people threaten and anger them, rather than touch their hearts with the opportunity to be generous, an opportunity espoused repeatedly and without ambivalence by Jesus of Nazareth? It is, I suggest, because wealth is power, and power is control, and most people do not want to relinquish whatever control they think they have over their own lives. Thus, corporate power's narratives about the dangers of big government and the horrors of higher taxes are designed to control the population by alienating millions of working- and middle-class

197

white people so that this corporate power structure can continue to run the nation, its economy, and its military. Any movement toward the creation of a more fully just and equitable society must challenge Big Money and debunk its lies about immigrants being dangerous criminals, poverty being a consequence of laziness, guns making us safe, and the federal government being the enemy of the people.

Any serious movement toward social transformation in history can be sparked only by the Spirit, who perpetually seeks ways to allay our fear and encourage us. Thus, generating spiritual and political encouragement is a primary responsibility of spiritual and religious leaders, including Pope Francis, who has made clear what he thinks of global capitalism. The pope still has much to learn and a long way to go when it comes to the full personhood and dignity of women and the LGBTQ communities, but he is showing himself to be remarkably committed to economic justice and environmental sustainability.

What neither the pope nor other patriarchal religious leaders understand is that global capitalism and the subordination of women (usually in the name of a Father God) go hand in hand. Sexism, of course, is universal. Sexist oppression does not belong solely to the domain of capitalism, but sexism takes particular shapes in a capitalist economy, beginning with the presumed right of the father to control most of his "private" wealth and the father's responsibility to protect and manage the women and children in his nuclear family, his primary domain of possession. This historically has been the capitalist ideal, most evident over the years wherever dynamics of male domination, white supremacy, and economic privilege have converged, as in many white middle- and upper-class families in the United States.

But the liberating Spirit will blow where She will blow. As I've noted, Bishop Robert DeWitt signed his letters "keep your courage" to the women he ordained in Philadelphia. There could be no more fitting a spiritual charge to religious leaders in the twenty-first century. Indeed, in years and decades to come, we must keep our courage as we work and pray for the great justice-loving Spirit to knock the wind out of corporate power and patriarchal religion. And we in the United States must keep our courage as we work and pray for the radical transformation of all three branches of the United States government, our state governments, and many of our local governing bodies as well.

I doubt I'll be around to celebrate the culmination of such bold spiritual adventures in justice-making, public well-being, and common sense, but I trust I'll be on several heavenly councils, encouraging my nieces, nephews, and their kids as they navigate the processes and weather the storms that will toss humanity onto new terrain in which categories like gender and race are opening up and being transformed into something new.

# Beyond Binary Categories

She spins beyond race and gender as fixed, binary categories.

From the perspective of a liberation spirituality, neither gender nor race is what it used to be as a legal or cultural means of defining people's place in society and granting, or denying, their rights. Not long ago, we thought we knew what being a woman or being a man meant. We assumed we could spot gender and racial differences by looking at someone. Times, however, have been changing. Today, many are moving beyond our attachments to rigid or even clear understandings of femaleness, maleness, blackness, brownness, whiteness.

What is a man or a woman? Who is male or female? What is a person of color? What is a white person? The lines often blur and shift and new images appear: Tiger Woods. Barack Obama. Michael Jackson. Beyoncé. They are widely perceived to be "black" or "mixed race," but might their racial identity be more complex than this? And what about Laverne Cox and Caitlyn Jenner? They were once men, or were they?—I am learning that even this question is misleading.[70] Laverne Cox challenges the assumption that many of us bring to conversations about transgender. She does not consider herself to have once been a man, but rather to have been incorrectly assigned a male gender at birth: "I was assigned male at birth is the way I like to put it, because I think we're born who we are and the gender thing is something someone imposes on you. And so I was assigned male at birth but I always felt like I was a girl."[71]

Recently I was introduced to a young trans person whom I asked to look at this section of my book. This person kindly read it and wrote back: "While I'm neither a transgender woman or a transgender man, I am still transgender, with a unique experience. I have experienced a trans masculine transition (from female to male) and a trans feminine transition (from male to androgynous). The challenges, barriers, and gifts I experienced in both of these transitions were very different, and both shaped the person I've become."[72] Because English doesn't have a non-gendered pronoun, this person had asked me, when we were speaking in person, to use the plural when referencing them. This rendered me speechless for a moment! I took a deep breath and realized how conventional I am in relation to gender identity. Indeed, most of us think we know who we—and others—are in terms of our gender and racial identities. I am no exception.

# Breaking Out of Sexual and Gender Boxes

She shakes up our senses of sexual orientation, sexual preference, and gender identity, moving us beyond binary concepts
toward accepting many dimensions and variations of gendered
and sexual being. . . .

You may recall from part two that, back in 1979, when I first came out as
lesbian, I wrote two essays. In one, I spoke of being bisexual and of sexuality as a fluid, changing dimension of who we are. At the time, that
essay seemed to most people less significant than the other piece, in
which I stated flatly that I wished to come out as a lesbian, because it
seemed to me important that some of us state publicly that we were
lesbian women and gay men in order to move the church and society
along in the mounting struggles for gender and sexual justice. Today,
however, more than thirty-five years later, I believe that the less-read
article in 1979 was, in fact, the more radical and potentially transformative regarding our experiences and views of sexuality, suggesting that
our understandings of sexual orientation, preference, and gender identity will become more multifaceted, textured, and nuanced.

In the early 1970s, Bev taught a course at Union Theological Seminary on "the sociology of knowledge" in which we studied the social
construction of what we know and of the language we use to describe
whatever we know. Ironically, the early post-Stonewall gay and lesbian
generations—that is, those of us coming out in the 1970s and 1980s—
were less clear about the social construction of our sexual orientations
than we were about the need to come out and state, unambivalently, that
we were gay or lesbian, not straight; homosexual, not heterosexual. Considerable peer pressure was asserted among gays and lesbians to declare
ourselves as either gay or straight, not as bisexual. Bisexuality was too
ambiguous, too easily dismissed as an in-between state that could slip in
either direction. The early lesbian and gay movement rooted itself in clear,
unambiguous definitions of sexual orientation. Everyone was either-or,
gay or straight, none of this in-between stuff, and nothing fluid or mal-
leable. Anything less than full identification as gay or straight was heard as
one's resistance to admitting he or she was, in fact, gay.

Similarly, the social theory that human sexuality is constructed rather than biologically and genetically based was also a red flag to gay and lesbian activists in the early post-Stonewall years. Because, in patriarchy, men are taken more seriously than women as subjects of their own lives and bodies, gay men, especially, feared that if their sexuality was thought to be socially constructed rather biologically given, intense pressure to be heterosexual would be exerted on them by parents, clergy, doctors, teachers, and others. Many lesbians also feared we would be told—as indeed we were by people who did not accept our sexual identities—that we could become heterosexual with the right therapy or the right sexual partner.

We have come far enough as a movement today that it is less threatening to many gay men and lesbian women in the United States to realize that Kinsey was probably right when he proposed in 1948 that human sexuality can best be understood as located along a spectrum. Those who experience themselves as fully heterosexual are at one end; those who experience themselves as totally homosexual are at the other end; and most of us are somewhere in between. Kinsey did not, however, study the extent to which men and women might fluidly move back and forth along the spectrum.

In the last several decades, increasing numbers of people have identified as bisexual. Many people today, as decades ago, continue to come out as gay or lesbian after having experienced productive, and reproductive, heterosexual relationships. Interestingly, some gay men and lesbians are finding themselves drawn to people of another gender identity and they enter into so-called straight relationships.

Over my last ten or fifteen years on the faculty of the Episcopal Divinity School—throughout the 1990s until 2005, when I retired—many students and alums shared their experiences of being basically bisexual, attracted to both men and women, and able to be partnered with either, or, in some cases, both. Increasingly during this time, I also had transgender students in seminary. Some of these trans students—men, women, or a combination of male and female—were gay, some were straight, some were bisexual, some were married, some were single. Some were sexually active, some were celibate. In other words, in terms of sexual identity, attraction, activity, and patterns of relational bonding, trans students were like everyone else—diverse and varied.

A point I always tried to make to my students was that, regardless of whether trans people were transitioning from male to female (as most were in the 1990s and 2000s, when I was teaching) or from female to male (less common), they needed to be mindful of the kinds of gender power and privilege, or lack thereof, that had to some degree shaped their lives. Trans women (male to female) needed to realize the power and privilege they were relinquishing; trans men (female to male) had to be aware of the power and privilege they were gaining in making the transition.

Like racial power and privilege, gender power and privilege are not assets or liabilities that can simply be chosen. It is likely that no one knows better how profoundly shaped our gender identities are by social power than those who are transitioning between, among, or beyond genders as we have traditionally understood gender. As well as anyone, trans people know how deeply we inherit gender power, or lack of it, and how deeply we are born, or adopted, into gender privilege, or lack of it. In terms of both race and gender, this is the case whether we like it or not. It is a social reality, not a personal choice.

I have always assumed that our sexual and gender identities are partially socially constructed, with probably some genetic basis. I still assume that this is most often the case. Many trans people experience themselves as wrongly identified at birth, or early in their lives, as male or as female. In these persons' experiences, their gender identification by parents, doctors, and others in their social world doesn't reflect an honest or healthy alignment between their biological, social, psychological, cognitive, and spiritual senses of self.

In all of our lives, our socializations and cultural understandings interact with our physical, cognitive, and psycho-spiritual constitutions to produce our sexual and gender identities as we grow from infancy through childhood toward adulthood. To assume that each of us must have primarily one of two gender identities—male and female, and their derivative "masculine" and "feminine" attributes—rather than multiple possibilities, is an uncreative, deeply untruthful, way of imagining who some—perhaps many—of us are or might be.

As I write, I'm aware of my age in relation to this discussion. Everything I am suggesting in these pages—especially about gender, sexual, and racial identity—is limited by the contours of my consciousness, which has been shaped over seven interesting decades that recede into the past even as I think about what I have learned. There comes a time when we realize that whatever we know, or think we know, about ourselves and others—especially in relation to gender, race, and other locations of social power in the world—is only partial and, if we aspire to be honest or creative, it must always be open to challenge and transformation.

My understanding of both gender (our experiences of being female, male, both, or neither) and sexuality (our experiences of sexual attraction and activity) is that most of us probably do live—and sometimes move rather dramatically and unexpectedly—along spectrums of gender and sexuality. All the while, our gender and sexual identities are being steeped in an interplay of biology and culture, nature and nurture. Each of us is a fascinating and unique embodiment of many social and biological factors. I suspect, in many cases, our genders and sexual identities are—or can be—shaped and reshaped again and again throughout our lives, often being reinforced, sometimes reformed, by social and biological forces working around, through, and within us.

In any case, neither gender nor sexuality can best be understood as static dimensions of who we are. Rather, each is a window into our unique self, our being the particular person we are today. We may have changed significantly over the years, and we may change again, and again. We are being socially constructed every day, and we are also complex biological organisms with our own organic histories and futures. We each embody particular possibilities and impossibilities. In the realm of Spirit and with Her help, we can move, or not move, in many gendered or sexual directions, or in very few.

I am biologically female. Socially, psychologically, and spiritually, however, I have always been ambivalent. Earlier in this book, I explored my adolescent confusion and unhappiness about being boxed into femaleness. It never occurred to me that I could become a boy or man, nor that I wanted to. But I did not like being a female in a sexist world in which girls and women are defined by men and kept under men's control. So, although biologically female, I became consciously less "feminine" through the years.

What, then, was my gender? By the time I was eleven or twelve, I was a fairly masculine, boyish girl-child and by the time I was grown,

I had become a happily androgynous woman, embodying traditionally masculine and feminine qualities, physically, psychologically, socially, and spiritually. Whatever my gender, I have never been very "feminine," never simply "female," always transgressive in appearance, behavior, and sense of personal identity, but clear that I am a transgressive *woman*.

The greatest spiritual and moral challenge for us in realms of gender and sexuality is to suspend our disbelief in whatever we do not understand and ask the Spirit to teach us how to embrace with open minds and kind, courageous hearts those who are different from us—and how to accept ourselves if we are different from who we once thought we were. Paraphrasing Pope Francis's remark about gay men and lesbians, "Who are we to judge?"

In relation to matters of gender, sexuality, and race, conservative Christian leaders are pushing hard to recreate a mythic past when "women were women," everyone was straight (at least publicly), and black and brown people "knew their place." In a fully just and equal society, our gendered, sexual, and racial identities wouldn't matter. But at this historic moment, in which many in our nation and world are pushing hard against justice for all, our gendered, sexual, and racial identities matter a great deal. In order not to be silenced or ignored, and in order to secure the gains we have been making in recent decades, we must continue to be outspoken and visible—as women, as queer (LGBTQ), as black people and folks of other racial-ethnic identities, as underpaid workers, immigrants, and as allies in the many struggles that unite us.

# Racial Identity and "Colorblindness"

She destabilizes assumptions about racial identity and challenges the foolishness of imagining that we are, or should be, "colorblind."

I was born more than seven decades ago to two Caucasian parents, which made me "white," or so I was told. Decades later, I discovered how often babies were born to slave women who were raped by their white masters or, perhaps, sometimes out of loving relationships with white men and boys. I concluded that I surely must have black relatives, "blood kin," as folks say down South. For all I know, I might have a great-great-grandparent who was a slave. I am reasonably sure I have black cousins in my ancestry.

So what does it mean for me to be white? Socially, politically, psychologically, and spiritually, it means I have enjoyed the privilege that has shaped every day of my life. "White" is a privileged legal status assigned me at birth because my parents and grandparents and great-grandparents were all legally branded as white. Being white has been a ticket into a world of economic and social benefits that neither I, nor my parents, nor their parents, nor theirs, earned, deserved, or chose.

My whiteness has shaped everything about me, including my spirituality. There is no way for a white person not to be white if, indeed, she has had access to the privileges that come with that racial identity.

Being a student at Union Theological Seminary and later a professor at the Episcopal Divinity School became the primary crucibles in which I learned a great deal about my racial identity and white privilege. My students and colleagues of color, more than anyone else, helped me accept my racial identity, rather than try somehow to climb out of it. They also helped me see that one of my chief vocations as theologian, priest, author, and activist would forever be to be an "anti-racist racist," the implication being that all white people are racists because, regardless of our personal awareness and commitments, racism is in the air we breathe. As Denise Ackermann, my South African feminist theological colleague, once remarked about apartheid, "You can't escape it. It's in the air. You wake up and breathe it in, racism." So, too, in the United States. It's in the air we breathe, regardless of our racial identities.

Believing that race shouldn't matter, many well-meaning people—black and brown people as well as white folks—claim to be "colorblind." From a positive, anti-racist perspective, which is often how it is intended, colorblindness refers to the progress we have made since the civil rights movement of the 1960s, such that many white people and some people of color genuinely try to see beyond race and not to even notice what color someone is. A number of white parents have said to me, for example, that they are so pleased that their kids don't even notice the colors of their classmates.

As well-intended and positive as this can be, we need to be clear that colorblindness is largely an aspiration among white people, not black or brown women and men, who often know better than white folks how far our society is from being truly colorblind. *As an anti-racist aspiration*, colorblindness is well-intended but it is also problematic in a society that continues to oppress and discriminate against black and brown and other people of color, a state of affairs laid bare by the vitriolic racist reactions against the presidency of Barack Obama.

In this real world, colorblindness can easily become lazy shorthand for a refusal to acknowledge the difference that race does in fact make today in law enforcement, criminal justice, voter suppression, public education, health care, housing, and other arenas of our life together. Race matters. Black lives matter. To pretend that race is not an issue, or that we are living in a world in which racism no longer exists to any significant degree, by insisting that we are colorblind, is to turn away from one of the most urgent challenges of our time. Among justice-loving people, the concept of colorblindness is not helpful, because it obscures serious efforts to promote and secure racial justice in a society and nation in which this worthy goal has not been met.

When the colorblind Republicans swept to power in North Carolina in 2010 and strengthened their numbers in 2012, North Carolina's NAACP took to the streets—not because Republicans rather than Democrats had come to power but because these particular Republicans were intent upon setting our state back fifty years in terms of voter suppression and more than a hundred years in the dismantling of our public schools and universities.

Initiating a weekly protest at the state house, including civil disobedience, NAACP president Rev. William Barber called upon justice-loving people throughout the state to join in this Moral Monday movement. Beginning in the spring of 2013, Moral Monday has stirred enthusiasm among people of all colors and cultures who have been looking for ways to protest the transparently racist, sexist, economically devastating, and environmentally damaging policies being put in place by a narrow-minded legislature and a feckless governor, who was defeated in 2016. Moral Monday has become a sign of the future in which justice will prevail. Those of us in North Carolina who have formed local chapters of the NAACP are experiencing this movement as a wellspring of community and hope, because there is such good energy and joy—such great Spirit—in struggling together for justice.

For many activists, there is also fear, grief, and exhaustion, consequences of years spent in struggle. For this reason, justice makers need to be attentive to everyone's needs for times and space to rest and play, meditate and pray, dance and sing, walk and talk, attend concerts and movies, hang out together and enjoy moments of solitude, writing, simply being.

# Beyond Human Beings

She transcends our humanity, moving us more fundamentally into our creatureliness. She soars above and beyond the struggles for human justice, weaving threads of energy among hawks and hemlocks, granite and geese, salamanders and sheep, all creatures great and small.

My friend Norene, a United Church of Christ minister and longtime social worker, suffered a massive stroke about a decade ago. She survived and has lived well, thanks to the generosity of friends who believe that the best use they can make of their resources is to share them, and thanks also to several hardworking home healthcare workers. But another reason Norene survived and has been able to live peacefully in the wake of her stroke is that she is seldom without her animal companions. Animals have always been family to Norene, but since her stroke, they have become indispensable resources of love and energy for life. I'd say her animal friends are Norene's primary daily resources of Spirit.

It is has taken most of my life to become, at times and in places, quiet and observant enough to notice that almost everywhere we turn, animals are with us, greeting, warning, hiding, reticent, aggressive, they are with us, communicating in their ways, not ours. I myself still do not know how to listen to most of creation, and I will continue to try to learn as long as there is breath in me.

We humans have no monopoly on God or spirituality.[73] In fact, we humans are the most spiritually complex and compromised beings on this planet and we are the only species with a clear capacity to make moral or immoral, good or evil, choices. I am not saying that other beings cannot make moral choices; other animals do make choices that reveal compassion and tenderness, sometimes across species. Think of the gorilla picking up and protectively cuddling the human toddler who fell into her enclosure in the Central Park Zoo. Think of assistance dogs and of horses that help humans heal. Think of elephants who gather round one another not only for protection, but also to console each other in grief, and of horses, dogs, cats, and other mammals who often quite obviously mourn their friends who have died. Goodness and kindness do not belong solely to human beings. Neither does "soul," the Spirit's presence in creation and all creatures.

A friend said to me years ago that the earth and some of its creatures will outlast humanity's recklessness. Her hope is for the earth, not for humanity, which she believes is self-destructing. My friend was neither especially sad nor cynical in her reflection. She was simply stating what she believes to be a fact. Through its greed, shortsightedness, and violence, humanity is destroying itself and much of the created earth as well, but creation will survive and go on without us. As Christian feminist theologian Sallie McFague has written, we need the rest of creation more than it needs us.[74]

The world's major religions, including the Western monotheistic traditions, have been not only dreadfully androcentric—putting males at the center of civilization—but also mindlessly anthropocentric—placing humanity at the center of God's realm.

Yet from my earliest years, something told me that this human-centered view of our life together is pure nonsense. This "something"—the Spirit—assured me as a child, and She tells me now, that all creatures are participants in the sacred processes of "godding" and that we ignore or exploit our other-than-human partners in creation to our great peril.

All creatures without exception are infused with Spirit and are involved in Her work. Creation is a sacred network of connections in which we humans depend on our brother and sister creatures—plants, animals, minerals—for our survival, and in which most of them are not dependent on us at all. The thing many creatures do need from us, since we are their self-appointed guardians, is for us to help them care for the earth and one another. Our strongest alliances with creation today are through a proliferation of non-profit organizations dedicated to the sustainability of creation; nearly all earth scientists throughout the world who testify to the reality and effects of climate change; governmental regulations of land use, energy, and other natural resources; and, increasingly, the voices of religious and spiritual leaders.

I am saying nothing here that Pope Francis did not say in a spirit of moral urgency to a far greater audience in his 2015 encyclical, *Laudato si* [Praise be to you].

# The Question of Meat

She urges us to give up "meat"—stop eating cows, pigs, lambs, chickens, fish, and other animals.

Do I believe that people like me—well-fed folks who can afford to buy nutritious food and whose health permits it—should be vegetarians or even vegans in order to be in right relation with the rest of creation? Yes.

Do I believe that we should stop slaughtering and eating meat in order to be faithful proponents of the earth's sustainability? Yes.

Do I believe that all creatures have souls, the meeting place between Creator and creature, in which we all are most fully who we are? Yes.

Do I believe that, in that a global capitalist economy, these questions are contextual—that is, questions for inhabitants of affluent cultures and contexts who have time, energy, scientific and moral resources, and economic space even to think about what we should eat, given many choices? Yes.

I personally have wrestled with the question about becoming vegetarian for decades. I understand how morally complicated and personally confounding it is. Around the world, there are religious communities and cultures in which vegetarianism is customary or required. In the United States today, however, the choice for most people to be vegetarian or vegan requires a fair amount of money, time, and energy, because preparing and eating a nutritious meat-free diet of vegetables, fruits, nuts, and grains is costly in time and money. Most people in the United States have grown up eating meat whenever we could, to the point that many of us imagine that we require it in order to be energized, happy, and healthy. I grew up on Southern fried chicken, hamburgers, steaks, and especially barbequed pork throughout the first half of my life.

About thirty ago, however, reading Albert Schweitzer and some feminist Christian theology and ethics about earth sustainability and animals, I began to consider becoming vegetarian to be as much in solidarity with animals and earth as possible. My aspiration has long been stronger, however, than my ability to actually turn away from meat, and I have only dabbled around with vegetarianism for many years, trying it on and taking it off like a coat.

And now, I am early in my eighth decade on this planet. It has taken me this long to stop eating mammals and birds. I still eat fish. To myself, I say, it's about time. Given my intense belief in the sacredness of these living creatures, and also my deep sense of our being connected and interdependent, it puzzles me that I ever in my life agreed to taste chicken or cow or pig or lamb or even fish. But for much of my life, I have enjoyed eating meat, echoing in my head what I have always been told—that the other creatures are here on this earth for our pleasure and nutrition.

Today I read my own words about animals being here for our use as the blabber of bad theology, self-justifying and mindless.

I believe that our indifference to the well-being of animals and the rest of creation feeds and strengthens our indifference to one another as human beings. For my participation in this indifference, I ask forgiveness from sister and brother creatures and from the Spirit who stirs among us all. I consider my step away from most flesh-eating a tiny token of solidarity but, more than that, a daily reminder to myself that we creatures walk together on sacred ground, and that the Spirit is with us, forever calling us to turn around and reconsider what we are doing.

There's no perfect way to do this, no one right path. Angela loved animals and also ate them, never failing to thank each animal for giving its life for our nourishment; and Bev cherished animals and earth and prayed before each meal, "Some have food. Some have none. God bless the revolution." Sue eats meat and spends as much time as she can caring for our land and animals, and for the flora and fauna and water and forests all around us in the mountains. Darlene, sister writer and dear friend with some serious health challenges, eats some chicken and is deeply devoted to animals and the sustainability of the earth. Each of us is on a path that makes sense to us.

The friend perhaps closest to me on the particular path I'm walking in relation to vegetarianism is Gerry, who also loves animals, especially rescuing old dogs and horses. Like Sue Sasser and my brother, Robbie, Gerry has no interest in spirituality and yet, like Sue and Robbie, she is grounded in a love of creation and a respect for all living beings. These and other agnostic, or atheist, friends of mine embody a spirit that I am inclined to call "God." Some eat meat. Some don't.

Some of us have the social and economic privilege—therefore, also some responsibility—to pursue issues of earth and animal well-being, and our vegetarianism or veganism may be one of the ways we shape this pursuit. Our privilege does not lessen the universality of the moral significance, even urgency, of earth and animal life. We should not trivialize these concerns by dismissing them as rich white or First World issues. Everyone on this planet has some responsibility to do whatever we can toward building and sustaining our common good. Those of us to whom much has been given, or to whom much has come, those of us with social and economic privilege, can and must speak on behalf of those who have no voice, including animals and earth. We need to realize, of course, that we will not always be wise or right in what we advocate, but this does not mean we should say and do nothing for fear of being wrong or dismissed as privileged people.

Regardless of whether I can, or do, live out the rest of my life as a vegetarian or vegan, I would be morally dishonest and remiss not to state, unequivocally, that I believe we humans ought not to eat animals, period. That we do consume the flesh of our fellow creatures suggests that we, as a species, have a long way to go spiritually. Be clear that I am not judging anyone more than myself. We are all deluded by an ignorant, anthropocentric—human-centered—view of what is right and what is wrong, what is good and what is evil. God, have mercy on us, each and all.

# Limits of Language

Animals, art, and music call us beyond human words in our efforts to communicate: We have to rely on silence, our senses, and body language—our own and that of other creatures. We have to build new strengths physically and psychologically, emotionally, cognitively and socially. For many people, animals and art and music connect us to people of other cultures, times, and places, and to creatures of other species, expanding our consciousness and deepening our appreciation.

Like gazing out the window of a train, we can easily zip by everything and everybody without seeing who we are in relation to them. We can be oblivious to the fact that our lives are connected, or we can be attentive to our vast network of relationships as we move along our way on this earth. Animals, artists, and musicians can help us slow down and pay attention to what is going on within, between, and around us in the world.

For some of us, our relationships with animals can expand our world and sharpen our senses of the Sacred even more intimately than our love of art and music. One afternoon about ten years ago, I was having a difficult ride on my horse Red. She was stubbornly resisting everything I was trying to get her to do. I wanted to go left, she turned right. I wanted to slow down, she sped up. I wanted to canter, she preferred to trot.

My teacher Linda Levy was watching us struggle from the other side of the arena in Littleton, Massachusetts. As I was getting more and more frustrated, Linda yelled to me, "Communicate with your horse, Carter!" I sighed and began to talk to Red much as I would have talked to a child. "Come on, girl. Cut it out!" Hearing my chatter, Linda yelled again, "I didn't say 'talk' to her—I said 'communicate'!" I was stunned. But I knew immediately what Linda meant, so I began to give Red nonverbal cues—with my thighs and hands, the posture of my body and even the tilt of my head. Within seconds, my horse and I were in sync, working together, having a good time.

My primary horseback riding teacher in North Carolina was Liz Galloway, a strong, smart, gorgeous younger woman not formally schooled as an equestrian but stunning in her connectedness to horses with a seasoned ability to read their behavior and respond to them in their own language. Over about a decade, Liz worked with Sue, me, and our horses, sometimes several times a week, building our confidence in ourselves as horsewomen. During this time, Liz—about twenty years my junior—became one of my dearest friends as we spun a deeply mutual relationship, Liz my equine coach, me her spiritual mentor.

One of the most sorrowful tragedies I've ever experienced personally was the death of Liz's only child, Jason, a twenty-three-year-old young man, in the summer of 2014, and the depth of Liz's ongoing grief. Liz's own horses and dogs, and a handful of human loved ones, beginning with her husband, have been partners in her processes of coming to terms with this terrible loss. More than anything, Jason's death and Liz's grief plunge me into deep pools of empathic sorrow and the broken-heartedness of all creation, and of the Spirit.

I know the Spirit intimately and intelligently in my heart and bones and brain when I am walking my dogs, riding my horse, playing the fiddle, listening to music of many different kinds, becoming aware of my friend Janine's loving attentiveness to words and her whimsical, colorful images of horses and women, observing the movement in my cousin Marsha's lively painting of my horse Feather with her mom, Red, in our pasture. I am filled with Spirit through being close to my animal companions and jamming with the Bold Gray Mares, our old-time band. Filled, that is, with zest and gratitude, and energized for whatever may come next. These resources—the animals, the art, the music, the people—make me spiritually larger than my one small self. Through them, the Spirit connects me with creatures and cultures that have existed before me, in times and places that are not mine. The animals, the art, and the music become part of me and transport me into realms of time and space beyond this moment and this place. This is what the Spirit does. She immerses me in radical mutuality with others. Experiencing myself connected at the core with others—painters and poets, composers and musicians, horses and those who turn to them for help and joy—I become better able to give and receive empathy and kindness, compassion and respect.

Linda, my former riding teacher and mentor, once said to me about Red, "*As long as you're afraid of that horse, she'll scare you.*" In these words, the Spirit was speaking through Linda, and this message was as wise as anything I have ever heard about our fears of one another, especially our fears of creatures and of people from cultures and religions that scare us. As long as we are afraid of them, they will scare us. What does this mean to me? It means that our fear of the unknown and our fear of "the other" is a common, natural dimension of our human and creaturely experience. It means that only insofar as we move through our fear, which is so often irrational, can we be healed and liberated. The movement through fear is courage. Without courage, we stay stuck in fear, which maintains a dysfunctional hold on our hearts and minds. "As long as you're afraid of that horse, she'll scare you."

It took me five years of hard work with my horse Red to begin to be able to hear and see her in her "horse-ness" and accept her unique horse being. She was not just any horse. She was my Red. After much time and energy had passed between us, it became clear to me that Red knew me to be her special person, not just any human, nor by any means the most talented equestrian in her life. But she knew that I was there for her. Red and I developed a mutual relationship rooted and grounded in love through our years of working patiently together. This helped me understand what love requires in all contexts, with any and all species— attentiveness, hard work, presence and patience, moments of pure joy and ever more gratitude.

Red died in December 2013, almost exactly a year after Bev's death. Like Bev's departure, Red's leaving was as great a loss as any I have experienced. These two beings—one so deeply my beloved human, the other so fully my horse—took pieces of my heart with them, or so it has felt. And yet, they are here. In the wake of Red's death, she has accompanied me more fully into my relationships with her special friend Patience and especially with Red's daughter, Feather. Like Red, Feather and I are taking plenty of time to see each other through our mutual fears and distrust of the "other" species— and that is exactly what we are doing.

It is always a sacred process, building mutual relation with anyone of any species. In this ongoing process, horses have become my priests. These days I often sit on a mounting block in the round pen and read while Feather or Patience or our whimsical rescue horse, Sundance, mills around, poking at me with a big soft nose or standing by my side, sometimes listening to my words when I speak, and always attuned to my heart. For whatever time I have left on this planet, the horses will be nearby, wellsprings of peace, resources of wisdom.

Intimations of this wisdom led me, along with a few other women, to found Free Rein Center for Therapeutic Riding and Education in 2000. Free Rein has become a place in which, as its motto reads, "horses help humans heal." Of course, I have long believed that humans help horses heal as well and that it is, in fact, the mutuality of the connection between the humans and the horses that generates the healing, liberating energy. At Free Rein, parents, teachers, volunteers, and others observe with wonder as "something" happens between the students and their equine companions. At least twice over the years at Free Rein, children have spoken their first words to the horse. Several times, children have begun to walk again, thanks to the stimulating movement of the horse and its impact on the rider's body. Amazing relational transactions are routine at Free Rein and other centers of therapeutic work with horses. I am persuaded that it is all about mutuality and the courage to step through fear, crossing boundaries and cultures—in this case, between horse and human—and learning to listen and speak in ways new to one another.

Here's the primary spiritual lesson I've learned from the horses themselves: Don't hold on too tightly, Don't try too hard, or you'll tumble off and break or give up, or maybe you'll plod along, but you won't relax or enjoy yourself. You won't see much beauty, you won't laugh or cry soulfully. I find myself thinking also about advice I've received from my fiddle teachers and my friend Albert, himself a marvelous fiddler. These friends and musical mentors keep telling me that my problem as a musician is that I hold on too tight. Loosen up. Relax. The fiddle will play itself![75]

# Life and Death

On the morning of Sunday, October 18, 2009, my mother, Mary Ann Carter Heyward, slipped away peacefully. In that moment, I was seated at the foot of her bed eating a croissant and sipping coffee. Ofa Tonga had put a baby blue smock on her, and some liptick, which mama would have wanted, and was standing at the head of the bed, running a brush gently through Mama's white hair. Brother Robbie and sister Ann were right outside the room updating their spouses via cell phone on how things seemed. Nephew Rob and niece Isabel were sitting on another twin bed, next to my mother's bed. Their faces reflected tiredness from not having slept all night as those of us gathered in Charlotte had taken turns sitting with Mama over the past few days. I had spoken a few minutes earlier to Bev, and Sue was nearby but not in the room when Ofa nodded to me, Rob, and Isabel—"She's gone."

Ofa Tonga, originally from the island of Tonga, was a most amazing helper who had moved my mother into her own home during the last year of her life so that she could take better care of her than regularly visiting her in the retirement community where Mama had lived for about a dozen years prior. During the eleven months Mama lived in Ofa's home, she was visited daily, usually by our family and also by Ofa's children and grandchildren and her African American soldier husband, Simon. On one occasion when I arrived to spend a weekend, I found several small children sitting on the edge of my mother's bed, singing to her. On another occasion, Mama phoned my sister, Ann, from Fort Jackson, South Carolina, to say that she was spending the night in an army barracks with Captain Simon Tonga and his wife and was having a fine time. Another time, Mama came to supper with my siblings and me sporting a lei from a luau she had attended with the Tongas. Among the most moving tales of all were those about how extremely hospitable and kind Ofa and Simon Tonga's Mormon congregation had been time and again to our mother, when she attended church with this generous and adventurous family.

Six days before her death, Mama suffered a massive stroke that destroyed her capacity to speak, but she was still able to communicate through her eyes, smile, and touch. We had figured that a stroke would probably take our mother, as is it had her mother as well, and a number of little TIA's (transient ischemic attacks) over six years had prepared us, as well as folks can be prepared, for this passage. The night before her death, when it was clear that Mama had hours, not days, left, we had gathered round her bed, taking turns sitting with her and administering morphine whenever she became restless or agitated. At one point during the night, Ofa and Simon Tonga had come into the room together and, assuming that Sue and I were asleep on our pallets on the floor, had begun to sing quietly to our mother, and to pray over her.

Shortly after her death the next morning, the entire Tonga family joined all the Heywards in forming a circle around Mary Ann's bed, and Simon asked us Heyward siblings if he could pray, which he did in the form of a song. He told us that the song was often sung in the Army when a soldier had been lost. I don't remember the words or the tune, but I do recall that Simon Tonga and his eighteen-year-old son, Sea, stood in the circle weeping as Simon sang. Before long, all of us were weeping and prayers were being lifted up spontaneously. I cherish this occasion as a tiny window into the realm of God in its fullness, the heavenly community of siblings that crosses all boundaries and cultures and religions and races and genders and sexual identities and ages and abilities and all creatures great and small.

For about a decade at the time of Mama's death, Sue and I had been reading the Harry Potter series aloud to each other. Along the way, as the volumes have become more nuanced and the characters more mature, the plot has thickened and I have read Harry Potter as a rich, textured story of theological imagination and ethical lore.

The series is about life and death, good and evil, courage and fecklessness, loyalty and betrayal, greed and generosity, wisdom and foolishness, intelligence and downright stupidity. It's about doing wrong and making amends, hurting and being hurt, showing kindness and bullying, healing and being healed. It's about interdependence of people like ourselves and those different from us, humans and the rest of creation living together with ease, and unease. The Harry Potter books explore the mundane and the magical, the extraordinary power of imagination, the willingness or refusal to sacrifice oneself on behalf of others, and how people and places and things are not always what they seem to be.

Harry Potter is about growing up, growing old, and staying young at heart. It is about the Spirit's magical mysterious ways of transporting us through time in its several dimensions into unknown places, close by and far away, places inside us as well as other lands and worlds and galaxies. In Harry Potter, the Spirit of life and love and courage introduces us to wonders beyond belief, opportunities beyond our wildest dreams, risks and challenges we would not choose, and friendships that endure. For me, the Harry Potter books have been a reintroduction to the Spirit herself, she who transforms us and everything else and flies on.

My nephew Rob says that J. K. Rowling wrote the series as a way of helping children deal with death. Children like me, perhaps. About the time I began reading the story about the boy wizard, my cherished friend and colleague Sue Hiatt was diagnosed with a terrible cancer and given a few months to live, a prognosis she beat by a year. What I didn't know at the time Sue's oncologist made the diagnosis in February 2001 was that, starting then and there, the rest of my life would involve accompanying sick and dying loved ones and being pastor to them and their families through and beyond the end.

This was not a vocation I would have chosen, nor one for which I felt equipped. I had never been around much human death, nor had I really come to terms with the fact that my own peers and closest friends would die. Through the deaths of animal companions along the way, I knew what it was to lose a friend through death, and to grieve. But I did not know much about being a pastor to a critically ill human companion like Sue Hiatt, and I did not know how best to be with her family who, unlike Sue, were not people of faith. During Sue's illness, I found myself coordinating her care as well as being as present to her as I could, going to doctors' appointments, waiting in hospitals with her, helping her eat and walk.

Sue Sasser, Sister Angela, sister priest Alison Cheek and many others joined in this care-giving effort, including many of Sue's former students, like Jean Austin and Libby Kennedy, Janie van Zandt and Webb Brown, whom Sue had taught in a course on "Death and Dying" at Episcopal Divinity School. As it happened, Webb Brown had become chaplain in the hospice residence which Sue entered twice over a period of sixteen months.

Strange as it may sound, Harry Potter became a primary spiritual resource for me during this ongoing crisis of death. A story of "good magic" (as well as evil magic), the Potter books spoke to my heartbreak time and again as friend after friend took leave through death—and as the world around us seemed to be flying apart, through violence and death.[76]

The attacks of September 11, 2001, occurred several months before Sister Angela herself "jumped the twig" following a massive stroke, in January 2002, and before Sue Hiatt finally succumbed to the anaplastic thyroid cancer that had robbed her of her voice before taking her life in May 2002. Bob DeWitt and Dorothee Soelle both passed away in 2003, just about the time Bush and Cheney launched the war in Iraq, which to this day is taking thousands of lives. My whimsical basset hound, Flower, had died in 2001, my first horse, Sugar, and my Labrador retriever, Brennan, died in 2003, and my twenty-three-year-old cat, Rubyfruit, two years later. In 2005, my sister priest Katrina Swanson succumbed to cancer just as the massive hurricane bearing her name devastated New Orleans, becoming a symbol of death and grief, as did the Indonesian tsunami the following year. In 2007, my sister, Ann's, first child died of cystic fibrosis at age thirty-eight. Sue Sasser's mother, Doris, died the same year, and my own mama, Mary Ann, left us in 2009. During the decade, we lost several beautiful Dominican sisters in Adelaide, Australia, women close to my beloved friend Angela Moloney, and Angela herself lost a very dear brother.

In the past few years, too, not only did we lose Bev in 2012, but also my dear dog Buddy a year earlier, my horse Red a year later, my friend Jim's wife, Judy, in 2013, Liz's son, Jason, and my sister's close friend Celeste in 2014, and our most empathic therapy horse, Macho, in the winter of 2015. So much death, and these are only the most personal instances, a sharp, painful tip of a huge, bottomless iceberg. There are countless millions, nay billions, of strangers—siblings of all species on this planet, more than anyone can know—who have taken their leave and are gone, and many more who share the grief and sorrow that transcend generations.

St. John Chrysostom's words come to my mind again and again. He is said to written this poem for his own epitaph in the second century CE:

He whom we love
and lose
is no longer
where he was before.
He is now
wherever we are.

The Harry Potter series secured my confidence in the last six words of this poem of Spirit: "He is now wherever we are."

Somehow, J. K. Rowling's "magic" has clarified and sharpened what the church has been teaching me for seventy years:

Our loved ones go with us, forever. We go with them, forever. Death is not the end, but a passage we share.

Those who have gone on are now wherever we are. And that, dear reader, gives us power. Through the legacy of our ancestors generation upon generation further back than we can know, we ourselves embody resources that empower us to join in the Spirit's everlasting spinning and sparking of justice and compassion and kindness. A sharpened sense of our connections over time and space, and the great power that we share, in its depths and fullness, was a gift to me from Harry Potter.

My Christian faith had long ago opened my mind and heart and soul to our ongoing-ness beyond death. Then, just as my confidence was lagging and the world was crashing around us in the early days of this century, along came J. K. Rowling with her Harry Potter books and their engaging, multi-dimensional characters like Lily and James Potter, Albus Dumbledore, and Dobby, Hedwig, and Severus Snape. These people and creatures had big feet of clay. They could be erratic and unattractive. But their courage to live with purpose and steadfastness—and to die when the time came—helped me see those around me, as well as myself, more clearly through the eyes of God. The Potter story helped me accept—with gladness and gratitude—my own capacity to stay on the path we are walking and to experience the ongoing presence and literal inspiration of those who have died.

I thank my sister in Spirit, Joanne Rowling, for helping me wake up. Without her, I doubt I would even have noticed my "heavenly council"! Rowling, whom I do not know, helped secure my faith in myself and the Spirit as I move on with friends and loved ones, struggling for social justice, celebrating small victories, loving each other as well as we can, accompanying one another toward death, and beyond.

I also thank Alison Cheek, my beloved friend and sister in the struggle for women's ordination and all things just, for deciding to join us as part of Redbud Spring's "off campus" community. A better friend there has never been, not to mention the fact that Alison Cheek is among the most treasured and admired feminist women priests in Anglicanism, including her native Australia. Alison is cherished for her wisdom and kindness as well as for her sharp feminist biblical analytical skills, which she learned primarily from her friend and mentor, renowned feminist biblical scholar Elisabeth Schüssler Fiorenza.

In 2014, as we moved around from one place to another, celebrating the fortieth anniversary of the Philadelphia ordinations, Alison and I were amazed again and again by the enthusiasm with which we and our "irregular" sister priests were met. For four decades, it had seemed to us that the Episcopal Church had all but forgotten that particular struggle and the women who were on the front lines. We were mistaken. While some of our Episcopal colleagues would just as soon have swept the whole feminist movement under the ecclesial carpet, there are many women and men still working in the church as lay and clergy, deacons, priests, and bishops who do seem to know what happened in Philadelphia in 1974 and a year later in Washington and, as important, what questions these ordinations raised for the Christian church—questions that, for the most part, have not yet been addressed by many Episcopalians, women or men.

Such questions sparked this book in your hands and have led Alison and me beyond patriarchal religious practices. I pray that, over time, long beyond our brief life spans, these concerns may lead greater segments of humanity than we see today—Christians, Jews, Muslims, others—to repent the grievous sins of male domination, white supremacy, economic exploitation, environmental degradation, and an androcentric view of creation, so that humans and other creatures can live, love, and die more confidently in the Spirit of genuine healing and durable liberation.

It seems wonderfully appropriate that Alison and I are sharing some precious moments in our senior years and are becoming steadfast spiritual companions as we fly on!

And when I do fly on beyond this life, when I take leave of this body, I will gratefully pass over in the company of those who love me, animal companions and human friends, trees and waterfalls and, if in early June, the magical blue ghosts in the North Carolina mountain night air. I want music around me and horses and dogs and fresh air and enthusiasm for social justice and a sweet, sweet Spirit that is carrying me more fully into God, who is our heavenly home.

One thing I know for sure—my heavenly council will be there, attending us, dancing and singing and encouraging the justice-makers. Something else: I will be swirling around with you, perfectly balanced and unafraid, in the spirals of the One who flies on, carrying us with Her. I will know then what I catch only in glimpses along the way, something I believed once upon a time, and will again: the box turtle I helped across the road tonight—she is God.

# Resources

## Selected Books by Carter Heyward

*A Priest Forever: Formation of a Woman and a Priest.* New York: Harper and Row, 1976.

*The Redemption of God: A Theology of Mutual Relation.* Foreword by Janet L. Surrey. 2nd ed. Eugene, OR: Wipf and Stock, 2010 [1982].

*Our Passion for Justice: Images of Power, Sexuality, and Liberation.* New York: Pilgrim, 1984.

*Touching Our Strength: The Erotic as Power and the Love of God.* San Francisco: Harper Collins, 1989.

*Speaking of Christ: A Lesbian Feminist Voice.* Edited by Ellen Davis. Cleveland: Pilgrim, 1989.

*When Boundaries Betray Us.* Foreword by Roy SteinhoffSmith. 2nd ed. Cleveland: Pilgrim, 1998 [1993].

*Staying Power: Gender, Justice, and Compassion.* Cleveland: Pilgrim, 1995.

*Saving Jesus from Those Who Are Right: Rethinking What It Means to Be Christian.* Minneapolis: Fortress, 1999.

*God in the Balance: Christian Spirituality in Times of Terror.* Cleveland: Pilgrim, 2002.

*Flying Changes: Horses as Spiritual Teachers.* Cleveland: Pilgrim, 2005.

*Keep Your Courage: A Radical Christian Voice.* New York: Seabury, 2010.

*The Spirit of the Lord is Upon Me: Writings of Suzanne Hiatt.* Edited with Janine Lehane. New York: Seabury, 2014.

## Modern (Twentieth Century) and Contemporary (Twenty-first Century)

Alexander, Michelle. *The New Jim Crow: Mass Incarceration in the Age of Colorblindness.* New York: New Press, 2012.

Althaus-Reid, Marcella. *Indecent Theology: Theological Perversions in Sex, Gender, and Politics.* London: Routledge, 2000.

Allen, Danielle. *Our Declaration: A Reading of the Declaration of Independence in Defense of Equality.* New York: W.W. Norton, 2014.

*The Gospel of Christian Atheism.* Philadelphia: Westminster, 1966.

Altizer, Thomas J.J., and William Hamilton. *Radical Theology and the Death of God.* Indianapolis: Bobbs-Merrill, 1966.

Amanecida Collective, Carter Heyward and Anne Gilson, eds. *Revolutionary Forgiveness: Feminist Reflections on Nicaragua.* Maryknoll, New York: Orbis, 1986.

Aslan, Reza. *No god but God: The Origins, Evolution, and Future of Islam.* New York: Random House, 2006.

Bonhoeffer, Dietrich. *Letters and Papers from Prison.* Edited by Eberhard Bethge. Enlarged edition. New York: Touchstone, 1997 [1953, 1971].

Bozarth-Campbell, Alla. *Womanpriest: A Personal Odyssey.* San Diego: Luramedia, 1988 [1978].

Bozarth, Alla Renee. *A Journey Through Grief.* Center City, MN: Hazelden, 1990.

———. *This is My Body: Praying for Earth, Prayers from the Heart.* New York: iUniverse, 2004.

Carlson Brown, Joanne and Carole R. Bohn, eds. *Christianity, Patriarchy, and Abuse: A Feminist Critique.* Cleveland: Pilgrim, 1989.

Brown, Dan. *The DaVinci Code.* New York: Random House, 2003.

Buber, Martin. *I and Thou.* Translated by Ronald Gregor Smith. New York: Scribner, 1958.

Cannon, Katie Geneva. *Katie's Canon: Womanism and the Soul of Black Community.* New York: Continuum, 1995.

Cannon, Katie Geneva, Emilie M. Townes, and Angela D. Sims. *Womanist Theological Ethics: A Reader.* Louiville: Westminster, 2011.

Carroll, James. *Constantine's Sword: The Church and the Jews, a History.* New York: Houghton Mifflin, 2001.

Cheng, Patrick S. *Radical Love: An Introduction to Queer Theology.* New York: Seabury, 2011.

———. *Rainbow Theology: Bridging Race, Sexuality, and Spirit.* New York: Seabury, 2013.

Clinton, Hillary Rodham. *It Takes a Village and Other Lessons Children Teach Us.* New York: Simon and Shuster, 1996.

Combahee River Collective, "A Black Feminist Statement." In *The Second Wave: A Reader in Feminist Theory,* edited by Linda Nicholson. New York: Routledge, 1997.

Crenshaw, Kimberle. *On Intersectionality: Essential Writings.* New York: New Press, 2016.

Daly, Mary. *Beyond God the Father: Toward a Philosophy of Women's Liberation.* Boston: Beacon, 1973.

Darling, Pamela. *New Wine: The Story of Women Transforming Leadership and Power in the Episcopal Church.* New York: Seabury, 1994.

De La Torre, Miguel A., ed. *Handbook of US Theologies of Liberation.* St. Louis: Chalice, 2004.

Douglas, Kelly Brown. *The Black Christ.* New York: Orbis, 1993.

———. *Sexuality and the Black Church.* Maryknoll, New York: Orbis, 1999.

———. *Stand Your Ground: Black Bodies and the Justice of God.* New York: Orbis, 2015.

Driver, Tom F. *Christ in a Changing World: Toward an Ethical Christology.* New York: Crossroad, 1981.

———. *Patterns of Grace: Human Experience as Word of God.* New York: Harper and Row, 1977.

Ellis, Marc H. *Encountering the Jewish Future—with Wiesel, Buber, Heschel, Arendt, and Levinas.* Minneapolis: Fortress, 2011.

———. *Unholy Alliance: Religion and Atrocity in Our Time.* Minneapolis: Fortress, 1997.

Ellis, Marc H., and Otto Maduro. *The Future of Liberation Theology: Essays in Honor of Gustavo Gutierrez.* Maryknoll, New York: Orbis, 1989.

Marvin M. Ellison, *Making Love Just: Sexual Ethics for Perplexing Times,* Minneapolis: Fortress, 2012.

———. *Same-Sex Marriage? A Christian Ethical Analysis.* Cleveland: Pilgrim, 2004.

Ellison Marvin M., and Kelly Brown Douglas, eds. *Sexuality and the Sacred: Sources for Theological Reflection.* 2nd Edition. Louisville: Westminster John Knox, 2010.

Ellison, Marvin M., and Sylvia Thorson-Smith, eds. *Body and Soul: Rethinking Sexuality as Justice-Love*. Cleveland: Pilgrim, 2003.

Friedan, Betty. *The Feminine Mystique*. New York: W.W. Norton, 1963.

Gawande, Atul. *Being Mortal: Medicine and What Matters in the End*. New York: Metropolitan/Henry Holt, 2014.

Gilson, Anne Bathurst. *The Battle for America's Families: A Feminist Response to the Religious Right*. Cleveland; Pilgrim, 1999.

———. *Eros Breaking Free: Interpreting Sexual Theo-Ethics*. Cleveland: Pilgrim, 1995.

Goodwin, Doris Kearns. *Team of Rivals: The Political Genius of Abraham Lincoln*. New York: Simon & Schuster, 2012.

Gottlieb, Roger. *A Spirituality of Resistance: Finding a Peaceful Heart and Protecting the Earth*. New York: Crossroad, 2003.

Greenspan, Miriam. *Healing Through the Dark Emotions: The Wisdom of Grief, Fear, and Despair*. Boston: Shambhala, 2003.

Harrison, Beverly Wildung. *Justice in the Making: Feminist Social Ethics*. Edited by Elizabeth M. Bounds, Pamela K. Brubaker, Jane E. Hicks, Marilyn J. Legge, Rebecca Todd Peters, Traci C. West. Louisville: Westminster John Knox, 2004.

———. *Making the Connections: Essays in Feminist Social Ethics*. Edited by Carol S. Robb. Boston: Beacon, 1985.

———. *Our Right to Choose: A New Ethic of Abortion*. Boston: Beacon, 1983.

Harvey, Jennifer, Karin A. Case, and Robin Hawley Gorsline, eds. *Disrupting White Supremacy from Within: White People on What WE Need to Do*. Cleveland: Pilgrim, 2004.

Hicks, John. *Evil and the God of Love*. New York: MacMillan, 2010 [1966].

Hunt, Mary E. *Fierce Tenderness: A Feminist Theology of Friendship*. New York: Crossroad, 1991.

Isherwood, Lisa. *Liberating Christ: Exploring the Christologies of Contemporary Liberation Movements*. London: United Church, 1999.

Kazantzakis, Nikos. *The Saviors of God: Spiritual Exercises*. Trans. Kimon Friar. New York: Touchstone/Simon and Schuster, 1960.

Keller, Catherine. *On the Mystery: Discerning Divinity in Process*. Minneapolis: Fortress, 2008.

Kohanov, Linda. *The Tao of Equus: A Woman's Journey of Healing and Transformation Through the Way of the Horse*. Novato, CA: New Library, 2007.

———. *The Five Roles of a Master Herder: A Revolutionary Model for Socially Intelligent Leadership*. Novato, CA: New Library, 2016.

Pui-lan, Kwok. *Postcolonial Imagination & Feminist Theology*. Louisville: Westminster John Knox, 2005.

LeGuin, Ursula. *The Left Hand of Darkness*. New York: Penguin, 1987 [1969].

Light, Gordon. "She Flies On!" ("She Comes Sailing on the Wind"), No. 2122. *The Faith We Sing*. Common Cup Company, 1986.

Linzey, Andrew. *Why Animal Suffering Matters: Philosophy, Theology, and Practical Ethics*. New York: Oxford University Press, 2009.

Lorde, Audre. *Sister Outsider: Essays and Speeches*. Berkeley: Crossing, 2007 [1984].

McDaniel, Jay B. *Of God and Pelicans: A Theology of Reverence for Life*. Louisville: Westminster John Knox, 1989.

McFague, Sallie. *The Body of God: An Ecological Theology*. Minneapolis: Fortress, 1993.

———. *Life Abundant: Rethinking Theology and Economy for a Planet in Peril*. Minneapolis: Fortress, 2001.

———. *Super, Natural Christians: How We Should Love Nature*. Minneapolis: Fortress, 1997.

McIntosh, Peggy. "White Privilege: Unpacking the Invisible Knapsack" (1988). [PDF] White Privilege: Unpacking the Invisible Knapsack—DeAnza College—https://deanza.edu/.../White%20Privilege%20Unpacking%20t

Manji, Irshad. *The Trouble with Islam: A Muslim's Call for Reform in Her Faith*. New York: St. Martin's, 2003.

Marable, Manning. *Race, Reform, and Rebellion: The Second Reconstruction and Beyond in Black America, 1945–2006*, 3rd Edition. New York: Macmillan, 2006 [1984].

Martin, Joan M. *More than Chains and Toil: A Christian Work Ethic of Enslaved Women*. Louisville: Westminster John Knox, 2000.

Mollenkott, Virginia Ramey, and Letha Scanzoni. *Is the Homosexual My Neighbor? Another Christian View*. New York: Harper and Row, 1978.

———. *Omnigender: A Trans-Religious Approach*. Cleveland: Pilgrim, 2001.

Morrison, Melanie Shelton. *The Politics of Sin: Practical Theological Issues in Lesbian Feminist Perspective*. Groningen, Netherlands: Rijkuniversiteit, 1998.

Morse, Christopher. *The Difference Heaven Makes: Rehearing the Gospel as News*. New York: T & T Clark, 2010.

Mud Flower Collective. *God's Fierce Whimsy: Christian Feminism and Theological Education*. Edited by Carter Heyward. Cleveland: Pilgrim, 1985.

Mukherjee, Siddhartha. *The Emperor of All Maladies: A Biography of Cancer*. New York: Scribner, 2011.

O'Dell, Darlene. *The Story of the Philadelphia Eleven*. Foreword by Carter Heyward. New York: Seabury, 2014.

Patte, Daniel, ed. *The Cambridge Dictionary of Christianity*. Cambridge University, 2010.

Plaskow, Judith, and Carol P. Christ, eds. *Weaving the Visions: New Patterns in Feminist Spirituality*. San Francisco: Harper Collins, 1989.

Pollan, Michael. *In Defense of Food: An Eater's Manifesto*. New York: Penguin, 2009.

Rasmussen, Larry L. *Earth Community, Earth Ethics*. Maryknoll, New York: Orbis, 1996.

———. *Earth-Honoring Faith: Religious Ethics in a New Key*. Oxford University Press, 2013.

Rich, Adrienne. *On Lies, Secrets, and Silence: Selected Prose 1966–1978*. New York: W.W. Norton, 1979.

Robinson, John A. T. *Honest to God*. London: SCM, 1963.

Rowling, J. K. *Harry Potter and the Sorcerer's Stone*. New York: Scholastic, 1997.

———. *Harry Potter and the Chamber of Secrets*. New York: Scholastic, 1998.

———. *Harry Potter and the Prisoner of Azkaban*. New York: Scholastic, 1999.

———. *Harry Potter and the Goblet of Fire*. New York: Scholastic, 2000.

———. *Harry Potter and the Order of the Phoenix*. New York: Scholastic, 2003.

———. *Harry Potter and the Half-Blood Prince*. New York: Scholastic, 2005.

———. *Harry Potter and the Deathly Hallows*. New York: Scholastic, 2007.

Ruether, Rosemary Radford. *Integrating Ecofeminism, Globalization, and World Religions*. New York: Rowman and Littlefield, 2005.

Russell, Letty. *Just Hospitality: God's Welcome in a World of Difference*. Louisville: Westminster John Knox, 2009.

Sennett, Richard, and Jonathan Cobb. *The Hidden Injuries of Class*. New York: Norton/ Knopf, 1972.

Shange, Ntzoke. *For Colored Girls Who Considered Suicide When the Rainbow Was Enuf*. New York: Scribner, 1975.

Soelle, Dorothee. *Beyond Mere Obedience*. Translated by Lawrence W. Denef. New York: Pilgrim, 1982 [1968].

———. *Christ the Representative: An Essay in Theology after the "Death of God."* Translated by David Lewis. Philadelphia: Fortress, 1965.

———. *Essential Writings*. Selected with an introduction by Dianne L. Oliver. Maryknoll, New York: Orbis, 2006.

———. *Political Theology*. Translated with an introduction by John Shelley. Philadelphia: Fortress, 1974 [1971].

———. *Revolutionary Patience*. Translated by Rita and Robert Kimber. Maryknoll, New York: Orbis, 1977 [1974].

———. *The Silent Cry: Mysticism and Resistance*. Translated by Barbara and Martin Rumscheidt. Minneapolis: Fortress, 2001 [1997].

———. *Suffering*. Translated by Everett R. Kalin. Philadelphia: Fortress, 1975 [1973].

———. *Thinking about God: An Introduction to Theology*. Translated by John Bowden. London: SCM, 1990.

Sotomayor, Sonia. *My Beloved World*. New York: Random House, 2014.

Spencer, Daniel T. *Gay and Gaia: Ethics, Ecology, and the Erotic*. Cleveland: Pilgrim, 1996.

Steinem, Gloria. *My Life on the Road*. New York: Random House, 2016.

SteinhoffSmith, Roy Herndon. *The Mutuality of Care*. St. Louis: Chalice, 2004.

Surrey, Janet L., and Samuel Shem. *The Buddha's Wife: The Path of Awakening Together*. New York: Atria, 2015.

Thistlethwaite Susan Brooks, and Mary Potter Engel, eds. *Lift Every Voice: Constructing Theologies from the Underside*. San Francisco: Harper and Row, 1990.

Tillich, Paul. See website for listing of his books, including *The Courage to Be* (1952) and the three-volume *Systematic Theology* (1953–1961) https://www.goodreads.com /author/list/42343.Paul_Tillich

Townes, Emilie M. *Womanist Ethics and the Cultural Production of Evil*. New York: Palgrave Macmillan, 2006.

Tutu, Desmond. *No Future Without Forgiveness*. New York: Doubleday, 1999.

Vargese, Winnie. *Church Meets World: Church's Teachings for a Changing World*, Vol. 4. New York: Morehouse, 2016.

Walker, Alice. *The Color Purple*, New York: Mariner/Houghton Mifflin Harcourt, 1982.

Washington, James Melvin, ed. *A Testament of Hope: The Essential Writings and Speeches of Martin Luther King, Jr*. San Francisco: Harper Collins, 1991.

West, Traci C. *Disruptive Christian Ethics: When Racism and Women's Lives Matter*. Louisville: Westminster John Knox, 2006.

Wiesel, Elie. *Night*. Preface by Robert McAfee Brown. New York: Bantam Edition, 1986 [1956]. For the entire series of Wiesel books, see: www.eliewieselfoundation.org /booksbyeliewiesel.

Williams, Charles. *Descent into Hell*. Grand Rapids: Wm. B. Eerdmans, 1966 [1937].

———. *Many Dimensions*. Grand Rapids: Wm. B. Eerdmans, 1993 [orig. 1930].

———. *War in Heaven*. Grand Rapids: Wm. B. Eerdmans, 1949.

For information on Charles Williams's books, see: *www.charleswilliamssociety.org.uk*

Williams, Delores S. *Sisters in the Wilderness: The Challenge of Womanist God-Talk*. Maryknoll, New York: Orbis, 2013 [1993].

Zoepf, Katherine. *Excellent Daughters: The Secret Lives of Young Women Who Are Transforming the Arab World*. New York: Penguin, 2016.

## Earlier Periods

Saint Augustine. *Confessions*. New York: Penguin, 1961.

Lincoln, Abraham. "Second Inaugural Address." See *https://www.loc.gov/rr/program/bib /ourdocs/Lincoln2nd*.

Maurice, Frederick Denison. *Theological Essays*. London: BiblioLife, LLC Reproductions, 1957 [1853].

Christopher Ricks, ed. *Oxford Book of English Verse, 1250–1900*. Oxford University Press, 1999.

# Notes

1. Isabel Carter Heyward, *The Redemption of God: A Theology of Mutual Relation*, 2nd ed. (Eugene, OR: Wipf and Stock, 2010).

2. Martin Buber, *I and Thou* (New York: Charles Scribner's Sons, 1937).

3. "Identity politics" is an academic term that refers to a way of understanding, and grouping, human beings by race, gender, sexuality, religion, nationality, cultural background, or other demographics. The term likely originated among groups such as the black feminist Combahee River Collective and others working for social change, beginning in the early 1970s. A classic example of the use of the term "identity politics" can be found in critical race scholar Kimberle Crenshaw's *Mapping the Margins: Intersectionality, Identity Politics, and Violence Against Women of Color, Stanford Law Review*, vol. 43, no. 6 (July, 1991), 1241–1299.

4. Janet Surrey's most recent book is *The Buddha's Wife: The Path of Awakening Together* (New York/Eugene, OR: Atria Books/Beyond Words, 2015), co-authored with Samuel Shem. In it, Surrey and Shem imaginatively explore the relational role of Siddhartha's wife Yasodhara as "She who stays" while her husband travels on the path to enlightenment.

5. Commonly shared among Christian worshippers in the more "catholic" churches (Roman, Orthodox, Anglican) as the basis of their belief in the Trinity (Father, Son, Spirit), the Nicene Creed originated in 325 CE at the First Council of Nicaea and was amended to its present form in 381 at the First Council of Constantinople. The Athanasian Creed is a lengthier, more tedious theological statement that details the early catholic church's Trinitarian basis. Its exact origin is unclear but it is thought to have originated in the late-fourth-century-CE teachings of St. Athanasius, archbishop of the Eastern church at Alexandria and an ardent proponent of the Trinity. By many traditional catholic theologians, the Athanasian Creed would likely be considered the "gold standard" of Trinitarian thought.

6. Augustine's *De Trinitate* was written between 399 and 421 in defense of the Trinity against its various critics, most notably the Arians who did not accept the full identity and equality of Father, Son, and Spirit.

7. "Ode 536: Intimations of Immortality from Recollections of Early Childhood," (1804), William Wordsworth, published in *The Oxford Book of English Verse: 1250–1900*, ed. Arthur Quiller-Couch (Oxford: Clarendon, 1919).

8. Siddhartha Mukherjee, *Emperor of All Maladies: A Biography of Cancer* (New York: Simon and Schuster, 2010).

9. Elie Wiesel, *Night*, was first published in1956. Widely considered Wiesel's masterpiece, it describes his experiences as a teenager in Auschwitz. Published in 2006 with translation by his wife, Marion Wiesel (New York: Hill and Wang).

10. Along the way, influenced by the work of Paul Tillich, I began to use the term "godding" to stress the active character of the Sacred. Philosopher Mary Daly, also influenced

by Tillich, makes the same point throughout her body of work, as does queer Christian theologian Virginia Ramey Mollenkott.

11. Womanist Christian ethicist Katie Geneva Cannon and I were students at Union together in the 1970s and later served together on the faculty of the Episcopal Divinity School.

12. See my essay in *Staying Power: Reflections on Gender, Justice, and Compassion* (Cleveland: Pilgrim Press, 1995).

13. The moral problem and theological mystery of evil has always interested me. It was one of the driving intellectual challenges behind my work in graduate school and continues to disturb me. Along with several of Elie Wiesel's novels, especially *The Town Beyond the Wall* (New York: Atheneum, 1964), a resource I found especially helpful during my doctoral research was John Hicks, *Evil and the God of Love* (New York: Macmillan, 1966).

14. I'm aware, of course, of the ugliness of this word in its violent, destructive historic context and of the danger of it being actually written out rather than coded ("n-word") as it usually is among white people in the United States who are conscious and mindful of our racist history. I've left the word in, as I used it when I was a child, to underscore its moral repugnance and relational destructiveness, even from the lips of a child who didn't mean to offend. I had never heard my parents use this word, and Elliott had never heard it from her parents. And yet we had heard the word.

15. I'm especially grateful to Valerie Batts, PhD of VISIONS, Inc.: "Taking Diversity and Inclusion to the Next Level," for lifting up this extremely important distinction in her work with the community of the Episcopal Divinity School, beginning in the 1990s.

16. Here, too, I spell out the "n-word" in this story rather than code it, in order to press upon the reader its socially destructive power.

17. Richard Sennett and Jonathan Cobb, *The Hidden Injuries of Class* (New York: W.W. Norton & Co., 1972). Until reading this book and listening to Dr. Harrison's lectures on "class," I had never thought seriously about "class" not just as a way of stratifying our society but, more radically, as an historic, multifaceted creation of invisible "communities" of human beings in our society.

18. Anne Hutchinson (1591–1643) was a spiritual leader among the Puritans in the Massachusetts Bay Colony who—defying the authority of the colony's governor John Winthrop and other Puritan leaders—taught that people can communicate directly with God's Spirit rather than having to rely on either the Bible or those who preach and teach from it, sparking what became known as the Antinomian Controversy. She was banished from the Colony in 1638 as a heretic.

19. I think of Delores S. Williams, Rosemary Radford Ruether, Aung San Suu Kyi, Alice Walker, Katie Geneva Cannon, Judith Plaskow, Ada Maria Isasi-Diaz, Kwok Pui-lan, Hyun Kyung Chung, Gale Yee, Joanna Dewey, Angela Bauer-Levesque, Rita Nakashima Brock, Catherine Keller, Susan Thistlethwaite, Joan Martin, Janie Spahr, Melanie Morrison, Selisse Berry, Reinhild Traitler, Denise Ackermann, Mercy Oduyoye, Delores Huerta, Hillary Clinton, Gloria Steinem, Julianne Moore, Meryl Streep, Michelle Obama, Elizabeth Warren, Malala Yousafzai, Ayaan Hirsi Ali, Fatima Mernissi, Irshad Manji, Bridget Rees, Angela Moloney and her Dominican sisters who have created the Sofia Center

in Adelaide, AUS, Cecile Richards of Planned Parenthood, Rev. Delores Berry, Bishop Barbara Clementine Harris of the Episcopal Church, and Sr. Simone Campbell of "Nuns on the Bus," to name only a few of the most outspoken advocates of women and girls in today's world.

20. I'm especially grateful to Cameron Partridge and Andrew Amanda Leigh-Bullard for reading an earlier draft of this manuscript in fall 2015, with an eye toward helping me speak accurately and respectfully of trans people. For example, the use of the term "bigender sibling" in this paragraph signals a sibling who is neither simply a sister or a brother.

21. Bonhoeffer's letters and papers in prison, written from 1943 to 1945 from prison, prior to his execution by the Nazis, was first published in German 1951 as *Widerstand und Ergebung*. It was translated for English publication in 1953. A fine contemporary translation was edited by John W. deGruchy and translated by Lisa E. Dahill, Reinhard Krauss, and Nancy Lukens (Minneapolis: Fortress, 2010). New Testament Scholar and English Bishop J.A.T. Robinson's *Honest to God* (London: SCM, 1963), was an effort to bring theological discourse down to earth by focusing on the social dimensions of Christian faith rather than the other-worldly. The "Death of God" theologians whose works were interesting to me in the late 1960s (in my later-college and early seminary years) were Thomas Altizer (*The Gospel of Christian Atheism*, Philadelphia: Westminter, 1966), Thomas Altizer and William Hamilton (*Radical Theology and the Death of God*, Bobbs-Merrill Co., 1966) and Paul van Buren (*The Secular Meaning of the Gospel: Based on an Analysis of its Language*, 2nd ed., New York: Macmillan, 1963, 1966).

22. Several of the most attentive Christian feminist theologians and ethicists of my generation to the well-being of the earth and to our relationship to other creatures have been Sallie McFague (*The Body of God*, 1993; *Super, Natural Christians*, 1997), Jay McDaniel (*Of God and Pelicans*, 1989; *Earth, Sky, Gods, and Mortals*, 1990), and Larry Rasmussen (*Earth Community, Earth Ethics*, 1996; *Earth-Honoring Faith: Religious Ethics in a New Key*, 2013).

23. My doctoral advisor and good friend Tom F. Driver wrote two theological books that helped shape my work: *Patterns of Grace: Human Experience as Word of God* (New York: Harper and Row, 1977); and *Christ in a Changing World: Toward an Ethical Christology* (New York: Crossroad, 1981). That "transcendence is radical immanence" is the core of Driver's theological conviction, and mine too.

24. See James H. Cone, *The Spirituals and the Blues* (Maryknoll, New York: Orbis, 1992), for a powerful description of this spirituality and its life-affirming value among African Americans.

25. Dorothee Soelle's magnum opus, *The Silent Cry: Mysticism and Resistance* (Minneapolis: Fortress, 2001), explores connections between God and world, good and evil, past and present and future, this world and other realms.

26. Notice that Augustine's *City of God* was published in 426 CE, about three decades after his *Confessions*.

27. A colorful print of this whimsical piece of wisdom by Andreas (1994) hangs on my wall, a gift from me to my mother and, after her death, from my mother to me.

28. In addition to Muffie Moroney, whom I discuss in these pages, two other friends from Randolph-Macon Woman's College have become especially good friends of mine over the last half century: Sissi Loftin and Anna Belle (Corbin) Ambrosen. In each case, we've become closer as we've aged and been involved together in a number of struggles for justice.

29. Betty Friedan, *The Feminine Mystique* (New York: W.W. Norton, 1963).

30. The "first wave" had been the women's suffrage movement in late nineteenth and early twentieth centuries.

31. "[Norman's wife ]Anne received a letter the next day penned by Norman: "Dearest Anne, I have been praying only that I be shown what I must do. This morning with no warning I was shown, as clearly as I was shown that Friday night in August 1955 that you should be my wife . . . Know that I love thee but must act for the children in the priest's village. Norman.'" Quoted in *Popular Resistance: Daily Movement News and Resources*, in a piece by Brian Wilson, Nov. 2, 2015—fifty years to the day after Norman Morrison's death in front of Robert McNamara's office outside the Pentagon.

32. I'm using the term "privilege" the way it's been used since the 1970s by feminist social theorists. One of the most helpful resources to me, in my work as a feminist liberation theologian, was Peggy McIntosh. See, for example, "White Privilege and Male Privilege: A Personal Account of Coming To See Correspondences through Work in Women's Studies" (1988), by Peggy McIntosh; available for $4.00 from the Wellesley College Center for Research on Women, Wellesley, MA 02181.

33. The Rejoice Mass was a folk mass written in the 1960s by Herbert Draesel, an Episcopal priest, primarily for experimental liturgical use in parishes, youth groups, and colleges.

34. I will be forever grateful to the women in our consciousness-raising group, which began meeting in 1970 at Union Theological Seminary. Seven of the women from this group continue to meet annually almost a half century later. Bunches of love to Linda Clark, Emily Jean Gilbert, Sarah Bentley, Maurine Doggett, Susan Savell, and Barbara Gerlach.

35. The Christology implicit in this book and these pages, in particular, is informed by interactions and growth in my thinking between eleventh-century French philosopher Peter Abelard's "moral influence" understanding of atonement; nineteenth-century Anglican/English teacher Frederick Denison Maurice's understanding of the primacy of a relational Trinity; Jewish social and mystical philosopher Martin Buber's comprehension of the radical relationality of all that is; the lives and teachings of modern German theologians Dietrich Bonhoeffer (d. 1945) and Dorothee Soelle (d. 2003) in their deeply moral—non-religious and a-theistic—appreciations of Jesus's neighbor-love as the root of all christological meeting; and contemporary feminist and womanist Christian theologians and ethicists, especially Delores W. Williams, Kelly Brown Douglas, Rita Nakashima Brock, and Beverly Wildung Harrison.

36. For a good summary of the three main historical understandings of "atonement," see Eugene TeSelle and Daniel Patte's brief discussion in *The Cambridge Dictionary of Christianity*, D. Patte, ed. (Cambridge: Cambridge University, 2010), 81–82.

37. For discussions of the christological controversies in the early church, see Richard A. Norris, ed. and trans., *The Christological Controversy* (Philadelphia: Fortress, 1980); also

Eugene TeSelle, "Christology in Western Church History," in *The Cambridge Dictionary of Christianity* (see previous citation), 214–217. Moving on about seventeen hundred years to the present day, if you are interested, notice the great variety of contemporary christologies in the "Christologies" sections, 218–225 in *The Cambridge Dictionary*— pieces by Ukachukwu Chris Manus ("Christologies in Africa"), Anne Nasimiyu ("Christologies in Africa: Images of Christ"), Peter C. Phan ("Christologies in Asia"), Muriel Orevillo-Montenegro ("Christologies in Asia: The Jesus of Asian Women"), Noel Leo Erskine ("Christologies in the Caribbean Islands: History"), Lesley G. Anderson ("Christologies in the Caribbean Islands: Present Day"), Nancy Elizabeth Bedford ("Christologies in Latin America"), Douglas John Hall ("Christologies in North America"), Marit Trelstad ("Christologies in North America: Feminist and Womanist"), Michelle Gonzalez ("Christologies in North America: Latino/a"), and Clive Pearson ("Christologies in South Pacific and Australia").

38. See James Carroll, *Constantine's Sword: The Church and the Jews* (New York: Houghton Mifflin Harcourt, 2002) for an important discussion of church and state collusion in the growth and spread of anti-Semitism, beginning with the Constantinian settlement of the fourth century.

39. The Book of Common Prayer, and Administration of the Sacraments and Other Rites and Ceremonies of the Church, according to the use of the Episcopal Church (New York: Seabury, 1977), 358.

40. See the varieties of christologies cited above, note 37, in *The Cambridge Dictionary of Christianity*. Also Dorothee Soelle, *Christ the Representative: An Essay in Theology After "The Death of God"* (Philadelphia: Fortress, 1967); Tom F. Driver, *Christ in a Changing World: Toward an Ethical Christology* (New York: Crossroad, 1981); Carter Heyward, *Saving Jesus from Those Who Are Right: Rethinking What it Means to be Christian* (Minneapolis: Fortress, 1999); Jon Sobrino, S.J., *Christology at the Crossroads* (Maryknoll, New York: Orbis, 1978); Jacqueline Grant, *White Women's Christ, Black Women's Jesus: Feminist Christology and Womanist Response* (Atlanta: AAR Academy Series, 1989); and Kelly Brown Douglas, *The Black Christ* (Maryknoll, NY: Orbis, 1993).

41. Those interested in my christological work and my understanding of "christic power" might consult several of my books: *The Redemption of God: A Theology of Mutual Relation*, 2nd ed. (Eugene, OR: Wipf & Stock, 2010); *Saving Jesus from Those Who are Right: Rethinking What It Means to Be Christian* (Minneapolis: Fortress, 1999); *Flying Changes: Horses as Spiritual Teachers* (Cleveland: Pilgrim, 2005); and *Keep Your Courage: A Radical Christian Feminist Speaks* (New York: Seabury, 2010).

42. See Darlene O'Dell, *The Story of the Philadelphia Eleven* (New York: Seabury, 2014); Carter Heyward, *A Priest Forever: Formation of a Woman and a Priest* (New York: Harper and Row, 1976); Alla Bozarth-Campbell, *Womanpriest: A Personal Odyssey* (New York: Paulist: 1978); Carter Heyward and Janine Lehane, eds., *The Spirit of the Lord is Upon Me: The Writings of Suzanne Hiatt* (New York: Seabury, 2014); Pamela Darling, *New*

*Wine: The Story of Women Transforming Leadership and Power in the Episcopal Church* (Cambridge, MA: Cowley, 1994).

43. Carter Heyward, *A Priest Forever: Formation of a Woman and a Priest* (New York: Harper and Row, 1976), 143.

44. Nelle Morton was a mentor and friend to several generations of feminist and womanist theologians. Her book *The Journey is Home* (Boston: Beacon, 1985) has been widely read not only among Christian feminists but among feminists of diverse spiritual identities, including post-Christians, among whom she counted herself in the last decades of her life. Nelle Morton is well known for the term "hearing to speech," first published in the essay "Beloved Image" (1977), which appears in *The Journey is Home.*

45. This is from Ntozake Shange's theatre piece, *For colored girls who considered suicide/ when the rainbow is enuf* (1975), which ran on off-Broadway for six months.

46. For Beverly Harrison's thinking about fascism and other social and economic challenges in our time, see Beverly Wildung Harrison, *Making the Connections: Essays in Feminist Social Ethics*, ed. Carol S. Robb (Boston: Beacon Press, 1985), and Beverly Wildung Harrison, *Justice in the Making: Feminist Social Ethics*, ed. E. Bounds, P. Brubaker, J. Hicks, M. Legge, R. Peters, T. West (Louiville: Westminster, 2004).

47. Michelle Alexander, *The New Jim Crow: Mass Incarceration in the Age of Colorblindness* (New York: The New Press, 2010).

48. Nikos Kazantzakis, *The Saviors of God: Spiritual Exercises* (written 1921–23; New York: Simon & Schuster, 2012).

49. Beverly Wildung Harrison, *Making the Connections: Essays in Feminist Social Ethics*, ed. Carol S. Robb (Boston: Beacon Press, 1985).

50. The Amanecida Collective, *Revolutionary Forgiveness: Feminist Reflections on Nicaragua*, ed. Carter Heyward and Anne B. Gilson (Maryknoll, NY: Orbis, 1986).

51. A book that grew out of such conversations among black, Hispanic, and white women was the Mud Flower Collective's *God's Fierce Whimsy: Christian Feminism and Theological Education* (Cleveland: Fortress, 1985). Working with me on the book were Beverly W. Harrison, Katie G. Cannon, Nancy D. Richardson, Mary D. Pellauer, Ada Maria Isasi-Diaz, and Delores S. Williams.

52. Kwok Pui-lan's *Postcolonial Imagination and Feminist Theology* (Louisville: Westminster, 2005), was one of the earliest feminist resources in postcolonial studies. Kwok Pui-lan continues to be a leading voice in Asian feminist and postcolonial religious studies.

53. The three of these children who are now adults—Rob, Isabel, Katie—have read, and given their permission, for this section to be published. The younger Kate's parents have given theirs.

54. In the realm of religious ethics and feminist theologies, Beverly Harrison's *Our Right to Choose: A New Ethic of Abortion* (Boston: Beacon, 1983) continues to be one of the most esteemed studies of women's reproductive history and moral choices in the Christian West.

55. *Les Miserables*, based on Victor Hugo's 1882 novel, is a musical by Alain Boublil, Claude-Michel Schönberg, Herbert Kretzmer, James Fenton, John Caird, and Trevor Nunn. My mother, brother, and I saw it in London shortly after it opened in 1986.

56. Delores S. Williams wrote a poem for Beverly Harrison for Bev's fiftieth birthday, on August 4, 1982. The poem's title, conveying the difficulty flowers have growing in mud, provided the name of the collective that wrote *God's Fierce Whimsy* (1985):

## MUD FLOWER

How will I walk this rope?
My foot size ten
   broad, careening
Woman I am
   black,
I have held her in my gaze
   white woman
Smile slashed across her face
   like the great pumpkin
   friendly
Asking to know me and
   I her
Should we together
   probe our-
   selves mythed
In the strength of
Men we've forgotten
   Should I say
Fuck the guilt
   Should she say
Fuck accusing
   Should we say to each other
Your people will be my people
Where you go I will go
   Shall we together
   admit alone
   We
Are the people  . . . ?

57. Among these friends were Demaris Wehr, an inquisitive educator and psychotherapist herself who was on a spiritual path and wanted company. Another was Peg Huff, a pastoral psychotherapist and bold Southern woman eager to share her own questions about God and the world. Demaris and Peg had joined the faculty of the Episcopal Divinity School to teach pastoral psychology. Another new friend was Ann Wetherilt, a woman from New Zealand and former nun who had come to the Episcopal Divinity School and went on to Union Seminary to study feminist liberation theology. Someone else who helped me navigate some of these questions, a few years later, was Peggy Hanley-Hackenbruck, who lived in the Pacific Northwest, a woman I had met at a professional conference in 1990. Peggy was a psychiatrist but, more importantly to me, a "birder" and lover of nature who was committed to living simply and frugally in relation

to money, food, possessions, and time itself. Peggy and I cultivated what I would now call a "slow time" relationship—in which I did not feel frazzled or hurried. The coast of Oregon became for me a refuge from busy-ness and a lovely place of retreat.

58. Sonia Sotomayor, *My Beloved World* (New York: Random House/Vintage, 2014).

59. Dan Brown, *The DaVinci Code* (New York: Doubleday, 2003).

60. Episcopalarchives.org. September 19, 1985.

61. https://www.poetryfoundation.org/poems-and-poets/poems.

62. Dorothy Samuels, "Wrong on Gun Rights," *The Nation* (Oct 12, 2015): 17.

63. Frederick Denison Maurice, *Theological Essays*, initial pub. 1853 (Cambridge, UK: J. Clarke, 2002).

64. Doris Kearns Goodwin, *Team of Rivals: The Political Genius of Abraham Lincoln* (New York: Simon & Shuster, 2006).

65. Shortly after I wrote this piece on "empathy," I received a call from Mark Burrows, director of Transylvania County Planning and Community Development, who wanted to put together an "empathy" project in our county, which is nestled in the southern Appalachian mountain range not far from Asheville, North Carolina. He and a number of us began to talk about what such an empathy project might look like. About a year later, as I was sending this revised manuscript back to the publisher, this group sponsored a dinner at a local church to begin discussions across lines that historically have kept us apart—racial, ethnic, religious, economic, gendered, ideological, political, rural, urban. This "empathy" dinner was quite a hit, and those seventy people who attended agreed that we need more of this kind of thing. Thanks to Mark Burrows and others working with him, Transylvania County, its townships and local communities, may be launching an empathy project to help us reach out and listen to one another in new ways as well as to work together to help generate and fund educational and employment opportunities for local youth.

66. Nelle Morton, *The Journey is Home* (Boston: Beacon, 1985).

67. My dear friend and colleague Darlene O'Dell does, however, respond to people much like my brother does: quite honestly and yet respectfully, demonstrating considerable personal courage and integrity—always an opening to mutuality.

68. Several trans colleagues have suggested that the term "sibling" might helpfully accompany or, sometimes, replace the terms "brother" and "sister" when referring to human family members since not all of our human siblings experience themselves as either male or female.

69. See Danielle Allen, *Our Declaration: A Reading of the Declaration of Independence in Defense of Equality* (New York: W. W. Norton, 2014).

70. Cameron Partridge, a trans man, brother priest, and former student, and Andrew Amanda Leigh-Bullard, a trans sibling who was introduced to me as I was finishing this manuscript, helped me think about trans issues in ways that were new to me. I asked them to read this section of the book and tell me where my concepts and language were problematic for them as trans siblings.

71. http://www.huffingtonpost.com/2014/08/04/laverne-cox-gayle-king_n_5647816.html.

72. Andrew Amanda Leigh-Bullard.

73. Mohandas Ghandi, Albert Schweitzer, Diane Fosse, Jane Goodall, and modern/contemporary Western theologians Andrew Linzey, Jay McDaniel, Carol Adams, Sallie McFague, Catherine Keller, Kwok Pui-lan, Larry Rasmussen, and Dan Spencer are a few among many who have known well that all created life is as Spirit-filled as human life.

74. For extensive attention to the sacredness of all creation from a Christian perspective and for connections between ecology and political economy/advanced global capitalism, see Sallie McFague, *The Body of God: An Ecological Theology* (Minneapolis: Fortress, 1993); *Super, Natural Christians: How We Should Love Nature* (Minneapolis: Fortress, 1997); *Life Abundant: Rethinking Theology and Economy for a Planet in Peril* (Minneapolis: Fortress, 2001).

75. Gratitude in bunches to my first, remarkable fiddle teacher Hilary Dirlam, and to those who followed, each a wonderful musician and caring teacher—Mary Jordan, Beverly Smith, Jon Singleton. Thanks also to my musical inspiration and beloved friend Albert Dulin; and to Rhonda Gouge, my guitar teacher; Melissa Saxton, who played banjo to my fiddle for several fun years; and of course my bandmates in the Bold Gray Mares, each a most cherished friend: Peg Hall on banjo, Gerry Azzata on mandolin, Gerrie Kiley on bass, and when, we're lucky enough to have her with us, Marion Sprott-Goldson on guitar.

76. The Harry Potter novels by British author J. K. Rowling were published over a ten-year period: *Harry Potter and the Philosopher's Stone*, 1997 (published in the U.S. as *Harry Potter and the Sorcerer's Stone*); *Harry Potter and the Chamber of Secrets*, 1998; *Harry Potter and the Prisoner of Azkaban*, 1999; *Harry Potter and the Goblet of Fire*, 2000; *Harry Potter and the Order of the Phoenix*, 2003; *Harry Potter and the Half-Blood Prince*, 2005; *Harry Potter and the Deathly Hallows*, 2007.